Last Waltz in Vienna

George Clare

Last Waltz in Vienna

THE DESTRUCTION OF A FAMILY
1842 - 1942

Pan Books
in association with
Macmillan London

First published by Verlag Ullstein GmbH 1980 in a German translation entitled
Das waren die Klaars
First published in Great Britain 1981 by Macmillan London Ltd
This edition published 1982 by Pan Books Ltd.,
Cavaye Place, London SW10 9PG
in association with Macmillan London Ltd
19 18 17 16 15 14 13 12 11
© Verlag Ullstein GmbH 1980
ISBN 0 330 26780 9
Printed and bound in Great Britain by
Hazell Watson & Viney Limited,
Member of the BPCC Group,
Aylesbury, Bucks

Contents

Part One

'*Klaar!*' There was a note of rising anger in Sergeant Lowe's voice.

And again: '*Klaar!* Where the bloody hell are yer?' Now he was using his loudest barrack-square roar.

'Coming, Sarge,' I shouted back, crawling out from behind the stack of jute sacks filled with Bailey bridging clamps where I had been spending my lunch-break reading my newspaper. If one knew how to shake the contents of these sacks into the right position one could build them into surprisingly comfortable seats, almost easy chairs. Having spent two weeks unloading them off railway trucks and stacking them I knew how to do it.

'At the bloody double, you!' the sergeant shouted.

'Been sitting on yer bloody ears again,' he grumbled when I had reached him. 'Been calling your name four times.'

'Sorry, Sarge.'

He held out a white oblong envelope. ' 'Ere that's for you, in't it?'

Of course it was. It was clearly addressed to

> 13805783 Pte. G Klaar
> 77 Coy. Pioneer Corps
> APO 1387

When I arrived in Britain in 1941 from neutral Eire, where I had been living since my escape from Nazi Austria, to volunteer for the army, I had hoped that I would be allowed to join a fighting regiment instead of the Pioneers, which was just a labouring unit.

No such luck. When I asked to join the Royal Artillery the reply was 'Where were you born?' 'In Vienna, Austria.' 'Have you been naturalised?' 'No.' 'Report to No. 3 Pioneer Corps Training Centre,

Ilfracombe.' Obviously I had no choice. But I searched for ways and means to get out of the Pioneer Corps again.

Eventually I thought of writing to 'William Hickey'. I read his column in the *Daily Express* regularly and knew that Tom Driberg, who wrote under the 'Hickey' pseudonym, liked to take up servicemen's grievances. On some days the grey slabs of print of his column almost looked like a wailing wall for unhappy soldiers, sailors and airmen. With great interest I had read Driberg's reports of his battles with red-taped or red-tabbed blockheadedness. Perhaps he could help me.

I wrote to him that I was twenty-one years old, Austrian born, able-bodied, keen to fight, that I spoke fluent German and good French and that I was wasting mine and the army's time working as a navvy. I said that there were at least thirty young men like me in 77 Company and many more in other 'A' companies who felt and thought as I did.

Driberg had just been elected Independent M.P. at the by-election for the New Malden constituency when I sent him my letter in July 1942.

And now I held Tom Driberg's reply in my hand. 'Daily Express, Fleet Street, London E.C.4' was printed on the top left-hand corner of the envelope Lowe had given me. Taking a deep breath I opened it.

'Dear Klaar,' Driberg had written. 'Thank you for your letter. The points you raise interest me. Next time you are in London come and lunch with me at the House of Commons. Let me know when you are due for leave.'

It was one of the great, one of the truly happy moments of my life. I shall never forget my feeling of elation. Had Lowe not scampered off to the Sergeants' Mess for another few pints before I had finished reading my letter I might even have embraced and kissed the old blighter there and then.

I, a young Jewish refugee from Vienna, a nobody without any connections whatsoever, had been asked by a Member of Parliament to lunch with him at the House of Commons!

It was fantastic! Could it be true? It was! How can I explain the enormous emotional impact this invitation had on me? For a young refugee in 1942, who knew that his survival depended on Britain, the House of Commons was the very centre of world and imperial power. In my eyes an almost superhuman, a God-like, aura surrounded every Member of Parliament.

When our lunch-break finished I went back to work dizzy with happiness, but, though my mental balance was so joyfully out of kilter, my physical one, fortunately, was not. For my job that afternoon was to add a fifth layer of Bailey bridge girders to a stack already four storeys high.

On a late October 'Indian Summer' day I entered the House of Commons by St Stephen's Gate. I went up to the policeman on duty and told him with what must have been quite a lot of self-importance that Tom Driberg, M.P., expected me for lunch. He appeared singularly unimpressed by my news and directed me to a nearby porter's lodge. There I was asked most politely to fill in a green visitor's card and wait till Mr Driberg came out to meet me. The porter even called me 'sir'. Me, wearing the uniform of a private in the Pioneer Corps!

I was, of course, very excited, but I took in my unique surroundings nevertheless. I looked at the vaulted ceilings, enjoyed the whole neo-gothic splendour, examined the busts of former Prime Ministers, all looking strangely alike as if high office, or perhaps only mediocre sculptors, extinguished most traits of individuality, spotted Jennie Lee talking to a visitor. She was so close to me that I eavesdropped unintentionally. He and she were – of all things – discussing Austria's post-war future. It's a small world, I thought. even in the House of Commons.

I had been waiting for some twenty-five minutes when Tom Driberg appeared. I recognised him immediately from the photographs I had seen. Still fairly slim in those days, he looked taller than I had expected. He had a pleasant smile and his dark good looks were attractive. The tightly curled receding black hair over his high forehead reminded me a little of my father.

He apologised for having kept me waiting and offered me a drink. I declined because I simply would not have known what to ask for.

Compared to what they must have been like pre-war the dining-room of the House and the food available were marked by austerity. But to me everything seemed the height of luxury. The white starched table-cloth, the highly polished silverware and the sparkling cut-crystal glasses made me feel transported into an almost magical world. Everything was bathed in a golden glow. Even the air tasted of history and tradition. Maybe it was merely stale, but for me it was a heady draught. The same air Winston Churchill breathed I was breathing now. I needed no wine to feel intoxicated.

I had never lunched with an Englishman before and did not know the ritual. So I was surprised when Driberg talked about the weather, fascinated when he talked about Fleet Street, the shining goal of my own post-war ambitions, about the theatre, about this and that but not at all about the subject of greatest importance to me.

When the coffee had arrived Driberg came to the point.

'I made some enquiries at the War Office after receiving your letter,' he said, 'and they tell me that chaps like you can now volunteer for the Glider Pilot Regiment or the Commandos. Why don't you. It solves your problem, doesn't it?'

'No, it doesn't,' I said. 'My Company Commander who's thought me a trouble-maker ever since I wrote to the Air Ministry asking to join the R.A.F., sent me to a hush-hush interview about joining the Commandos.'

'How did it go?'

'I said "No, thanks" to the major who interviewed me.' 'But why? You say you want to join a fighting unit. There was your chance.'

'We are not allowed to join just any Commando unit, you know. The one we can go to is No. 10 Commando, and all the men in it are non-British-born soldiers. In a way it's just another ghetto. But if the War Office suddenly considers us suitable for near-suicide units why shouldn't we be suitable for ordinary fighting units as well? I want to get into the Royal Artillery, others want to join the tanks. If they trust us with gliders why do they not trust us with guns? Why can't we slog along with the infantry or rattle about in tanks?'

'What you are saying is that the War Office is unfair?'

'Exactly.'

'Haven't you got a bit of a chip on your shoulder about all this?'

'Quite likely, but how would you feel if the people you admire most in the world, in our case the British, distrust you? Did you know this: The first alien companies were formed shortly after war began. They were shipped to France. They were unarmed. When the Germans broke through they were given some rifles. And they fought their way through to St Malo. They were evacuated from there. But the moment they were back in England their arms were taken from them. That was not all. It was touch and go whether these men, British soldiers who had taken the oath to the King, who had fought with the B.E.F. in France, would be interned or not. Mind you, I was still in Ireland then. But is a chip on one's shoulder all that surprising under these circumstances? And don't forget, officially we are all still "enemy aliens".'

'Enemy aliens?' Driberg asked with some surprise.

4

'Oh yes,' I said, 'and we'll stay enemy aliens until after the war. All naturalisations have been stopped for the duration. It is ridiculous. Any refugee who joins the U.S. forces automatically becomes an American citizen after six weeks.'

'So if you are taken prisoner of war you really are without protection?'

'Yes. That's a risk we just have to take. All I ask for is some British fairness, and I believe that even the War Office is still British.'

Driberg laughed. I had paraphrased in my last sentence something he had written in his column.

'I'll see what I can do,' he said. 'I really can see no reason now why you should not be able to get out of the Pioneer Corps and join any unit you like provided you are otherwise suitable. I'll make some further inquiries and I'll write about it in my paper.'

He was as good as his word. Some weeks after our lunch he published quite a long paragraph about us in his column suggesting that we had proved our loyalty and should now be treated with greater fairness.

Driberg's voice was not, of course, the only one raised on our behalf at that time. Nor was I the only one in the Pioneer Corps searching for the support of prominent and influential people. Eventually the War Office gave way, and in the spring of 1943 a new Army Council Instruction was put up on our Company notice board stating that aliens serving in the Pioneer Corps could now apply for transfer to any regiment in the army. The doors were open at last.

In July 1943 I joined the Royal Artillery. With intense satisfaction I took the Pioneers' 'grave diggers' badge – crossed spade and pick-axe – off my uniform cap and threw it into the dustbin. Its place was taken by a lovingly polished little brass field-gun, the insignia of my new regiment.

I was one of a group of fifteen 'alien' ex-Pioneers at the Royal Artillery Training Centre near Harrogate in Yorkshire. As we had all arrived on the same day we were also all billeted together.

The last one to leave our barrack-room in the morning was given the job of checking that our beds were properly made up in the approved army fashion, the blankets neatly folded and the kit-bags, stuffed with newspaper so that they looked like well-filled sausages, at the head end of each bed so that the owner's name and army number painted on them in white were uppermost.

On the first morning when it was my turn to check that everything was in order I suddenly remembered something Tom Driberg had said to me. 'So if you are taken prisoner,' he had said, 'you are really without protection.'

What had made me think of that? After a few seconds I understood. The army numbers on each kit-bag began with the same four digits: 1380. Of course, that was it! Each member of the 'alien' companies had an army number starting with 1380, and our numbers had not been changed when we transferred to the artillery. That was not only stupid, I thought, but dangerous. There was every likelihood that German intelligence would know that those four figures marked a soldier who was not a British national and most likely a Jew as well. If one of us was taken prisoner that number was the perfect giveaway.

Most of us had German-sounding family names as well, but that, I thought, was less dangerous. There were British as well as German Goldsteins and Rosenbergs, and indeed the General Officer Eastern Command, British Home Forces, was one Lieutenant-General Schreiber. One could hardly have a more German-sounding name.

I talked to the others about my discovery that same evening. They all shared my view, and as I was the one to have spotted this they thought I should be the one to see the Battery Commander about it.

I asked for an interview with him and my request was granted.

I marched smartly into the major's office, stamped my feet in regulation manner, saluted, and, after being asked what I wanted, I said: 'Sir, I and all my comrades transferred from the Pioneers have kept our old army numbers. All these numbers start with 1380. We are now in a fighting unit, we may go into action and could be taken prisoner. If the Germans should capture me, I am not worried about my name. Klaar is neither specifically Jewish, nor specifically German. I could be of Dutch ancestry. But surely German intelligence must be aware that any prisoner whose army number starts with 1380 is not British. This could be very dangerous. I should, therefore, like to ask, sir, that I and my comrades be given new army numbers.' The major thought this request reasonable. He would put it up to regiment, he said.

What neither he nor I could know, was that somehow, somewhere, the 'Practical Jokes Department' of the War Office would get involved in the act.

A fortnight later I was called to the battery office again. 'Leeeft! right! leeeft! halt!' the Battery Sergeant-Major bellowed. Stamp feet. Salute.

'Stand at ease!'

The major looked up. 'I've heard from regiment, Klaar,' he said, 'there's no problem about changing your army number, but the colonel says you should change your name at the same time. So, if you change your name you get a new number. The colonel suggests "Clark".'

'With respect, sir,' I replied, 'not "Clark". Everybody pronounces "Klaar" as "Clare" anyway, so if the name has got to be changed for me to get a new number, I'd like it changed from "Georg Klaar" to "George Peter Clare".'

'Right,' said the major, 'you'll hear.'

''Tenshun, about turn,' the Sergeant-Major shouted; and the 'Klaar' that was marched out of the battery office to become the 'Clare' that is.

A document arrived in due course informing me that I was from now on officially 'George Peter Clare' and that I had been given a new army number, which, instead of the alien-pioneer 1380 began with the figure 1157. Problem solved. Or so I thought, not knowing anything about the 'Practical Jokes Department' in the War Office.

Within less than two weeks it had arranged for every non-British-born soldier in the Royal Artillery to be given a new army number. All those numbers started with 1157, indicating to friend and foe alike that we were all bloody foreigners.

When I discovered that bit of nonsense I was not at all amused. But there was nothing to be done about it now, and in any case my feelings were also somewhat ambivalent. On the one hand I wanted to 'pass', to assimilate, to become English and for that purpose 'Clare' was of course much better than the foreign-sounding 'Klaar'. By then I had begun to speak with what I imagined was an Oxford accent, and when, eventually, I found myself smiling, sometimes even laughing, at cartoons and articles in Punch I thought I had finally made it. I was much too young to realise that one can never eradicate one's background, that it is an essential part of one's identity and one to be cherished, and that all one can eventually achieve is a happy form of double-vision which enables one to see England and the English, perhaps slightly blurred, but from the inside and the outside at the same time.

But on the other hand I was sad to have lost for no good reason at all the family name of which I had been so proud. My pride in being a Klaar sprang from my father's pride in his family, from the stories about the Klaars he and his mother, Grandmother Julie, told me. And being a very Austrian little boy the fact that my great-grandfather, according to family lore, had been the first Jew to rise to Regimental Surgeon First Class in the Imperial army, and that his son, my grandfather, had been one of the senior Medical Officers of the city of Vienna, had a lot to do with my growing up believing our family to be special.

But that military background (grandfather had also been a Captain-Surgeon though in the army reserve, not a regular like his own father) might well have had something to do with my dislike of the Pioneer Corps and that strong wish to become a proper soldier.

In many ways the Klaars were also typical of Central European Jewry, of people who, within a short space of time, moved from the narrowness of the East-European ghettos into that wide and glamorous world of West-European culture, absorbed it, became an essential part of it, climbed to new heights during the enlightened nineteenth century only to fall so deep into the dark abyss of extinction which our own century had so thoroughly prepared for them.

So let me start this story of the Klaars, of Austria and Central Europe, of that whole world which has disappeared forever, with Herrmann Klaar, my great-grandfather. He was born in Stanislau, a small town in the Bukovina, now part of Russia, but then the Habsburg Empire's most eastern province, in 1816, when Napoleon was still fretting his life away on St Helena, when Beethoven had yet to ascend to the summit of his genius, and when clever and arrogant Prince Metternich was the undisputed ruler of Austria, ruthlessly suppressing progress, liberalism, the rights of man – in short, all those ideas which had spread across Europe in the wake of the French Revolution. For Metternich the three vilest words in any language were 'Liberty, Equality, Fraternity'. He was the staunchest propagator and defender of 'Legitimacy', the Habsburgs' and their fellow-monarchs' God-given right to rule. The only right Prince Metternich was prepared to allow the citizenry was to live in peace, provided they did not interfere in politics, exhibit any desire to participate in government and keep its mouth shut. That 'oval opening' was for singing hymns and consuming Backhendl, but not for talking about politics.

Austrian history knows this period as the Backhendl ('baked chicken') era. But in spite of Metternich's thought-police it was a time when only the very few actually felt oppressed. The vast majority was quite content to leave politics to its 'betters' and restrict itself to making a living as best it could. Money kept its value and was the foremost symbol of stability; and the whole period looked as if it were destined to be one of economic and political permanence. On the whole it was a happy and secure era, because – as Henry Kissinger described it – Metternich's policy was a reflection of a fundamental certainty : that liberty is inseparable from authority, that freedom is an attribute of order.

It was also a time of hope for Jews. It was the time when a young Jew like Herrmann – unlike his father Eisaak, a well-to-do wine merchant, but still caftan-clad and bearded – could grow up in an orthodox Jewish home and yet eventually become a quite new species : a Jewish Austrian military gentleman.

Of course he was neither dashing dragoon nor flamboyant guardee, for no Jew still professing the faith could be commissioned into one of Austria's élite regiments. His was not a purely martial army career. He joined the army's newly expanded medical corps and became one of the first, if not the first, Jews in the Imperial Army to rise to the rank of regimental surgeon first class.

In a photograph taken long after he had retired from active service Herrmann certainly looked the part of the former military gentleman. His stern face and ramrod posture betrayed not only the ex-officer, but also the lifelong disciplinarian. I do not know whether little Ludwig, his younger son and my grandfather, or his brother and sister, actually had to click heels and salute when they returned from the barracks in the evening. Presumably matters were not taken quite that far, but I am certain that the barrack-square manner was not unknown in the family home.

Herrmann Klaar was twenty-five years old when he finished his medical studies and married Rosalie Goldberg on 14 November 1841. He received his degree as Doctor of Medicine and Obstetrics from the University of Vienna on 25 January 1842.

Herrmann Klaar could now stand on his own feet. The scion of a line of village innkeepers who had risen to become wine merchants, he had availed himself of the first opportunity for ghetto dwellers from what the Austrians considered the almost 'Asian' part of their Empire to acquire a Western European education and to train for a vocation from which Jews had been previously barred.

The newly fledged doctor began to practise medicine in Czernowitz, and in due course his and Rosalie's marriage produced three children, two boys and one girl. Ludwig, my grandfather, born on 1 November 1849, when his father was thirty-three, was the youngest.

The seeds sown by the French Revolution, fertilised by changed economic patterns, began to sprout in the Habsburg monarchy in

1848 and 1849. Opposition to the authoritarian monarchy grew into a revolutionary movement that left few parts of the European continent untouched. The highly contagious and vigorous movements of nationalism and liberalism seriously threatened the re-established European authoritarianism of Metternich.

The former ghetto-dwellers who had emerged into European secularism were caught in a dilemma. To a great extent they owed their emancipation to awakening European nationalism and liberalism. Nationalism in the first half of the nineteenth century was fighting for self-determination and did not yet have the chauvinistic traits it acquired during the second half. Nor was early liberalism the political agent of unrestricted business interests: it also advocated political equality and the extension of the franchise.

For Jews nationalism harboured dangers. Theoretically nationalism and liberalism implied greater tolerance of minorities. But this was not true in practice. One section of the population saw the Jew in league with the central government, while the other looked at Jews in the revolutionary movement and condemned them as destroyers of the established order.

As so often happens with revolutions, once the first impetus had passed, the revolutionaries began to fight among themselves. Some wanted to overthrow everything, others counselled a more cautious approach. But while they squabbled, the forces of Legitimacy, which had first fled before the revolution in terror, began to organise and reassert themselves. In Austria the eighteen-year-old Franz-Josef replaced the imperial imbecile, his uncle Ferdinand, on the throne.

His troops put down the revolution mercilessly. For hangman and execution squad those were hectic days. On 11 March 1849, just nine months before the birth of Ludwig, Herrmann Klaar locked the door of his Czernowitz surgery and joined the army.

Why? Was he trying to defend the system of Legitimacy which had emancipated him? Was he afraid that popular nationalism would eventually deprive him of equality? Or was he just rebelling against his orthodox father and his Jewish background with its ancient rules and superstitions of the ghetto?

To some extent this was probably true, but when Klaars rebelled they did not go to extremes. Herrmann did not abandon his Jewish faith and convert to Catholicism. Yet, though remaining a Jew, he also wanted to be a true Austrian; and nothing was as truly Austrian in the polyglot Empire as its army. Austria's greatest dramatist, Grillparzer, said it in one sentence: 'The army is Austria.'

The army was composed of soldiers and officers from many nationalities, and its loyalty was direct to the Habsburg Crown. That Crown was Austria. Until 1918, when the Habsburg Empire collapsed, Austria was spoken of as 'The Monarchy'. There were many monarchies in Europe, but the countries their monarchs ruled were called Germany, France, Italy, Great Britain; only Austria was 'The Monarchy', quite correctly, for Habsburg Austria never was a national ethnic entity.

Herrmann was accepted for army service by a Dr Bürtl, the medical corps colonel in the Lemberg area command. The thirty-three-year-old doctor was given the rank of 'First Lieutenant Medical' and posted to Field Hospital No. 11.

On Herrmann's army conduct sheet one of the questions reads: 'Mental faculties?' The officer who filled in the answers wrote: 'Very many.' The new lieutenant was a good linguist. He spoke and wrote German, French, Polish and Ruthenian, the last two being the languages of the area where he grew up. He must also have spoken Yiddish, the language of the ghetto, and he also had a good command of Latin. In addition to these languages he later learned Italian, which he picked up in the course of his army service in that country.

He was both intelligent and ambitious. While serving with the 29th Infantry Regiment – admittedly garrison duties were far from strenuous in those days – he continued his medical studies, and in February 1851 he qualified as a surgeon at Cracow University. He remained a lieutenant-surgeon for a further four and a half years and then resigned his commission to return to civilian practice. After six years' service he was entitled to a pension, and, of course, he remained on the reserve.

The Klaar family returned to Czernowitz. It was the town where Herrmann was known, where he and his wife had both family and friends, and which he therefore regarded as home. But the army did not allow him to enjoy the life of a civilian for very long. On 1 March 1858, only two and a half years after getting out of uniform, he was, in the language of the Austrian army, 're-arbitrated' and posted to the 'Prince Lichtenstein' 5th Infantry Regiment. Franz-Josef was putting his army on a war footing. The young emperor wanted to teach his rebellious subjects in Italy a lesson.

The Revolution of 1848 in Poland and Hungary had been bloodily put down with the able and willing assistance of the Tsar and his cossacks, but in Austria's Italian possessions unrest grew from day to day. The Italians would not be pacified. The time of the 'Risorgimento', the resurgence of Italy as a nation, was at hand. National unity for Italy was the ideal that fired the hearts of the Italians. Garibaldi and his red-shirted legions had given Italians a new pride in their nation, and the dazzling political manoeuvres of Cavour, Prime Minister of the Piedmontese Kingdom, showed that astute political leadership was not lacking. In a brilliant political coup Cavour concluded an alliance aimed against Austria with Napoleon III, the Emperor of the French. One Italy, united under one crown, was no longer a distant dream.

Cavour played his cards well. His trump card was the inexperience of the twenty-nine-year-old Franz-Josef and the bone-headedness of his advisers. Austria declared war. France declared war. The Italians declared war. The French marched, the Italians marched, the Austrians marched, and with them marched the newly promoted surgeon-captain Dr Herrmann Klaar.

He did not wear the bright white tunic, visible mark of Austria's military might for centuries, of the officers and men of the Imperial infantry regiments. The army's medical officers – there were altogether 972 regular ones in the Austrian army – wore medium blue tunics with black facings on collar and sleeves and two rows of brass buttons, charcoal trousers with red braid along the legs, the long officer's sword with golden tassels, and a gold braided cocked hat with green feathers. On the black tunic collar sparkled the three captain's stars of Herrmann's new rank.

There they were, pouring into Italy, a mass of men in white and gold. Gold glittered on their black shakos, the bright metal scabbards of their sabres glistened in the sunlight, every man as smart as a polished button, every man a perfect target for the marksmen of the enemy.

Reading about the wars and battles of the last century, reading about the soldiers' deeds of valour and derring-do, about men advancing and retreating to the sound of the bugles, picturing young ensigns breathing their last, while their hands, stiffening in death, still clasp the flag, all this makes our wars of yesteryear seem so heroic, so clean – almost nice. The reality for those who took part in them was very different from all this panache and excitement. Wars were always a bloody, sickening shambles. To Surgeon-Captain Herrmann Klaar and his colleagues the dying and the wounded were dragged, to him and his colleagues the injured crawled for help.

Hour after hour they wielded the scalpel and the hacksaw; and the blood flowed bright red over those splendid white uniforms.

But the shambles at the dressing stations and in the field hospitals was as nothing when compared with the overall chaos created by the Austrian commanders. Austria's soldiers were good soldiers. There were brave men in the ranks and dashing junior officers; but their senior commanders had developed bone-headedness to a fine art. They firmly believed that ten loud-mouthed sergeant-majors and a handful of gruff colonels were more valuable in battle than any number of brilliant staff officers.

Take General Gyulai, who commanded at Magenta on 4 June 1859. He had risen to high rank because the Archduchess Sophie, the Emperor's mother, liked him. He was a welcome guest at her salon, his manners were impeccable and he always said the right thing. He commanded his men to look like proper soldiers and wear black moustaches. The blond ones had to dye theirs black, and those who hadn't any were told to paint them on their faces with burnt cork.

At six o'clock on the morning of 24 June 1859, the day of the battle of Solferino, the Emperor, who had personally taken command and thus added inexperience to ineptitude, sent his staff forward. He and his chief of staff were to follow later. That decision was the start of a comedy which turned into a tragedy. By about nine in the morning the staff officers were looking for their Emperor, while the Emperor was looking for his staff. In a style which would have done credit to an English fox-hunt, sixty or seventy staff officers dashed across ploughed fields and over hedges and ditches, desperately searching for their Emperor and commander-in-chief. By the time the two parties caught up with each other it was, of course, too late.

Herrmann Klaar retreated with the Austrian troops into those parts of Italy which remained Austrian. The regiments to which Herrmann was subsequently transferred were stationed there. Herrmann's daughter married one of the Princes of the Colonna family whom she met in Italy. One did not meet Princes of the Colonna blood in Czernowitz.

Herrmann Klaar was still in Italy in 1866, the year when Austria lost its war against Bismarck's Prussians, who believed a few brilliant staff officers to be worth more than any number of loud-mouthed sergeant-majors and gruff colonels.

Austria's difficulties with Bismarck's soldiers encouraged the Italians to have another go. This time the Italians lost. One of the places they attacked was Fort Palmanova protecting the approaches to Trieste, the Monarchy's most important seaport. Italian troops cut off the garrison and besieged the fort commanded by General Corte. Being in a fort under siege can never be a pleasant experience, but for great-grandfather Herrmann, the garrison's senior medical officer, it must have been hellish. Cholera broke out amongst Palmanova's defenders. Herrmann's efforts to bring this epidemic under control were outstanding. He was mentioned in dispatches and promoted to Surgeon-Captain First Class. The official citation says: 'On 10 October 1866 Surgeon-Captain Dr Herrmann Klaar was officially mentioned in dispatches and highly commended for his unceasing devotion to duty during the siege of Fort Palmanova and the ensuing cholera epidemic. General Corte wrote a personal commendation for this officer.'

So, at last, aged fifty, Herrmann Klaar received his third promotion after serving in the army for almost twenty years. True, promotion in the peacetime army was slow, but Herrmann had taken part in the Italian campaigns, had seen war service and yet his way up the ladder of the hierarchy was not a climb but a crawl.

The army officers under whom he served had a good opinion of him. Colonel Franz von Brznina and Major Gustav Lorenz, commander and adjutant of the regiment to which Herrmann belonged, recorded on his army conduct sheet that he was 'of friendly disposition, respectful and obliging to his superiors, kind and just to those under his command, exact and highly reliable in carrying out his duties'.

But Herrmann's medical superior, a Colonel Zimmermann of the army medical corps recorded a very different view. 'Weak character', he wrote on Herrmann's conduct sheet, 'easily influenced, of unpleasing outward appearance, diligent and active enough in ordinary, formal service, but not capable of satisfying higher demands. Not suitable for promotion.' Translated into plain language 'of unpleasing outward appearance' meant 'the man's a Jew', and 'not suitable for promotion' 'Jews ought to be kept in their place.'

Zimmermann obviously did not like Jews, but professional jealousy also influenced his negative judgment. More and more Jewish students with first-class medical degrees were leaving the universities, more and more Jewish doctors were opening successful practices in Vienna and other Austrian cities. Zimmermann could not stop that trend, but he could see to it that the same thing did not happen in the army. Zimmermann did not have to state his views openly. His meaning was quite clear, anyway, and the way he put it was in keeping with the Austrian way of doing things.

But to be fair: Zimmermann's Austria was also the Austria in which a young Jew could free himself from the shackles which had kept Jewry in bondage for centuries. It was this Austria which allowed him to study, to become an officer, to accomplish in a single lifetime the enormous transition from Jew of the ghetto to respected citizen of Vienna, the most glamorous capital on the whole continent. And because Herrmann could and did do this, he is, in many ways, the crucial figure in our family history. He was the first Klaar to become fully westernised, the first to absorb in his person the culture of Austria, the first to be completely assimilated, and undoubtedly also the first to make the tragic mistake of believing himself to be wholly Austrian, no different from other Austrians, except perhaps for the relatively unimportant fact of practising a minority religion.

Herrmann lived in a world which had its Colonel Zimmermann, true enough, but even the Zimmermanns of his time were, on the whole, civilised human beings. They had their prejudices and their dislikes, but they were no murderous beasts. There was anti-semitism, there were anti-semites; they could, and did, create difficulties for Jews, but their anti-semitism was mostly religious, not yet racial. If a Jew 'converted', then virtually all professional doors opened to him. It was a time when the world seemed in order.

As Stefan Zweig, the famous Austrian writer, said in his autobiography, *The World of Yesterday* :

Everything in our almost thousand-year-old Austrian monarchy seemed based on permanency, and the State itself was the chief guarantor of this stability ... Everyone knew how much he possessed or what he was entitled to, what was permitted and what forbidden. Everything had its norm, its definite measure and weight. He who had a fortune could accurately compute his annual interest.

An official or an officer, for example, could confidently look up in the calendar the year when he would advance in rank, or when he would be pensioned ... Whoever owned a house looked upon it as a secure domicile for his children and grandchildren; estates and businesses were handed down from generation to generation ... In this vast empire everything stood firmly and immovably in its appointed place, and at its head was the aged emperor; and were he to die, one knew (or believed) another would come and take his place, and nothing would change in the well-regulated order. No one thought of wars, of revolution or revolts. All that was radical, all violence, seemed impossible in an age of reason.

Yet in that 'vast empire' hardly anything actually stood immovably in its place, except one man – Franz-Josef. Nationalist movements acquired a new dimension besides the desire for self-determination, *hate*. The Hungarians hated the German-Austrians, the Czechs and the Croats; the German-Austrians hated the Hungarians above all others; the Czechs hated everybody. Crisis followed crisis, government followed government.

But above this cacophony, 'immovably in its place' stood the Monarchy. Franz-Josef was not a great man; at times jealous of others to the point of pettiness, he was stiff and unbending; far too often he viewed the problems posed by the nineteenth and early twentieth century through the eyes of an eighteenth-century monarch; he made innumerable mistakes including the final and most tragic one in 1914, when he signed away millions of lives at a corner desk in his shabby little room in his hunting lodge in Bad Ischl. Nevertheless, simply by remaining 'immovably in his place' for so long he created that psychological climate of permanence and security Stefan Zweig described so well.

The arts – music, literature, the theatre – flourished in this climate as they had never done before. Hardly anywhere in the world was artistic achievement more appreciated and so concentrated in time and place as in Franz-Josef's Vienna. The audience which the artist needs if he and his work are to flourish existed in Vienna. Sigmund Freud – no sharper and more analytical observer of this period can be quoted – said about Franz-Josef's empire long after it had collapsed: 'Austria-Hungary is no more, but I would not wish to go elsewhere; emigration is not for me. Instead I shall go on living with the truncated body, *clinging to the illusion that it is still complete*.' The permanence Zweig speaks of was also an illusion, but when an illusion is believed it becomes reality.

It was an age of reason in which Herrmann Klaar lived, it was an age of durability which was equated with stability. It made the Klaar family feel, in spite of its religion and background, that it was equal among equals.

But nothing is so impermanent as permanence, nothing is so insecure as security. If Jews, as the saying goes, are like other people, only more so, then they are more so because their permanence is as impermanent as that of the others, only more so, their security is as insecure as that of the others, only more so.

The fates of Herrmann's grandchildren, Paul, Fritz, Pepi, Sally and Ernst, prove the folly of identifying durability and absence of change with stability and security. They were born fully integrated Viennese and grew up in the state which seemed so secure and permanent. They were born and grew up as Austrians amongst Austrians. They belonged to the same generation as Stefan Zweig, who wrote about his and their time:

It was reserved for us, after centuries, again to see wars without declaration of war, concentration camps, persecution, mass robbery, bombing attacks on helpless cities, all bestialities unknown to the last fifty generations, things which future generations, it is hoped, will not allow to happen. But, paradoxically, in the same era when our world fell back morally a thousand years, I have seen mankind lift itself, in technical and intellectual matters, to unheard-of deeds, surpassing the achievement of a million years with a single beat of its wings ... Not until our time has mankind behaved so infernally, and never before has it accomplished so much that is godlike.

When Herrmann retired from the army in 1868 after almost twenty years' service, he was fifty-two years old, young enough to set himself up in practice in Vienna. His army pension, if not providing riches, did provide security. He was placed on the army's reserve list and at last promoted to major, which meant an increase in pension of 60 guilders a year. Life flowed gently and easily.

A photograph of Herrmann Klaar's younger son, Grandfather Ludwig, taken in his old age shows kindness in his dark Jewish eyes as well as sadness, but the deep lines cutting diagonally across the skin over his sharp nose betray a quick, hot temper and the very bushy eyebrows over them give him a look of determination. Moustache and beard hide his mouth, the ends of his moustache pointing down towards his bearded jowls enhance his sad expression.

Ludwig is marked in the family history as an authoritarian. His attitude towards the child of his first marriage was for years a matter for family speculation.

Grandmother Julie was not Ludwig's first but his second wife. His first wife Hermine was the daughter of Dr David Winternitz, the renowned founder and editor of the *Österreichisches Journal für praktische Medizin*.

Hermine, born in 1859, was one year younger than Ludwig. They married in 1881 and had one child, a son named Felix, born a year later. Ludwig divorced Hermine in the spring of 1884, two years before he married Julie. The first marriage failed because Hermine was mentally unstable. The last twenty years of her life she was an inmate of the Steinhof, Vienna's psychiatric hospital, to which Felix was also committed in 1919, the very year his mother died there.

I learned about Ludwig's earlier marriage for the first time in 1938 after the *Anschluss*, when I went with my father to Vienna's town hall to get a certificate stating that he owed no taxes. Without such a certificate one could not emigrate.

The official, a youngish man with a little Hitler moustache, welcomed us with an almost friendly sounding *Heil Hitler*, but after looking at us, added, 'Oh well, as you aren't allowed to say that, good morning, and what can I do for you?' He even asked us to sit down. Father explained that he needed his tax clearance certificate. 'Have you paid everything?' the man asked. Father said he had, and the official started to rummage through his files. 'Ah yes, Klaar, Ernst, here we are.' He took out the file, opened it, wrinkled his forehead as he read for a moment and then, with a sarcastic smile on his lips, he looked up at Father. 'Well, well, well,' he said, and you could see that whatever he had found pleased him no end. 'I can't give you that certificate.' 'Why not? I've paid all my taxes,' Father replied. 'Now, have you really?' the man said, clicking his tongue against his teeth with glee. 'Haven't you forgotten something? What about your brother, then?' he asked. 'Which of my brothers are you talking about?' Father replied. 'I'm talking about that nut half-brother of yours. The one the Christian taxpayers of this city have been maintaining in the loony bin for the last twenty years. Aryans don't pay for insane Jews any more, you know. You Jews have the money anyway. It's up to you. You either pay for his keep or you don't get your certificate. Please yourself.'

Under Austrian law my father could never have been held financially responsible for a half-brother. But law or no law, the Nazis were the masters now, and what they said went. And when Father pleaded that he had never even seen that poor step-brother of his, that did not cut any ice either. Father had no alternative. He paid up.

Only after the war did we hear that the same official forced Uncle Paul and Uncle Fritz to pay for Felix Klaar all over again.

His file, still kept in the Steinhof, says about Felix's further fate that he was moved to an 'unknown institution' on 1 August 1940. Most likely that 'unknown institution' was Hartheim Castle near Linz, where the Nazis murdered the mentally handicapped and called it 'euthanasia'.

Grandfather Ludwig's birthplace was the same as grandmother Julie's: Czernowitz. It was then the capital of the Bukovina province, but for all that no more than a smallish market town of some 24,000 inhabitants. Half the population was Jewish, the other half was made up of Ruthenians and Poles, Austrian civil servants and soldiers. Ludwig, though he was very much head of the household, and that in a period when these words meant much more than a convenient description on a census form, had a much less dynamic personality than Grandmother Julie. Outwardly he compensated for this lack of true 'leadership' by exaggerated outbursts of temper. It did not take much to make Ludwig rant and shout and yell his head off: Grandmother in tears, the children hiding in fear, Annitschek, the maid, red-faced and sniffling, shuffling off into the kitchen, all pretty regular occurrences in the Klaar family. He was a father in those happy and balmy days for fathers, when they and their wishes were immediately obeyed, when they were the ostensible focal point of the family's existence and their commands were never ignored. No one had heard of children's rights or Women's Lib. If there was any cosseting going, then it was for Father and not for the children. The universal family motto was: the best is for Father! He got the choice cuts of meat, the asparagus tips, and was entitled to take an undisturbed afternoon nap with his feet on the shoulders of one of his sons. That, he believed, was good for his circulation.

Every night, when Dr Ludwig retired, a freshly baked chocolate cake, Annitschek's version of the famous *Sachertorte*, had to stand on his bedside table. He must have been more worried about night starvation than about tooth decay, or perhaps the doctors and dentists of his time had not yet discovered this problem. Next day, when the cake was not quite so fresh, the children were each allowed a slice of the remainder, while Annitschek was already slaving away over the hot oven, baking that evening's new gooey chocolate delight.

All this was perfectly normal and accepted paternal behaviour in those days. My own father, Ludwig's son, apparently accepted this 'divine right' of fathers. According to him there were fathers who went much, much further. I have never forgotten the story he told me about the husband of Aunt Thalia, Grandmother Julie's sister. This gentleman took a keen pleasure in taking his children to that excellent pastrycook's shop across the road from my grandmother's flat, owned by Herr Beisiegl. Herr Teller – that was the gentleman's name – used to settle himself behind the conventional little marble table, group his children around it and order coffee with whipped cream, two or three cakes or anything else he fancied. Father Teller drank his coffee and ate the cakes, after which, satisfied with himself, he lit a fine cigar. All the while his children sat around the table with not even a glass of lemonade to share between them. Their treat was that they were allowed to come into the cake shop at all. And they knew well enough from bitter experience that their roles were limited to those of observers. After gently stroking his protruding stomach, Herr Teller would raise his right hand, point his forefinger at his eldest son Erwin and pronounce the immortal words, 'There you are, my dear boy, one day when you are a father, you too, will be able to eat as many cakes in a patisserie as you like.'

Ludwig did not go quite that far. His children did get the asparagus stalks to suck, they were allowed their slices of dried-up chocolate cake. But in spite of all this generosity, there is a tale about Ludwig and his son Fritz, which makes Herr Teller appear by comparison in a better light. Young Fritz, then twelve or thirteen years old, was ill, suffering from rheumatic fever. Not a minor illness then or even now. One morning – everybody else had gone out and he was alone in the flat with his father – Ludwig suddenly needed something from a shop in Josefstädterstrasse. Instead of getting his coat and hat and going out himself, Ludwig ordered the sick boy to go and buy whatever it was he wanted. That young Fritz could have become even more dangerously ill through this shopping expedition and might have had to stay in bed for many months – which is exactly what happened – apparently did not occur to his doctor father.

How can one explain this? How can one explain Grandmother's interminable pregnancies following so rapidly after one another? Even allowing for the attitudes of the time Ludwig must seem a complete egotist. He was a contemporary, indeed a colleague, of Sigmund Freud, and practising medicine in the very same city. He had seen madness getting its vicious grip on his first wife, a woman he must have loved, or at least been close to, but he seems to have gone through life unaffected, not understanding, seeing nothing. He knew all about the functions and malfunctions of the human body, but shut himself off from the functions and malfunctions of the human mind. Was this because he was afraid to face this knowledge and ultimately his own personality? How else can one explain the way he treated his second family, and, above all Felix, the unfortunate child of his first marriage. When his parents were divorced Felix was three or four years old. His mother was committed to a mental institution twelve years before her death in 1919. How long did Felix grow up in the care of this manic depressive mother before his Aunt Laura took him to live with her? I know that my father had never seen his half-brother. The only Klaar boy who may have met Felix when he was a grown man, was Fritz. His daughter remembers Fritz telling her that another Klaar was posted to his regiment during the First World War, that he sought him out and spoke to him. Most likely that man was Felix. But why was this child never brought to Josefstädterstrasse, to meet and play with his father's other children? Did the stigma of divorce, in those days, put the child of a failed marriage beyond the pale? Did little Felix ever see his father? As I said, there is something mysterious about Ludwig Klaar's early life.

That Ludwig determined his sons' professional future without the slightest reference to their own wishes, was also in the spirit of his time. It was he who decided that the eldest, Paul, and the youngest, Josef, were to study medicine. There was not enough money to allow all four sons to go to university. Ernst and Fritz could eat their hearts out to become doctors as well: both regretted all their lives that they had no academic degrees, but there was nothing they, or even Grandmother, could do about it.

Probably the disappointments Ludwig suffered in his professional life because he was a Jew contributed to make him a difficult man in his middle years. His wife and children made plenty of allowances for him, particularly on that score. The way they talked about him after his death even when telling the stories of his severity and foibles, made it quite clear that they had loved him.

Those thick, bushy eyebrows in his photo betray also a strong streak of tenacity. Even though greatly tempted he refused to abandon the religion of his forefathers. Yet he was certainly not a religious man. He entered a synagogue only when family occasions demanded it. But although he was advised – such was his reputation as a diagnostician – that he would be appointed a court physician were he to convert to the Roman Catholic faith, Ludwig stuck to his convictions and refused.

That he did not get this appointment did not embitter him. He had been given an option and had made his own decision. What did embitter him was that his career in the medical service of the Vienna municipality was dogged by anti-semitism. Here he was supposed to be treated as an equal, and promotion was supposed to be based on merit. His misfortune was that his career coincided with the rise to power in Vienna of the lawyer Dr Karl Lueger, who used anti-semitism, ever popular with the mass of the people, to achieve his political goal. 'Beautiful Karl', as the Viennese nicknamed their handsome idol, became the most beloved and also the most efficient Burgomaster Vienna ever had.

But in those days there were also men, foremost among them Franz-Josef himself, who despised anti-semitic rabble-rousing, and on occasions even a Lueger had to be careful not to show his anti-Jewish policies too openly. One such occasion is recorded in the minutes of the meeting of the Vienna City Council held on 25 June 1907:

City Councillor Dr Hein submits the following question: 'Recent events in connection with the appointments to the city medical department have created considerable unrest in the circles concerned. One District Chief Medical Officer, who has for some time performed the relevant functions to everyone's satisfaction, though recommended by his colleagues, was not promoted because of his Jewish origins. Instead the position went to a medical officer junior to him, who, however, is the fortunate holder of two papal decorations. That doctor was promoted over the heads of many other colleagues of greater seniority. How can the Herr Burgomaster justify this discrimination against so many deserving and hard-working medical officers in the city's service?' Burgomaster Dr Lueger: 'The City Councillor is fully aware that the promotion of municipal servants, in this case of medical officers, is a matter for the City Council. When this subject was discussed in Council I was not present. I absolutely refuse to accept any responsibility whatsoever for City Council decisions made in my absence. I have nothing to justify as I am absolutely innocent of the whole affair.' City Councillors: 'Hear, hear!'

For sheer effrontery, but also for political guile, this remark of the all-powerful Burgomaster was difficult to beat. He was not present at that particular Council meeting, because it was far more astute to manipulate such delicate matters from behind the scene. Lueger had anticipated that this decision to appoint a Catholic junior doctor to the office of City Physicus – the three City Physici were the most senior medical officers in Vienna's medical service – over the head of a Jew much senior to him, had all the makings of a first-class public scandal and that the press would make a meal of it – which it did. It was all there in the newspaper cuttings Grandmother Julie had carefully preserved, for the Jewish district medical officer who should have had that promotion was her husband Ludwig.

But, whatever the newspapers wrote, Lueger could plead innocence. He had not been there, he had had nothing to do with it. It was all just the usual cheeky speculation of the Jewish-controlled gutter-press.

A little while later, after a suitable diplomatic delay, Ludwig was given the title *Ober-Medizinalrat*. But this, a state not a municipal award, was probably another one of the many tiny barbs with which the Emperor, who intensely disliked Lueger and was also jealous of his immense popularity among the Viennese, chose to prick the Burgomaster from time to time.

Even after Lueger had died it took another two years before Ludwig Klaar was at last appointed *Stadtphysicus*. However, even then he got this appointment only as a result of a special and somewhat surprising petition which was submitted to the city authorities by three leading members of Lueger's own Christian-Social party. This deputation was led by one Michael Hersan, a Catholic priest, who was supported by the town clerk of the Josefstadt district, Herr Bergauer, and the district councillor, Herr Walter. They argued that Ludwig had been intentionally passed over for promotion for seventeen years merely because he was a Jew, and that it was high time that his services to the city received the recognition they deserved.

The three submitted their case to the City Council early in September 1911 and were successful. The minutes of the Vienna City Council meeting of 12 January 1912 recorded: 'Town Councillor Dr Haas reported on the new appointments in the City Physic Department. *Ober-Bezirksarzt* Dr Ludwig Klaar receives the title of a City Physicus, and his pension will be increased by the sum of 500 Kroner per annum.' So, in the end, Grandfather Ludwig got his title, but only that. He never got the function as well.

Two years later, aged sixty-five, Ludwig retired from the municipal medical service. The only official function he retained until the end of his life, was that of medical supervisor of the city orphanage in the Josefstadt.

In the end, Grandfather Ludwig had achieved the dignities he had wanted and deserved. He was seventy-three when he died of cancer of the throat on 24 March 1922; and Austria's leading newspaper, reported:

The funeral of *Ober-Medizinalrat* Dr Ludwig Klaar took place at the Döbling cemetery on Sunday morning. Among the mourners were the president of the Jewish community, Professor Alois Pick, Police Chief Surgeon Dr Merta, Hofrat Dr Munk, *Oberstadtphysicus* Dr Boehm, Hofrat and University Professor Dr Lelewer and many other personalities. At the open grave Rabbi Dr Bauer described in moving words the meritorious life's work of the deceased.

It must have been quite a funeral, and all the worthies came, including – be it noted – Dr August Boehm, he of the two papal decorations.

Though he had to wait for so long for recognition, status and dignities, Ludwig could eventually enjoy them. But financial security eluded him. He left Grandmother Julie 120,000 Kroner in cash, a gold watch and chain, a signet ring, some medical instruments and books, three white shirts, two black overcoats, two suits, four pairs of shoes, one black hat, one umbrella and, of course, the furniture in the Josefstädterstrasse flat. The medical books, the inventory of his possessions noted, were mostly outdated. When everything had been added up and set against the medical fees incurred during his illness, the cost of his grave, bought in perpetuity, and his funeral, the balance was written in red figures. Grandmother and her children were left with a debt amounting to 108,510 Kroner. That sounds an enormous sum. But in 1922 Austria's post-war inflation had almost reached its peak. By the time the estate was settled the debt was no more than the price of ten packets of cigarettes. Ludwig shared the miserable financial results of his life with most of his fellow-countrymen, particularly those who had to live on fixed incomes or pensions. He certainly was no Jewish capitalist speculator making money out of the misery of inflation, that favourite bogey-man of the anti-semites. In many ways the inflation of the twenties was not all that different from the inflation of our time. The retired were the chief victims of inflation, then as now. The pension Ludwig received in 1922 was the same on which he had retired in 1914, but its purchasing power in 1922 was only sixteen per cent of what it had been in 1914. The war loan certificates into which he, the patriotic Austrian, had put his savings were not worth the paper they were written on. Grandmother Julie was left with a nearly worthless pension. Had she not been supported by her sons her situation would have been desperate. Without their help she would have had to leave the flat in which she had lived so long, in which her children had grown up and her husband had died.

Efroim Schätz was a lucky man and a happy one. In his early thirties, good-looking and with ample means, he was one of the few, one of the privileged Jews. Vast estates, large herds of cattle, huge forests, all these were his. Well, not quite: he was entitled to the income from these holdings. The true owner, a member of the local Polish gentry, up to his neck in debt to Efroim, was far away from his native Bukovina squandering money on wine, women and above all on the fall of the cards and the whirr of the roulette wheel in Monte Carlo or Vienna, or some other place where the stakes were high and the morals low. And as his debts to Efroim grew and grew, new parcels of land, with everything that stood and lived on them, whole villages with their peasants, their Jews, their inns and saw-mills, their rivers and rolling fields, came under Efroim's control.

With pride and confidence in the future, he and his young wife Pauline, _née_ Baltinester, looked into the cradle where their little girl slept. Born on 7 April 1861, she had been given the name Jochewed-Julcze, and to Efroim and Pauline, as to all parents, their first-born looked the most angelic, the sweetest, the prettiest baby ever.

To me, Jochewed-Julcze's grandson, this scene is difficult to imagine. How could our female 'patriarch' at any time of her life have been other than the pear-shaped old lady I knew? How did this rosy baby-face develop into that strong head, reminding one a little of Goethe in old age, with the sharp, aquiline nose, which the mysterious ways of genes projected onto the face of her sons, their children, onto those of some of my children and which, in due course, will appear and reappear in further generations?

Efroim's hopes and calculations for the future were astute enough, but there were two or three factors he had not, and could not have, allowed for. The first was the still common danger of puerperal

25

fever. His young wife Pauline died of it in 1865, having given birth to another little baby girl. Jochewed-Julcze was not yet five when she lost her mother and had to accept responsibility for her younger sister. The only keepsake her mother left Julcze was the pathetic little myrtle wreath she had worn on her wedding-day. A sad little souvenir, it hung under glass in a heavy gold frame in Grandmother's living-room.

The second unforeseen factor was the determination of Bismarck, the Prussian Chancellor, to push Austria out of Germany, for only then could he establish Prussia as the leading power in Germany and thus in Central Europe. In 1866 the Austrian troops faced the Prussian army at the battle of Sadowa. The Prussians with their modern training and arms, above all the new firing-pin rifle, which the Austrian general staff had found much too new-fangled and unreliable compared to the dear old muzzle-loaders already in use in Napoleon's day, won the battle and with that the war. The Austrian army fled in disarray.

According to Grandmother it was this war which nearly ruined Efroim Schätz. Huge herds of livestock were sequestrated, whether by the advancing Prussians or by the fleeing Austrians, I cannot say. Nor can I explain how the men of either soldiery got from Moravia, where the battle was fought, to the area around Czernowitz in the Bukovina where Efroim's estates were. But somehow Efroim must have recovered at least some of his fortune. In spite of the lost war this was the period of industrialisation, and the Austrian economy started to boom. That bubble burst with the big stock exchange crash of 1873, but the foundation for economic growth had been laid.

Efroim must have been a wealthy man again by the time his daughter Jochewed-Julcze – whose Jewish first names had meanwhile changed to 'Julie' – married Dr Ludwig Klaar on 6 April 1886. This is proved by the bride's address on the marriage certificate: 'Opernring 3', one of the best addresses one can have in Vienna to this day. The house which Grandmother left to become the wife of Ludwig Klaar disappeared during the Second World War. In its place now stands one of the few modern post-war buildings in the centre of Vienna, which has otherwise miraculously survived virtually unscathed not only two world wars, years of occupation, but also most of the follies of modern town planners.

I wish I knew more about Grandmother's girlhood and her life as a young bride. In the life-story of this one woman, born in a Ruritanian corner of the old Empire, who lived for eighty-two years and died in April 1943 in the Nazi ghetto of Theresienstadt, the tale of not one, but several, vanished worlds could be told. Her life began in the world of eastern Jewry, not in that of the *shtetl* ghettos of eastern Poland and Tsarist Russia, but in an atmosphere not all that far removed from it. The most important difference was that the Jews in the eastern regions of the Austrian empire led a life free from fear of the pogroms unleashed every so often on their unfortunate brethren within the Tsar's power.

From this primitive world, where the caftaned Jews mixed with colourful peasantry and small-town folk on the fringes of the most slothful but most comfortable of empires, young Julie was translated to the imperial capital at a time when Vienna even outdid Paris as the focus of intellectual excitement and nineteenth-century elegance. From Opernring 3 she could see straight across Opera Square to the famous Sirk Ecke, that corner where the upper end of Kärntnerstrasse, Vienna's most elegant shopping street, meets with the 'Ring'. This wide, tree-lined boulevard shaped like a horseshoe, its two ends resting, as it were, on the banks of the Danube canal, embraces all the true beauty of the old city within its two arms: the baroque palaces of the long-vanished nobility, the old churches, the wide squares through which Mozart and Haydn, Beethoven and Schubert strolled, the narrow old lanes of the medieval city as well as wide roads flanked by the elaborately ornate buildings from which the Empire was governed for hundreds of years.

The Ringstrasse, to give the 'Ring' its full name, represents both a style and a period. In the last quarter of the nineteenth century Franz-Josef's reign had reached its zenith. There was unbounded confidence in the future coupled with a totally uninhibited display of wealth. The apartment blocks of the rich, which were to flank that grandest of European grand boulevards, shot up with amazing speed. Nothing could be too ornate, nothing too overladen. A house was not fit for the 'Ring' unless it had caryatids and all the curlicued garlands, urns, figures, the stonemason's art could produce. The official buildings vied with the private houses in opulence and variety of styles. The Opera House was built as an Italian renaissance palazzo, the university as a French castle, the new town hall looked like a neo-gothic cathedral, and the parliament like a Greek temple. The Viennese duly noted that Pallas Athene, the Greek goddess of wisdom, whose gold-helmeted statue was erected in front of the parliament building, did not face it, but turned her back on the Austrian diet's new home.

The Ringstrasse was uniquely Franz-Josef's own creation. In 1858 the Emperor, who wanted a capital worthy of the Habsburg Empire, determined that Vienna needed to grow outward beyond the narrow confines of the old inner city. He ordered the destruction of the moats and bastions that had surrounded the city for centuries. But before Franz-Josef could realise his plan, he had to overcome the determined opposition of his generals. The shock of the 1848 revolution was still embedded in the very marrow of their bones. In the end a compromise solution was found. The Emperor could have his grand boulevard, the generals agreed, if they could have the last word in its design. The elegant squares and attractive open spaces which interrupt the Ringstrasse at intervals and give it lightness, air and variety pleasing to the eye, are the creation of Franz-Josef's general staff. Once again the Austrian genius for hiding hard-faced decisions behind elegance and charm had asserted itself. Most of these open spaces are on the side of the 'Ring' from which the main roads radiate towards the outer districts with their crowded tenements of the proletariat. If one has one's infantry and artillery drawn up on the other side of the 'Ring', closer to the inner city with its ministries and palaces, then those lovely squares offer a clear field of fire at the rabble from the outer districts, should it ever dare to threaten the established order again. The very top of the 'Ring', its most select section, the centre of the upper curve of the horseshoe, is the Opernring.

Let us look out through Julie's window in that house on Opernring 3 and view the scene at the very heart of the Imperial capital through Julie's eyes. When evening came she looked straight across the Opera Square at the elegant carriages driving up the ramp to the main entrance of the Opera House, disgorging the gorgeously dressed and jewelled ladies of society, their husbands or lovers – or sometimes both – dressed in white tie and tails or in the splendid uniforms of the Imperial Army : the white tunics and gold lace of the dragoons, their blood-red breeches disappearing into the glistening patent leather of their black boots; the blue of the infantry officers; the chocolate-brown tunics and red collar flashes of the artillery; the short, fur-trimmed and golden-frogged cloaks of the hussars nonchalantly thrown over one shoulder; the staid, dark green uniforms of the higher echelons of the general staff, jangling spurs, sabre scabbards glinting in the light of the gas candelabra; golden belts and buckles, the whole panoply of operetta come to life. It was a scene of incredible richness and splendour; no stage setting anywhere in the world could compete with it.

How could young Julie know that all this was only stage glitter, that all the glory of the Empire displayed before her eyes was nothing but elegant futility and that underneath that sparkling surface was hiding the decay of the nineteenth century and of the Austro-Hungarian monarchy? How could she know that out of all this the foul creed of murderous envy and hatred was already worming itself to the surface of this lovely city, and would condemn her to die in poverty surrounded by terror? Race hatred and antisemitism were not invented by Adolf Hitler. He was only the executor of the vile thoughts of others before him. All the venom of the nineteenth century spurted into the mind of this one man. He was the personification of the evil of a whole century. He alone brought to a conclusion the thoughts and writings of others and thus arrived at the ultimate, the final, solution to the hatred of centuries: murder on a such a huge scale that the human mind cannot grasp it. We cannot identify with millions, we can only identify with single human beings. That is one reason why this book is not about the defenceless millions who were murdered in Hitler's holocaust and who, because of their numbers, must remain strange, shadowy, unreal, but tells the story of only a few men and women who were my ancestors. Their sufferings can be grasped because the victims can be described and named.

In 1882, four years before Julie Schätz married Dr Ludwig Klaar, the German-Austrian student fraternities passed the Waidhofer Resolution. It was one of the first occasions when that hateful worm gnawing at the vitals of humanity showed his head. The problem that concerned them was, whether a Jewish student was fit to duel with a non-Jewish student. In *My Youth in Vienna*, Arthur Schnitzler, the famous Austro-Jewish writer, quotes the Waidhofer Resolution. It said:

Every son of a Jewish mother, every human being with Jewish blood in its veins, is born without honour and must therefore lack in every decent human feeling. Such a person cannot differentiate between what is pure and what is dirty. Ethically he is the lowest of the low. It follows from this that contact with a Jew dishonours; hence any contact with a Jew must be avoided. It is impossible to offend a Jew and therefore no Jew can demand satisfaction for any insult he may have experienced.

One Jewish student, a member of the German-Austrian Students'

Organisation, proudly walking about Vienna university sporting the blue cap and ivory-handled black ebony stick which was the sign of membership, was the young Theodor Herzl. The impact of the Waid-hofer Resolution on the thoughts of the future founding father of the State of Israel went very deep. He resigned from his fraternity. It was his first step on the road to Zionism.

It is unlikely that young Julie from Czernowitz knew about the Waidhofer Resolution. She was captivated by life in the metropolis, so different from provincial Czernowitz. The glamour of the evening scene in front of the Opera House was, if anything, even surpassed by the view from her window during the daytime. From her flat on Opernring one could watch almost the whole length of the famous 'Corso', those five or six hundred metres of pavement, café terraces and luxury shops on that section of the 'Ring' which starts at the corner of the Opera Square and leads past the elegant Hotel Bristol to the end of Akademiestrasse. There, from eleven o'clock in the morning till lunchtime, elegant Vienna strolled, heel-clicked, hand-kissed, flirted. The most delicious intrigues began on this short stretch of pavement with glances bold or shy, with smiles half-hidden, but, oh, so meaningful, with whispers of promise or of despair.

Nowhere in the whole of Europe was there anything to compare with the Vienna 'Corso' of the last two decades of the dying century and the first decade of the new. It encompassed that whole bitter-sweet world, so brilliantly recorded in the plays and stories of Arthur Schnitzler and Hugo von Hofmannsthal.

It is easy to record the few facts I know about Grandmother Julie : where and when she was born and married, where and when she died. But the facts are less than nothing. I knew and remember an old lady. But who was this woman when she was twenty, thirty, forty? I see her before my eyes on her last visit to our flat. I was ill at the time, with measles or chickenpox, one of those illnesses one has at the age of nine or ten. Grandmother took a good ten minutes to walk up the two flights of stairs. Her legs, tightly laced in black half-length boots, could hardly support the weight of her huge body. Painfully she puffed her way up step by step. Finally, on my mother's arm, the old lady arrived at my bedside. There she was, dressed in a long, black silk dress, a black bonnet pinned to her grey hair, fighting to get her breath back as she settled in the chair by my bedside. She had brought me a present. One of Hugh Lofting's Doctor Dolittle stories. I adored Doctor Dolittle, and at that moment I adored my grandmother for bringing me this lovely book. Julie was my 'number one' grandmother, and not only because she, on the whole, provided better if less expensive presents than my mother's mother, who was the 'rich' granny, while Julie was the 'poor' one. There were also other reasons. Most important, I could talk to Grandmother Julie, or rather she knew how to talk to me. Indeed, much of what I remember about the family comes from tales she told me. But also on other subjects she could talk in a way that aroused and held the interest of a little boy.

Grandmother Adele, my mother's mother, did not possess this gift of talking to children. Julie I remember as an intelligent and educated old lady, Adele as a much more limited person and a moaner. I am probably quite unfair to that poor woman, and my memory of her may well be influenced by the lasting impression that of the two, Adele, in her behaviour and speech, punctuated by her never-ending sighs, was very much the East-European ghetto Jewess, while Julie in speech and manner appeared totally westernised, totally Viennese. Why Jochewed-Julcze from Czernowitz should have been so different from Udel-Leie, who Germanised her name to Adele and was born in Lwów, the capital of Austrian Galicia, I found impossible to explain until I came across an old history of the Jews of the Bukovina. Both apparently came from similar backgrounds, and yet the one seemed to have shed her eastern past entirely, while the other carried it with her to her dying day

This was why I liked Julie so much better than Adele. I was already second-generation Viennese, and Viennese-born Jews felt resentment towards the less assimilated Jews from the East. We were, or rather thought we were, quite different from that bearded, caftaned lot. We were not just Austrian, but German-Austrian. Little wonder that I resented the Yiddish singsong intonation with which Adele spoke German, a 'Yoich' sigh at the start and end of almost every sentence.

After that visit to my sickbed, Julie never left her home in Josef-städterstrasse except to visit Bad Ischl in summer. If she could go to Bad Ischl and also negotiate the steep steps that led from the house in Brennerstrasse into its garden and back, then her plea that she was too heavy and too old to go out in Vienna was not considered a very good excuse by the family. She walked slowly and always used a stick, but she managed quite well. The truth was, and the family guessed it, that she preferred being visited to visiting. It was more in keeping with her 'royal' posture. By staying at home and letting her sons come to her, she also diplomatically avoided Aunt Alice,

Uncle Paul's wife, nattering that she was being given the honour of grandmother's visits less frequently than my mother. Alice had been keeping the score for some time, and did not mind letting the family know about it.

So Grandmother preferred to stay at home and 'receive'. She was extremely good at it. Carpet-slippered Annitschek, the maid, was certainly not the most elegant 'Lord Chamberlain', but Grandmother's air as she sat on her chair in the living-room with that great halo of wispy grey hair round her head was very much one of pomp and circumstance.

Grandmother Julie's flat was furnished in the late 1880s when Franz-Josef was at the zenith of his glory as Emperor of the Austro-Hungarian monarchy. Almost fifty years later, when I was a little boy, nothing had been changed, nothing had been modernised. Not a chair, not one of the heavy plush burgundy curtains, not one anti-macassar had been replaced. Everything remained exactly as it had been on the day when Dr Ludwig Klaar and his young wife Julie moved into the house at Josefstädterstrasse 70 so many years before.

· Grandmother's flat passed through time as a haven of permanence, but the world outside raced through catastrophic and cataclysmic change. Franz-Josef, his glory and his empire, had vanished. Grandfather Ludwig had died. His young bride of 1886 had grown into an obese matriarch. No, that is the wrong word to describe Grandmother Julie. In spite of her sex, the absolute sovereign of the family, was a patriarch.

In the Twenties and Thirties of this century Austria was geographically and politically a rump of her former greatness. It was an unhappy country, the remnant of the huge Monarchy with a capital, Vienna, suitable for the Empire that had been, but far too big for the dwarf state that it became. Neither the country nor the city had come to terms with their dismal present. Most Austrians dreamed of their splendid past, disliked the world as it was, and feared the future – quite rightly, as it turned out. Theirs was now a country which one Austrian historian aptly called 'The state nobody wanted'.

The Vienna in which I grew up was a city still pretending to be a world metropolis of cosmopolitan elegance. But behind the imposing façade of former imperial splendour lurked defeat, poverty and fear. Behind the baroque masonry of superb elegance lay dark, dank corridors filled with the stale smell of over-boiled cabbage and human sweat and the indefinable but clearly discernible odour of hatred and envy. A world war, all too gaily begun, had been bloodily lost.

Millions had died, and new states, to die in turn a few short years later, had been built on the ruins of the Habsburg empire.

But in my grandmother's flat, in the territory where patriarch Julie ruled, time was under orders – her orders of course – not to change. The Franz-Josef, or, if you will, Victorian, atmosphere was carefully maintained. There is one room which reflects to this day almost exactly the look and feel of Grandmother Julie's flat. It has that comfortable shabbiness, it has the worn rugs and chairs, the same carpet pattern upholstery. That room is Emperor Franz-Josef's study in his hunting lodge in Bad Ischl, the old man's favourite holiday resort. This picturesque spa in Upper Austria was also the favourite holiday resort of our family sovereign. No *lèse-majesté* is intended in comparing Klaar family surroundings with those of the Imperial Family. As a matter of historical fact the bourgeois mustiness of the Klaar flat, like the flats of other representative Austrian bourgeois families, was similar in taste to the bourgeois mustiness with which the bureaucratic Emperor of the world's most bureaucratic Empire liked to surround himself. The fat old Jewish lady, my grandmother, was at heart just as much of an Austrian traditionalist bourgeois as the stiff and glittering Emperor.

By the time I was born the Habsburgs had gone, but in Grandmother Julie's flat everything remained as it had been when Franz-Josef had ruled. No matter how wide you opened the windows, that musty warmth remained. It made her home feel comfortable, safe and, above all, immutable. Her children, four boys and one girl, certainly sensed this. With one exception, that of my uncle Josef, whose wife forbade him to visit his mother more than once a year, the other three brothers and Aunt Rosalie, named after her paternal grandmother, but called 'Sally', were part and parcel of the Josefstädterstrasse establishment all their lives. After Ludwig's death Uncle Paul, the eldest, a G.P. and gynaecologist, had taken over Grandfather's surgery in the rear part of the flat. He was there every day. My father visited his mother and sister (Aunt Sally lived with Grandmother) at least once, but more often twice a week, and Uncle Fritz, though he had a wife and two children and a home of his own, seemed a permanent fixture in Grandmother's flat.

One entered the flat through a narrow corridor from the landing. This held a huge dresser and an ice-box : no new-fangled refrigerator in Grandmother's home. That ice-box had been put there when she moved in, and that was where it stayed. In summer the iceman called twice a week, humping huge lumps of ice upstairs and stuffing them into it. What Grandmother kept in the dresser I never knew. The narrow corridor led into the hall, a fairly big room with a big table, covered with a carpet, in its centre. Behind the table stood a wall bench, and on either side of it were carpet-upholstered easy chairs. Also in the hall was a water tap and bowl fixed to the wall. Why any Imperial Austrian architect should have put a water tap there instead of in the kitchen is a mystery I never penetrated. Another mystery which I did not solve till very much later was that other piece of apparently permanent hall 'furniture' – my Uncle Fritz.

'Officially', Uncle Fritz came to Josefstädterstrasse to visit his mother and sister. So he should have been, one would think, in the living-room with them. But I cannot remember ever seeing him there. In my memory he is screwed to the far easy chair in the hall, looking very decorative, smoking one Turkish cigarette after another. Maybe his smoking was why he had been banished from grandmother's throne-room. Dear Aunt Sally was of delicate health, and cigarette-smoke might have disturbed her. It could, of course, also have been that he fled from conversation with Grandmother, which tended to be somewhat restricted to the family's number one topic: dear Sally's health. Uncle Fritz, whose health, in spite of much illness, must have been quite amazing – he outlived everyone else and died in Melbourne, Australia, in 1972 aged eighty-four – did not really want to hear about Sally's woes. He needed someone to listen to his own. And he had plenty.

From his chair in the hall he could easily reach the ears of Annitschek, the family's most perfect listener, through the always open kitchen door. Annitschek resided in the kitchen. If Grandmother Julie was the family sovereign, reigning over the family from her living-room, then Annitschek was her prime minister. She ruled the family on the sovereign's behalf from the kitchen stove. Annitschek had entered the service of Dr Ludwig Klaar and his wife well before the turn of the century. An apple-cheeked young peasant girl from Bohemia then, she still spoke German, even forty years later, with the soft singing accent of the German-speaking Czech. In all those years she had never once been back home. She had shared the fortunes and misfortunes of the family, had helped to bring up the four boys and one girl, and her entire life had been devoted to the Klaars. There never were any men in her life: only the Klaar boys and the inevitable slap and tickle with which growing boys, in the days when one had servants, prepared themselves with the half-willing

34

assistance of the family maid for the bigger and better things to come.

Annitschek knew everything. She decided what the sovereign female patriarch should be told, and what not. Of course, she had heard Uncle Fritz's tales before – hundreds of times – but that did not prevent her from listening to them over and over again, for, though she was the true power behind the throne, Annitschek also knew her place. It would no more have occurred to her to tell Fritz to stop boring her than it would have occurred to her to sit down to a meal at the same table with Grandmother or any of the other members of the family. Never mind sitting down to a meal, in spite of over forty years' service, in spite of knowing everything there was to know about every member of the family, she would not, no matter how tired she might have felt, ever have sat down in the presence of a Klaar. I cannot remember ever seeing Annitschek in a chair. It was not that the Klaars were a reactionary crowd and insisted on that sort of servility. On the contrary, I often heard Grandmother say, 'Annitschek, why don't you sit down?' But such invitations towards greater ease and familiarity were quietly ignored. Annitschek, as they say, knew her place and felt comfortable in it. She was interested in power, not in the trappings thereof. And power, as Grandmother's chief counsellor, she certainly held.

Chain-smoking Uncle Fritz was a very handsome man. With his thin, fair moustache, trim figure, well-cut, if slightly fraying suits, he looked the very picture of an Austrian army officer in retirement. He had actually held a commission in the Austrian army and got as far as captain, which was pretty good going for a Jew. Though some years had passed since those heady days, he still looked as if he had just stepped out of a Strauss or Lehar operetta. His sharply well-cut profile had more of an aristocratic than a Jewish air about it. That and the smart army uniform must have been what attracted Aunt Hanna so much that she married him, in spite of the fact that he was a Jew.

Aunt Hanna was not over-fond of Jews. Eventually she even played some sort of minor role among the clerico-fascist ladies of society of the Dollfuss–Schuschnigg regimes. By religion Aunt Hanna was officially an Old Catholic. The Old Catholics split from the Roman Catholic church in 1871 in reaction to the 1870 papal encyclical which proclaimed papal infallibility. The Old Catholics refused to recognise this dogma. Some Austrian Jews therefore rationalised that in some ways it was closer to Judaism and therefore more suitable for Jews to convert to. My anti-Jewish Aunt Hanna was actually born an ordinary Jewish girl. Her maiden name was Hanna Valerie Weiss. Old Herr Weiss, her father, was a well-to-do director of one of Austria's biggest breweries. Hanna's 'flirtation' with anti-semitism was not the result of a strongly held conviction, but of her social ambition. She was a social climber, if ever there was one. When still unmarried the young lady had visiting cards printed which gave her name as 'Hanna v. Weiss'. The 'v' stood for 'Valerie' but was printed in lower case so that any Austrian reading her card would naturally assume that it was the abbreviation of the aristocratic 'von' and that the young lady's full name was 'Hanna von Weiss'.

Not altogether surprisingly the family patriarch had less than no time for this daughter-in-law. To tell the truth, she did not exactly adore any of her sons' wives, but with one exception she adored Hanna even less than the others. In her more outspoken moments, and Grandmother Julie had many of these, she referred to Aunt Hanna as the 'con-woman'. Malicious this may have been, but on the other hand quite a few grains of truth were contained in this disagreeable designation. For Hanna, highly intelligent as she was, was capable of doing the strangest things. She so desperately wanted to find out what her friends and acquaintances thought of her that one day she put her own obituary announcement into the newspapers. Whether it brought her lots of flowers and much pleasure or whether, when it was discovered that she was still happily in the land of the living, lots of problems, I do not know.

I liked the pretty, vivacious, red-head, and though she visited us but rarely (Father was so close to Grandmother that their views on people were usually almost identical), I always enjoyed seeing her. There was something warm and kind in her, even if overlaid by social ambition and a carelessness about money which came close to ruining her and her family. The advent of Adolf Hitler brought out her true self and did away with everything that had been pretence and folly. During the war, though she herself had very little money, she suddenly surprised me by sending very generous food parcels from Australia where she, Uncle Fritz and their daughter had emigrated.

Poor Uncle Fritz was supposed to be a victim of Austria's economic difficulties, one of the many thousands of genteel unemployed who had lost their jobs through no fault of their own. Fritz had been an employee of the Creditanstalt, Austria's biggest bank, which collapsed, or nearly collapsed, during the world economic crisis of the early Thirties. That he was out of a job was hardly his fault. Nevertheless the family's somewhat harsh point of view was that he might try a bit harder to find another one, and that, wherever jobs might be got, it certainly was not in the hall of Grandmother's flat. Did he spend so much time there because he felt safe in the presence of his dominating mother?

From the hall a glass-panelled double door led into Uncle Paul's surgery waiting-room. The surgery had been modernised by Paul after Ludwig's death. It was all steel and white paint, and even his desk was made of metal and new, but the Victorian stuffiness of the waiting-room had been preserved. It was a dark room in spite of two windows looking out into a back yard. There was a big couch, a heavy table, two or three easy chairs, a small table with old magazines, a big painting of Beethoven looking his stormiest, bits of greenery, rubber trees or aspidistras – plants of a sombre green which made this cheerless room look even more depressing. It was gloomy enough to keep the patients away. I never saw more than two or three people in it at a time, and most of them looked like faithful relics from grandfather's time. It was not a flourishing practice. Uncle Paul's main and most important source of income was his salary as a police surgeon.

It should by rights have been one of the most crowded surgeries in the district, because Uncle Paul was a very good doctor, a large, cheerful man, with a tremendous paunch. In spite of all that fat, he was also surprisingly quick and nimble on his feet. He weighed well over 130 kilos, but I shall never forget how fast he could move that enormous bulk when he had to. It was an unforgettable experience to see Paul jumping on a very fast moving tram. This huge man suddenly raced the tram, which gathered speed very fast indeed, and swung himself on to the driver's platform. It all happened at a tram terminal somewhere near the Vienna Woods, the famous and very beautiful area of woods, hills and meadows surrounding the city.

We had been on a country ramble – Paul, Aunt Alice his wife, Didi and Heinzi, their two boys, Leopold Klaar, a remote cousin, his wife Stephie and their fourteen-year-old son Herbert, my parents and I. I was eight or nine years old. We had spent a day walking in the sun and were fairly tired, although I am pretty certain that the day's mileage had been very modest. My father was not one of the great sportsmen of his day, and a short stroll in the woods in his terminology merited the description of a 'walking tour'. At the end of the day our tired and hot crowd stood by the stop waiting for the next tram. What possessed the driver when it finally arrived, the Lord only knows. The three tram coaches slowed down as they went into the curve before the actual stop, approached the stop still slowing as if to halt, and young Herbert Klaar jumped on. Suddenly the driver accelerated, the whole train shot forward, rapidly gaining speed, fast removing the sheepish-looking Herbert from the family party hysterically screaming, 'Stop, stop!' At that moment Paul hurtled his enormous person through the air, landed nimbly on the driver's platform and, after another hundred yards or so at high speed, the tram came to a very sudden stop. Uncle Paul, our hero, had flashed his big enamelled police badge with the Austrian eagle under the driver's nose, shouted that he would arrest him for attempted grievous bodily harm, and naturally the frightened man stopped his tram at once.

That was the Uncle Paul of my childhood, big, strong and always good-humoured, a very different person from the poor burnt-out, guilt-ridden hulk of a man who returned to Vienna from the Theresienstadt ghetto in 1945.

But, besides being a good doctor and attractive person, Paul was also the son of Ludwig Klaar, who had been one of the best known medical practitioners in the Josefstadt district, and its Chief Medical Officer as well. So one would have expected a full waiting-room, a steady stream of patients through those dark glass doors, a continuous ringing of the bell of grandmother's flat.

Was Paul's surgery so empty because of the flat's general atmosphere of days long past, or was it, perhaps, because of Annitschek? She was not a neat doctor's assistant in a white coat opening the door for the patients. Bulky, in a somewhat rusty old black dress, a not exactly spotless kitchen apron over it, Annitschek waddled to the door in her old carpet slippers. It was not her fault. The truth was that time and circumstances were against Paul. There were plenty of doctors in Vienna. The city, with its famous medical school and many doctors of world renown in every field of medicine, suffered from an inflation of physicians. A very few medical geniuses could hope to rise to the top of their profession and to material affluence. Paul certainly did not belong to that tiny group of aristocrats of medicine. In any case, much of his time was taken up by his duties as a police surgeon. It could not have been easy to get this appointment, particularly for a Jew. Possibly Ludwig's connections had helped and the fact that Paul had been the highly decorated medical commandant of a field hospital during the Great War – he was a Knight of the Military Order of Franz-Josef.

Working for the police was no sinecure. When on duty, you were on call at any hour of the day or night. I cannot recall Uncle Paul spending an on-duty evening at any of my parents' dinner parties without the phone ringing and poor Paul, who so loved his food, having to rush off without being able to finish his meal. He had one compensation, and it was one which counted a great deal in a country where to be anyone one had to have some sort of handle to one's name. Paul was gazetted a *Regierungsrat* – Government Councillor – in the mid-Thirties. In Austria a title really matters.

Paul did enjoy life. He loved company and, quite unlike my father, was an eminently clubable person. As a young student he had belonged to one of the university fraternities of the aggressive teutonic duelling and beer-swilling kind, with weird rites and early nineteenth-century uniforms. He had a ready wit and some facility in writing amusing doggerel verse, which made him very popular in his masonic lodge. That Paul should have chosen to join a lodge called 'Schlaraffia' from among the many in Vienna was most apt. Its name comes from the old German legend of Schlaraffenland, a country where scrumptious food and luscious drink are free, but which you can only reach after having eaten your way into it through a huge pudding mountain. For Paul's huge girth was not God-given, but man-made, along do-it-yourself lines. He ate hugely and preferably those goodies which build up layer after layer of fat. Of course, the cult of slim youthfulness (for that matter, the entire fetish of youth) had not yet become the fashion. A good paunch, or to put it more elegantly, a bit of *embonpoint*, added dignity to a man in those days. If he fed well and looked well then he was obviously a somebody. For breakfast Paul sloshed the butter on his crisp rolls, drank innumerable cups of coffee either at home or in selected coffee-houses, each cup topped with thick layers of sugared whipped cream, ate a hearty second breakfast mid-morning so that his system would hold out till he went home for a proper three-course lunch, followed by a little post-prandial snooze, to give all that good food a chance of settling properly on his ample frame.

His afternoons were not exactly austere either. Just across the street from Grandmother's house was the well-known pastry shop of Herr Beisiegl. Every afternoon Annitschek could be seen shuffling over there in her carpet slippers and returning with an assortment of chocolate, cream and other cakes, to be distributed among the family, the lion's share being Paul's, of course. After tea Paul started out on his visits, and as he was offered a little refreshment at every patient's home, he was fairly well sustained till it was time to go home for dinner.

One of my more hilarious memories is of Uncle Paul on a diet. He was nagged into 'fasting' from time to time by Aunt Alice, who was herself a huge eater, much envied by my chubby mother, for the more she ate the more she looked like a beanstalk. Then Paul had honey on his well-buttered breakfast rolls instead of lashings of jam, proudly maintaining that this was true dieting. He also halved the size of the whipped-cream mountains topping his coffees in his favourite café. That was a shrewd ruse, for Aunt Alice sometimes dropped into that coffee-house on a quick tour of inspection. He enjoyed his full portions of whipped-cream coffees in other cafés, which were less likely to suffer lightning visits from Alice.

The family which, of course, means Grandmother Julie, accepted Alice, unlike Hanna – but not uncritically. Alice was considered a bit hysterical and something of a spendthrift. She was certainly a highly-strung person, and this impression was much enhanced by her high-pitched voice. Her nervousness, her quick and somewhat jerky movements, her eardrum-bursting voice, these were enough to label her hysterical. She was an excitable lady, and it was this excitability which led her to make mountains out of molehills, such as the famous 'sex' row which centred on me and temporarily estranged our two families.

It happened when I was about eight or nine years old, and it involved Alice's younger son, Cousin Heinzi, who was roughly one year my junior. Heinzi and I were at my home playing fairly innocent games, like slaughtering my rocking-horse with my toy sabre, when Heinzi, getting tired of such harmless activities, suddenly asked me: 'Do you know what a whore is?' I had never heard that word before, so Heinzi told me that it was a woman you paid to do anything you liked to her – not that he could explain what that really meant. What he did know, though, was that it had something to do with undressing the lady and knocking her about. He had obviously overheard his father talking about the profession. Paul, as a police surgeon, was quite naturally professionally involved with these ladies, mostly after they had been knocked about, or possibly cut up, by their more demanding customers. We decided that Heinzi was to play the whore and I the client. He walked up and down in my room as if it were Kärntnerstrasse, Vienna's most elegant shop-

40

ping street, where the easy ladies strolled of an evening. I played the man-about-town, eager to investigate lady Heinzi's charms. We linked arms and thus approached the place of the 'orgy', my bed.

Although I acted the male, I had, of course, no clue what I was supposed to do. So the better-informed Heinzi took over the leadership. 'You undress me,' he commanded, and I obliged. By this time both of us had really entered into the spirit of this pseudo-heterosexual game with its underlying homosexuality. It all began to seem very real and rather thrilling. Neither he nor I had the slightest idea what was to happen next; all we knew, or rather Heinzi knew, was that beating up came into it. I was the man, I was one year older than my cousin, and quite a bit stronger, and I did what I was supposed to do: I thrashed him. Apparently, even as a child, I believed that if something is worth doing, it is worth doing well, so dear Heinzi got a pretty sound hiding. Under normal circumstances he would have howled the house down, but circumstances definitely were not normal. After all, he was a whore who had been 'paid' for her services. Like a proper professional he bore his thrashing quite stoically, and at the end of the day, when it was time for him to go home, we parted good friends. Little did we know what the future held in store for me.

That evening was Heinzi's bath night. When his loving mummy, Alice, undressed her little angel to put him into the tub she noticed that his pretty little bottom looked rather more colourful than usual. It showed bruises in red, green and black. Painful traces of our 'love-making' were also visible on other parts of Heinzi's body. It did not take Alice very long to get the truth out of Heinzi, except that what he told her was not the true truth. It was I who had seduced him, I who had had the idea of playing whores. It was all my fault. Alice put her angelic-looking son – he really was a pretty child with lots of blond curls – to bed, after having alarmed Uncle Paul that darling Heinzi needed immediate medical attention. Then she rushed out to create hell, havoc and damnation in my life.

When I heard her voice in our hall, pitched several octaves higher even than usual, I had a pretty good idea what her unexpected visit was about. I was in bed by the time Alice arrived, so I quickly switched off my light and shammed sleep. I need not have bothered. The door of my bedroom did not burst open, my outraged parents did not rush in, all I could hear was their voices, and naturally Alice's, which by that time had already started to slide down the scales a little. I fell asleep.

41

My cross-examination started next morning and I established my, at least comparative, innocence. Yes, I admitted, I had beaten up Heinzi; after all he had told me that this was what I was supposed to do, but the whole idea had been his, he had told me about whores, not I him, I had never heard that word before, and it was he who was lying and not I. I was believed. All the evidence indicated that it was much more likely that Heinzi had picked up this knowledge from his father, than that I was a somewhat premature pervert, as Alice claimed. Paul was far more sensible about the whole affair than his wife. My parents' relationship with him remained unaffected by this drama, but it took a while before Alice was again on speaking terms with us. Maybe the family did have a point, after all, and she was a little hysterical.

Paul was later to help my parents and me out of a rather difficult situation in 1936, when I was fifteen and had my first personal confrontation with the rising tide of Nazism. I was by then a pupil at the Schopenhauergymnasium, a rather strict grammar school with a low percentage of Jewish students. For each age group this school had two parallel streams, Form A and Form B. Form A was always the mixed one, Jews and Gentiles, while Form B was kept racially pure.

By this time Austria was a clerico-fascist state, though Kurt von Schuschnigg's regime was not openly anti-semitic. Officially there was no discrimination against Jews, but its power base consisted of various pseudo-military organisations, of which the most important one was Prince Starhemberg's Heimwehr, a fascist militia modelled very much on Mussolini's, and though it had some Jews, mostly baptised, among its officers and publicists, it had a very strongly racial anti-semitic wing.

Whatever assurances Chancellor Schuschnigg gave to Vienna's influential Jewish community, however honestly he might even have meant them, by 1936 the writing, had the Jews been able to read it, was on the wall. Anti-semitism permeated public life. Daily the activities of the illegal Austrian Nazis increased, with their secret S.A. and S.S. cells, and the special terrorist commando groups led by a Viennese gangster of slavonic ancestry called Odilo Globocznik. They planted bombs in Jewish shops and spread fear wherever they could. Globocznik later became the senior S.S. and police commander of Poland's Lublin district, and there he continued on a large scale what he had begun to practise in Vienna.

Great stress was laid in Austrian schools at that time not only on academic achievement, but also on pre- and para-military training. Once every six months the older pupils of fifteen and upwards, were supposed to spend one day on a route march combined with minor military exercises in the Vienna Woods. I had been in Schopenhauer-gymnasium for some five months when the first route march was due. We left the school in fairly smart marching columns under the command of our P.E. teacher. He was a small, wiry chap with close-cropped fair hair. Very tough in manner, looks and behaviour, he seemed the perfect Nazi. After a few hours' marching he ordered us to sing military songs, and we did as we were told. So far it was all good clean fun; it was enjoyable to be out in the open air, and I rather liked playing at soldiers, anyway. We were singing again, when I noticed that our parallel form, the one without Jews, was singing a different song. They yelled at the top of their voices the refrain, 'When Jew blood spurts from our knives,' from one of the vilest of the Nazis' songs, the *Horst-Wessel Lied*. I turned to the boy next to me, a Gentile I liked, and said, 'I'm not going to stand for this. When we get back to school I'll go to the headmaster and make a hell of a row.' 'Why don't you go and complain to the teacher?' the boy asked me. 'What's the use of that?' I replied. 'He can hear them as well as I can. He's doing nothing about it. He's a Nazi anyway.'

On our return, I asked to see the headmaster. I told him what had happened. He listened to what I had to say, promised he would investigate, and dismissed me.

Next morning I was called to the headmaster's office. He received me with the words: 'You'll pack your things this very moment and leave the school. I don't want to see you here again. Your parents will be informed in writing. Out with you!'

I did as I was told. My mother opened the door. I told her my story. She phoned father and he phoned Uncle Paul. Half an hour later Paul was at our flat. If anybody could help me, it was he, with his official title and government connections. And this Paul was more than willing to do. He went to see the headmaster immediately and that gentleman, duly impressed by the Herr Regierungsrat, explained for the first time why I had been thrown out. That Christian 'friend' of mine, to whom I had said that it would be no use complaining to the teacher because he was a Nazi himself, had reported my remark to the P.E. instructor on our return. Although I have no doubt to this day that he was an anti-semite and rather liked that 'Jew-blood spurting from our knives' bit, he was, at least officially, not a Nazi.

What I had not known was that he was actually a very senior officer of the 'Patriotic Youth Movement', Chancellor Schuschnigg's Austrian youth organisation.

The headmaster concentrated on my remark about him. Nothing else mattered, only that I had 'slandered' a teacher. The offending song and its singers were simply not mentioned. When Uncle Paul threatened that he would demand a police investigation into the political affiliations of the teaching staff, the headmaster climbed down and suggested that, provided my parents promised to take me voluntarily out of the school at the end of that term, he would withdraw my immediate dismissal for misbehaviour, which would have meant an end to my academic career, as no other grammar school in Austria would have accepted me with such a black mark against my character. That compromise was accepted. I had no choice but to leave the Schopenhauergymnasium in any case. Had I stayed on, the Nazi boys I had denounced and those teachers who were Nazis would have made life hell for me – for, even if the P.E. teacher was not one of them, plenty of others were. But without Uncle Paul's help no bargain could have been struck.

My father was closest to Paul. His relationship with Fritz was at best tenuous, and that with Josef, the youngest, called 'Pepi' in the Viennese vernacular, hardly existed.

Pepi was rarely at Grandmother's flat. This was because of his wife, Gisi, not any lack of affection for Grandmother and the rest of the family. Pepi, whose full names were Josef Pasquale, was an excellent and highly successful dermatologist. His name was mentioned with respect in professional circles. He was also a gifted cellist and much sought after by amateur chamber quartets. With his thick, curly black hair peeping out from under his wide-brimmed 'Verdi' hat, he looked much more like the musician he would have loved to be than the doctor he was.

I went to Uncle Pepi's surgery only two or three times, but what a difference between his and Uncle Paul's! It was always crowded, patients were constantly coming and going, the door was not opened by an Annitschek either, but by a proper assistant in a proper white coat; and if the assistant of the moment was young and pretty then one would inevitably meet a tall, stern-looking lady, also in a white

coat, busying herself around the surgery. That was Aunt Gisi supervising the practice – or so she claimed. In truth, she was supervising
her romantic-looking Pepi and his lady assistant to ensure that no
hanky-panky developed between them. Not that Pepi would ever
have dared: Gisi had made it absolutely clear that should he ever
get involved with another woman she would as soon kill him as look
at him. Pepi and the rest of the family knew that she was not joking.
This was not even a threat: it was a simple statement of fact. She
was a woman driven by many demons, and that of jealousy was by
no means the least of them. When their daughter Susi was six or
seven years old, Pepi only just prevented Gisi from throwing her
own daughter out of the window of their fourth-floor flat. It happened in the middle of a furious row between the parents. Gisi accused Pepi of loving their daughter more than her. Pepi was still
arguing that this was not true, when Gisi, absolutely beside herself
with rage, grabbed the child and dragged her to the open window.
Pepi managed to stop her just in time.

Gisi was much older than her husband, the official version said by
ten years, but more likely it was something like fifteen. When Pepi
met her he was in his early twenties. Gisi was a divorcee. By her first
husband Erich Störck, a well-known Austrian doctor, she had two
children. She was a woman of strong character and a much-admired
beauty, tall, willowy, elegant; she might have stepped straight
out of a painting by Gustav Klimt. Pepi fell head over heels in love
with her; but when he introduced her to his parents, the mutual
impact was immediate and striking. It ended with Grandfather
Ludwig slapping his future daughter-in-law's face. As later events
proved, old Doctor Ludwig was not a bad diagnostician of character.
I do not know whether it was just Gisi's personality that upset
Grandfather Ludwig so much. or whether the slap in the face had
something to do with the circumstances of Gisi's divorce? As the
court awarded Dr Störck custody of the children, there can be little
doubt that the verdict must have gone against Gisi. Had the husband
been the guilty party, no Austrian court in those days would have
given him the children.

The affair is mentioned in the memoirs of Stefan Zweig's first wife,
Friderike Maria, who writes: 'One of my childhood friends, Dr Erich
Störck, who has just been divorced, has asked me to look after his
children.' Later in her book, after describing the tragic death of Dr
Störck and his second wife, she refers to the bitter circumstances of
Gisi's divorce in these words:

Dear, good, faithful friends! I should have to write a book to describe the battles of your lives, to say something about the valuable human beings you were. You unfortunates, you victims of your sense of duty, you double victims of this terrible war. Your children, Erich, what a bloody battle you fought for them with your first wife, who is undoubtedly pleased now to possess them on her own. Death has given them to her. He was the stronger.

Yes, Gisi was good at fighting bloody battles.

Pepi had a mother-fixation of generous proportions. He was an absolutely classic case, one which did not need a Freud to diagnose. Gisi was the perfect mother-substitute. She gave Pepi some love, and plenty of punishment. The human psyche is a strange instrument, one whose many strings often sound very strange notes of yearning. As the youngest one, Pepi was the much-cuddled baby of the family, the apple of his mother's eye. But he was robbed of this privileged position by the arrival of a still younger sister, the only girl after four boys, the over-protected nestling of the family, Grandmother's undisputed darling. On her the intense and quite overpowering love of Grandmother Julie concentrated, and there was suddenly far too little left for the youngest boy.

All the Klaars seem to have inherited from Grandmother Julie this ability to love intensely but narrowly, to concentrate overpowering affection exclusively on one other human being, leaving too little for others. With Paul it was Alice. What was left was given to the younger of their two sons, Heinzi. Didi, six years older than Heinzi, was asked by his parents on his tenth or eleventh birthday what he would like for his present. 'That Mummy and Daddy love me as much just for one day as they love Heinzi all the time,' he said. This remark was much quoted with considerable wonderment by the whole family. How could the child say such a thing? Surely parents loved all their children equally? Not at all. Young Didi knew what he was saying.

The three elder Klaar boys, Paul, Fritz and Ernst were born in quick succession. Poor Julie had hardly given birth to one baby, when the next one was already on the way. Paul and Fritz were actually born in the same year. Ludwig was obviously very intense, if not in his loving, then in his lovemaking. For Grandmother this conveyor-belt production of sons must have been traumatic. I remember her telling me some forty years after the birth of her last child, still with much resentment, of her cruel fate as a young woman. From the arrival of Paul to the arrival of Sally she had at least one birth or miscarriage per year. She kept saying how much better off women of my mother's generation were, who refused to be mere breeding machines. There was, however, a gap in births, if not in pregnancies, of something like four years between Ernst and Pepi, and a further two years before Aunt Sally was born. For two years much love was lavished on Pepi and then, if I know the ways of the Klaars, there was suddenly nothing. Naturally the older boys were much less affected by this than Pepi, although they all had their mother-fixation too. Pepi's relationship with Gisi can only be explained against this background.

Gisi's great period as a society beauty was in the years before the Great War. And with that domineering determination so characteristic of her she willed time to stand still and remain forever in the period of her greatest glory. She only wore coats and dresses of 'Edwardian' style. Women might show their legs, bob their hair, but Gisi strode out in dresses that swept the ground, did not show a glimpse of ankle and were in complete accord with the fashions of 1908. Let others wear cloche hats: on Gisi's head, pinned to hair piled high, sat one of those huge bird-adorned cartwheel hat confections which were as much *de rigueur* at the court of Franz-Josef as at the Ascot of Edward VII. People stared at her in the street, children pointed and giggled, but Gisi swept past totally unconcerned. Wherever Pepi went, she went: a strange-looking couple indeed, he with his wide-brimmed artist's hat, she on his arm, much older and also much taller, dressed in clothes thirty or more years out of date. Everyone in the district knew them. Everyone made fun of them – behind their backs, of course.

One of the restaurants my father and I liked best was the Goldener Hirsch, a lovely old-fashioned inn which served excellent food. It was in the street in which Pepi lived and had his surgery. He also often ate there. I never forgot the embarrassed look on my father's face one Sunday, when he asked the waiter at the Goldener Hirsch whether Dr Klaar had been there. 'Oh yes,' the waiter replied, 'his gendarme took him away a minute or so before you arrived.' The 'gendarme' was the description by which Aunt Gisi was known throughout the district.

Relations between my parents and Uncle Pepi and his family were somewhat distant, but there was a time when I was about six or seven years old when contact seemed to become closer. I remember

47

being surprisingly invited to one of Susi's birthday parties. That in itself was unusual enough to be remembered, but two other events made that particular party unforgettable for me. The first and less important one was that we were shown some Chaplin films. To have moving film at a private party in those days was quite sensational. It impressed me immensely. More unforgettable even than the film show was that I fell deeply in love that afternoon with one of Susi's little girl friends. It was true love, nothing less. The little girl gave me a present, a chocolate coin wrapped in gold paper. I treasured it for many months. Nobody was allowed to touch this precious gift. It lived on my bedside table by day, and under my pillow at night. It must have been pretty inferior quality chocolate, because even in my hot little hand under my pillow it did not melt. Who knows, this love affair might have had a future had I been invited to Susi's next birthday party and met the object of my dreams again. But that was not to be. Fate struck once more, and for the second time, and no more justifiably than the first, my family reputation as a premature sex-maniac received another boost.

Susi was on one of her rare visits to Grandmother and Aunt Sally. Whether Grandmother had suggested that I should come too, so that we could play together, or whether it just happened that I turned up with one of my parents, I cannot remember. Anyhow, whatever the grown-ups were doing in the living-room, Susi and I withdrew into Aunt Sally's bedroom and played – happily and innocently. It was Susi who eventually suggested that we should play bride and bridegroom. So we fixed the furniture to look like a church altar, and Susi and I were about to march towards it side by side. We were not too well informed about the ritual at these ceremonies, but I suddenly remembered that brides always wear long white dresses with long trains, and that there always is a bridesmaid or a page to hold it up. That to me must have appeared the most important and impressive part of the whole ceremony. I quickly stepped behind Susi, grasped the hem of her dress – the imaginary train, you understand – lifted it up and looked straight at my little cousin's knicker-less bare bottom. Susi, thus desecrated, screamed. Sobbing, she stormed from the room to find sanctuary with the grown-ups from me, the would-be rapist. Grandmother and Aunt were so puzzled by Gisi letting her little girl walk around without knickers, that my part in that affair was overlooked – not by Susi or Gisi, though.

Never again was I invited to any party, birthday or otherwise, at Cousin Susi's.

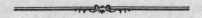

The living-room was the focus of family life in my grandmother's flat. As one entered it through the double door from the dining-room, the first thing one saw was the huge, black concert grand by the two windows. Against the far wall stood a big mahogany bookcase with Grandfather's books and the signed photographs of Sally's three principal saints on its ledge. One, showing an elderly, bearded gentleman, had a dedication – 'To my dear pupil Rosalie Klaar.' This was the great Leschetizky, the most famous music pedagogue and piano teacher of his time. All her life Sally's greatest pride was that this famous musician, himself a pupil of Czerny's, who in his turn had studied music with Beethoven, had accepted her as a student. In the second frame was a signed photo of Gustav Mahler. Sally was an early admirer of Mahler. In the third frame was the sad, aristocratic face of the second-rate Austrian poet Richard von Schaukal. Aunt Sally had set some of his poems to music. The Austrian radio occasionally broadcast her Schaukal *Lieder*. Those were the happiest moments in her short life, not otherwise much blessed with happiness.

One can only hope that Sally never saw an article her idol Richard von Schaukal published in the Austro-Fascist newspaper *Der Heimatschützer* in April 1934. In it he complained about 'the all-too-obvious Jewish influence on Austria's social and intellectual life'. He thought it a 'scandal' that 'Jewish arrogance should distort the true face of Austrian art into an ugly grimace. How can an Arthur Schnitzler, whose work is perhaps worth a tiny entry in the annals of Austrian literature, represent Austrian artistic achievement abroad, or a Sigmund Freud Austrian science?' Why Herr von Schaukal permitted a Jewess to perpetuate this 'scandal' by setting his words to music must remain a riddle.

Against the wall next to the door was the big couch where Grandmother slept. A big table, with three easy chairs grouped around it, stood before it. The surprise among all this heavy and solid Victorian furniture was the big oak wall table on the other side of the double door, the hand-painted Italian majolica mirror over it framed by two huge matching vases. Each vase showed a portrait of the poet

Petrarch, surrounded by ornamental flowers. The magnificent mirror and the vases were a wedding present to Grandfather Ludwig from his sister, the Princess Colonna. I loved looking at it in the evening when its white surfaces reflected the yellow-green tint of the gas-light. Gas-light? But of course! Grandmother thought it much superior to vulgar electricity. Every evening Annitschek shuffled from room to room, matchbox in hand, lighting the hissing gas-lamps.

Aunt Sally tried to earn money as a piano teacher. I was one of her pupils. She was not only an excellent pianist, but also a good teacher. That my piano studies with her were a waste of time, was not her fault. First, I had no talent. Second, she was my aunt, so I felt I could do as I liked. Third, my mother would not allow me to walk around with one of those big, black folders with 'Music' embossed on it in gold lettering, which I had seen other children carry. With that folder under my arm I should ha :e looked very important and artistic, or so I thought. But Mother put her foot down. That sort of display was in extremely bad taste, it was showing off. That was exactly why it appealed to me. With no gold letters it was to hell with music, tearful scenes at home, lessons with an angry aunt, nothing but cheek and laziness from the nephew. Had my vanity been satisfied, who knows, I might have tried long enough to develop a liking for the piano.

Sally's frequent migraines, which made regular lessons impossible, must also be mentioned. These headaches had started when she was a young girl and grew steadily worse as she became older. If I did not know what caused them, I could now indulge in writing pages of pseudo-analysis. But it was not her relationship with her mother, with my grandmother (and what a relationship that was!), nor with her severe Victorian father, that was to blame for her migraines. The cause was a slowly developing brain tumour. It finally killed her in 1942, perhaps mercifully, a short while before the last Jews were deported from Vienna, and Baldur von Schirach, Vienna's Nazi Gauleiter, sent his joyous wire to Hitler: 'My Führer, I report to you that Vienna has been cleansed of all Jews!' Though Sally was surrounded by doctors in the family and must have visited every famous specialist in Vienna in the course of the years, not one of them discovered this tumour until it was too late.

Grandmother lived only for Sally. She was the be-all and end-all of her own existence. No matter on what subject a conversation with Grandmother may have started, somehow, somewhere the subject of poor Sally always came up. Not surprisingly, as time went on, the daughter lived up to her role and came to play the part of 'poor Sally' with some relish. There was, of course, a physical cause, but many, many years before that tumour could have developed, and at a time when her migraine attacks were still intermittent and spaced out over very long periods, Sally realised how they focused her mother's attention and the sympathy of other members of the family on her.

Sally was in her mid-thirties, when Grandmother – who was not for nothing the widow of one physician and the mother of two – finally diagnosed what was really wrong with poor Sally. She was still a virgin. I was not, of course, present at that particular scene between Grandmother and Uncle Paul, but Paul's eldest son Didi was somewhere in the background, and he reported gleefully how Grandmother had been screaming, 'Sally needs a man, she needs a man!'

After that outburst the family scouts were given strict orders to 'find a man for Sally', and a man was found. The source of Sally's future happiness was Dr Robert Friedmann, a concert pianist, like her a former pupil of the great Leschetizky. Robert was tall and bald, with a long arty fringe of hair around his shiny pate, extremely thin, with an intelligent and sensitive face, and a very large, very Jewish, nose. He was a brilliant pianist, but he never made a great career for himself. He was, or at least appeared to me, a first-class nut-case. To hear him play the piano was a joy, but to watch him doing so was to see a performance of more than Chaplinesque eccentricity. His hands flew not only over the piano keys, but all over the place. His whole body went through the most incredible and horrible contortions. His face screwed up into an inexhaustible variety of grimaces. He hummed, sang, snorted, even screamed, while playing.

Robert sometimes played at my parents' dinner parties. He turned up in white tie and tails, which he must have bought when he was an infant prodigy. The trousers were too short, the coat too tight, his waistcoat swam around somewhere in the middle of his starched shirt front; its two pointed ends and the waistband of his trousers had not met in years. His erratic behaviour did not prevent people at private parties from enjoying the brilliance of his playing; but on a concert platform he would have been unacceptable, except, possibly, as a musical clown. His appearance in ordinary clothes was no less hilarious. Out in the streets he wore a wide-brimmed hat, the front of the brim turned up, the back down, and an overcoat a few sizes too large, which made his curious posture, his head between his shoulders and his shoulders hunched forward, even more stork-like. The impression was enhanced by his beak of a nose and trousers always several inches too short, showing his thin legs. That he was not killed very young walking into a bus or tram was nothing short of a miracle. He was always completely absent-minded, presumably engrossed in some symphony or sonata. His guardian angel, who kept him from falling under buses, must also have been a very good street guide, for without such heavenly guidance Robert Friedmann could never have found his way from A to B. Apart from music he had two other passions. He collected sweet-smelling soaps, *eau de Cologne*, all kinds of face creams and an endless variety of cigarette-lighters. He delighted in showing me his treasures, making me play with the lighters and letting me smell his collection of cosmetics.

Besides these passions, Robert had a non-passion : poor Aunt Sally. There was nothing personal in this. It was simply that this gentle-man, found by the family scouts to relieve Sally of her virginity, was impotent. Poor Sally, poor Grandmother. Not having been able to 'deliver the goods', Robert Friedmann was allowed to exist in the family circle very much on sufferance. The marriage, quite apart from not having been consummated, was kept up merely as a fiction, and not even a polite one at that. It ended with Hitler's march into Austria. Dr Friedmann emigrated to England, and the shock of Nazism changed him. It shook him out of the dream world in which he had lived for so long. He settled in Birmingham and married again. This time, however, he led an apparently perfectly normal married life. Possibly his impotence was not a physical, but a psychological malfunction. Probably he already had a tendency to nervous im-potence, and it was brought out by his mother-in-law's all-pervading presence.

Marriage therapy having failed, someone, probably Grandmother, suggested trying bridge therapy – I am talking about the card game. Bridge had become very fashionable in Vienna by then, and every self-respecting coffee-house had a lady bridge teacher on its staff. Naturally it was out of the question for Sally to go and learn the game at a public place. A private bridge circle was arranged; and twice a week a bridge mistress, Sally and two lady friends, spent their afternoons dealing cards in the living-room, their physical needs attended to by Annitschek shuffling back and forth with endless cups of tea, dainty sandwiches and a selection of Herr Beisiegl's delicious cakes.

Aunt Sally was, however, not merely an object of other people's feelings and actions, particularly her mother's, but also a person in her own right. When she felt well she was actually quite an energetic person, someone also with pretty decided views, though whether these were her own or merely echoes of Grandmother's opinions, I cannot remember. Her brothers treated her as the little sister who must not be upset at any cost. Whether this attitude was determined by Sally's state of health or was still part of the boys' Victorian upbringing, which automatically put every female member of the family on a sort of pedestal, I cannot tell.

In all her years Sally had not spent one day away from her mother. Summer and winter, in Vienna and on holidays, year in, year out, these two women stuck together. Every summer they went to Bad Ischl. They always rented the same flat for July and August. The satellite families, that is to say my father's and Uncle Paul's, were assembled in rented flats nearby. Pepi was missing, but so he was from the Vienna flat. In fact, the only real change from Vienna, apart from the better air, was that Fritz, the permanent Vienna fixture, was also missing. It was not lack of affection but lack of money that caused his absence. Sally lived with Grandmother, Annitschek looked after them, and everything and everyone circled round the three women, even more closely than in Vienna, as distances were that much shorter. Sally never had a chance of escaping from her mother's presence. All she did escape from in Bad Ischl were the non-existent affections of her husband. He never came. For Robert Friedmann July and August really were holiday months.

What this life must have done to Sally is only too obvious. No doubt she herself would have protested that she could want nothing better, and even have believed it.

I have a photo of my father showing him as a little toddler of about nine months or so on the arm of his nanny. She, a woman of about thirty, wears the head-scarf, dark coarse dress, over layers and layers of petticoats, and striped apron of the Ruthenian peasant, a family servant who had followed my grandmother from Czernowitz.

This picture must have been taken in late spring or summer of 1890, for Ernst was born in Vienna on 15 October 1889 in Stolzenthalergasse 26. This flat was only about a hundred yards away from that in Josefstädterstrasse. So, when the family moved to the flat I knew, the children remained in their familiar surroundings. It was and still is one of the better', but by no means the 'best', Viennese addresses. The Josefstadt goes right up to the 'Ring' at its patrician end; at its seamy end it disappears into proletarian Hernals. The Klaar residences – Grandmother's, and later also Uncle Paul's and Uncle Pepi's – were all located in the district's middle-class centre. The move from Stolzenthalergasse to Josefstädterstrasse was made when my father was still very young.

Although Grandfather Ludwig was a severe father and Grandmother Julie hardly progressive in the way she brought up her children, with four little boys around the place it must have been quite a lively household. And Ernst, the little boy with the intelligent, questioning eyes, certainly was no angel.

After elementary school he, like his elder brother Paul, went to the famous Piaristengymnasium in the Josefstadt, a grammar school formerly run by the pious monks of the Piarist order. The school building was, and still is, housed in one wing of their monastery. By the time young Ernst entered this school the state had taken over. The severe monks had been replaced by no less severe secular teachers. The school was, and remained, famous for strictness and also for the high quality of its academic standards. In Ernst's schooldays, as indeed in my own, an Austrian grammar school teacher was inevitably addressed as 'Herr Professor', and to a little boy, who, after having passed the not at all easy entrance examination, transferred to a Gymnasium from elementary school where the teachers were only called 'Herr Lehrer' and appeared more or less human, the Herr Professors were demi-gods who had deigned to descend from their Mount Olympus to impart knowledge to that sub-human species in short pants known as Gymnasiasten. I have never forgotten the shock I experienced when I saw one of my professors eat a ham sandwich during break. The thought that professors were real people, in fact minor civil servants, who ate and slept just as I did, had never occurred to me until that moment.

Paul was a first-class scholar, right at the top of his class, Latin and Greek verbs came trippingly off his tongue. Ernst was at best mediocre and battled in vain with Julius Caesar's account of his Gallic Wars. He certainly was not among the top scholars of his form. This tradition, begun by Ernst, was later ably followed by his son, though I, the son, was not told about father's school record until my own schooldays were nearly over. As Ernst knew that he would not be able to study medicine, this may have been the underlying reason for his rather dismal performance.

Ernst left the Piaristengymnasium with just about middling marks at fourteen, and entered the Handelsakademie in 1904. This school, also in the Josefstadt, just a few hundred yards from the family home, had the status of a *Gymnasium*, but specialised in business studies. It was attended by the sons of well-to-do families, often Jewish, who were to follow their fathers in the family business. In father's case there was, of course, no family business to follow. Here he knew that he was preparing for his future career, and he worked hard and well. I found my father's final report dated 1909 among my father's papers in the archive of the Länderbank, the bank where he spent all his working life; it states that he achieved distinction in his studies, that his behaviour was praiseworthy and his diligence persevering. Those were the highest overall grades obtainable. In most of the individual subjects he also got high marks. One teacher who felt that this pupil 'might have done better' was a Mr Henry S. Langridge who, of course, taught English. Ernst did not have a great gift for languages. In his own language, German, taught by a Dr Jerusalem, Ernst got a 'distinction'. Possibly Dr Jerusalem was one of those rare teachers who knew how to arouse their pupils' enthusiasm for their subject. In any case, Ernst grew up with a real love for German literature, for its classical writers and poets. He could recite long passages from Goethe, Schiller and other lesser masters. That I, as a schoolboy, did not share his devotion for classical literature, was a disappointment to him, but by that time the atmosphere had changed substantially from that of his own youth.

The world in which my father grew up was a highly romantic one, a world where young men, literally and figuratively, sat at the feet of writers and poets. Heatedly they argued about the latest poem from the pen of Rainer Maria Rilke, the newest polemic from the rapier-like brain of Karl Kraus; till late into the night they analysed the true meaning of a passage from the latest play by Hugo von Hofmannsthal. The list of writers, poets, musicians who fired their imagination is almost endless. There were few cities in the world where artists were held in such high esteem, enjoyed so much social prestige, as in Franz-Josef's Vienna. But in their art there was also, however subtly, a kind of death-longing, a decadent joy in the decline of Austria-Hungary and of Europe's last 'sunlit decades'. Their spirit of unrest and despair led them into a sick disgust with the civilisation in which they lived, made them yearn for its destruction.

Their writings, paintings, music contained within all their beauty some of the seeds from which grew the blood-soaked poppies of the Great War battlefields. They wanted war, some consciously, some unconsciously. The coming *Stahlgewitter*, the steely thunder of war, was to cleanse their time and them of the supposed evils in and around them. Even the North-German Thomas Mann, so much cooler in his judgment than those Viennese dreamers, shared in that death-wish. In 1914 he wrote:

This world of peace which has now collapsed with such shattering thunder – did we not all of us have enough of it? Was it not foul with all its comfort? Did it not fester and stink with the decomposition of civilisation? Morally and psychologically I felt the necessity of this catastrophe and that feeling of cleansing, of elevation and liberation which filled me, when what one had thought impossible really happened.

Thus the lemmings' suicidal instinct became the ideological aberration of my father's generation. Yes, the Great War was enthusiastically welcomed.

Ernst belonged to a generation profoundly influenced by men and women whose fanatical search for the higher values of mind and soul created an intellectual hot-house atmosphere. Its stifling, humid air produced not only luxuriant blooms, but poisonous weeds as well.

Adolf Hitler was born in the same year as my father.

The 'Imperially and Royally Privileged' Austrian Länderbank was a very distinguished banking institute indeed. It had an Imperially and Royally Appointed Governor, the noble Count Montecuccoli, who was so noble and so privileged that he did not draw a salary. The fee for his services was brought, nay presented, to the Count, only once every year. It was not paid by cheque and ledger entry, or, even more unthinkable, in mere banknotes. On the first working day of each year a leather bag made of the finest calf containing his annual emoluments in gold coins was placed on the Governor's desk. The man who actually ran the bank, its chairman, was somewhat less august a personality than the governor. His name was Herr Lohnstein, whose ancestors' cradles had hardly been standing in

Vienna for many generations, but more likely in places like Czernowitz.

To the Länderbank Ernst, after graduating from the Handels-akademie, sent his first job application:

To the highly esteemed Board of the Imperially and Royally Privileged Austrian Länderbank.

Highly Esteemed Board!
The humbly undersigned permits himself the privilege of begging the highly esteemed Board of the Imp. and Roy. Privileged Austrian Länder-bank, to have the kindness to accept him into the service of their Institute, and permit himself to support this request as follows:

The undersigned is in his 20th year and was born in Vienna. After four years in a *Gymnasium*, he continued his studies at the Handelsakademie, from which as per enclosed report, he graduated with good results. During his years of study he obtained a thorough knowledge of all business subjects, as well as great facility in shorthand and typing. Should the highly esteemed Board have the kindness of responding to the request of the humbly undersigned, then it will be his endeavour to achieve the trust and satisfaction of his superiors through diligence and devotion to duty.

The highly esteemed Board's humble

Ernst Klaar

Humble you had to be as an employee of this highly esteemed institute. The bank's little book, called *Service Rules for Employees*, leaves little doubt on that score. Here is what paragraph 10 had to say: 'Every employee must serve the interests of the bank during official working hours. If necessary he will, on the instructions of his superior, work additional hours.' No question of paid overtime or coffee-breaks. But even during those hours that were the employee's own, the eyes of the bank were still on him. Paragraph 12 enjoins the employees 'to lead a private life giving no cause for annoyance'; and, to make absolutely sure that none of their clerks fell for bar-maids, paragraph 19 specifies that 'No employee can enter matri-mony without the explicit consent of the bank. Such consent can be refused without the bank having to state any reasons for such refusal.'

The bank replied within three days, on 27 September 1909: 'You are hereby requested to present yourself at our offices at 09.30 a.m. on 20 October, in order to sit for an entrance examination.'

After three weeks of excitement and intensive preparations, a few hours of drawing up fictitious balance sheets and writing fictitious business letters at the actual exam, then the interminable waiting period, finally the bank's letter came saying: 'We are offering you employment for a six months' trial period at three crowns per day.'

Ernst's entire future career was decided by this letter. He liked the bank, and the bank liked him. After the six months' trial, he was 'promoted' to temporary employee, and after a further six months given permanent status. From then on life must have looked sweet to the young man. He had a good job, one that offered lifelong security, he earned his own money, but continued to live at home, he sported a smart moustache, making him look more grown-up and more handsome, and pretty girls were, as they always have been, plentiful in Vienna. Father was neither a young blade nor a rake. He had a great liking for female charms, which must have led to romances and affairs during his youth and bachelorhood. Possibly some fathers, as they get older, do tell their sons about their romantic adventures, re-living their early years in the telling. My father was not granted that innocent pleasure, he was not given the time to establish a mature relationship with his son.

The last time I saw him was within one month of my eighteenth birthday, and that was not the time to exchange such intimate memories and confidences. But even without these I knew that my father was 'not made of wood'. I had learned from him what the phrase 'I am not made of wood' meant. Apparently Austrian bosses did allow their employees, when travelling on business, some money for 'wine, women and song'. As long as the amount shown under that heading on their expense sheets was not too large, no questions were asked.

If there was no shortage of pretty young things in Vienna, there was one city in Europe where the supply was at least as plentiful and the ladies even more readily available. That was not the gay Paris of the *belle époque*, but Bucharest, the capital of Romania, the most 'open' city in the most 'open' country at that time in the whole of Europe. It was said that when a gentleman checked in at an hotel and booked a single room, the porter immediately asked whether he wished to sleep with one or two pillows. The curly head for the second pillow usually arrived at about ten at night, on two shapely legs. Father, from whom I have this titbit of information, was certainly an authority on life in Bucharest before the Great War. He was sent there in February 1914 to work for the Romanian Credit-Bank, a subsidiary of the Länderbank.

'What did you do in the Great War, Daddy?' I often asked my father this famous question when I was a little boy. I was then eight or nine years old. The time for these tales was always on a Sunday morning when I was allowed to lie between Mummy and Daddy in their big double bed. All honour to my father for never pretending that he had been one of the first to rush to the colours, that he had done great deeds, or been fired by a desire to lay down his life 'for Emperor and Fatherland'. I probably misquote the official phrase, for 'God' must also have come in somewhere as an incentive for men to have themselves blown to pieces in some filthy, muddy ditch.

The documents I have confirm my father's truthfulness. He went before the recruiting commission in November 1914, and not immediately war was declared, because the Länderbank had certified him an essential employee. His services were needed in connection with the issue of War Savings Bonds. On 27 January 1915, the Länderbank again applied to the Ministry of Finance to free Ernst Klaar from military service. Again they succeeded, but only for a further six months. On 1 August 1915, he put on uniform.

According to those Sunday morning tales, told in the safe and comfortable warmth of the bed, my head in the crook of Father's arm, they first put him into the infantry. The officer-candidate corporal did not enjoy those three months of square-bashing, and even less a short spell with the artillery at the front. So, with his accounting and business background a useful argument, Father applied for a transfer to the Service Corps. Strings were pulled. One of Grandfather's patients, possibly one that Ludwig himself had inherited from his own father, was a certain *Feldzeugmeister* (General of Cavalry) Ballasz. Whether His Excellency was retired or still on active service at that time, I do not know, but he knew the right strings, pulled them, and Father was promptly transferred to the Service Corps. Ballasz was always referred to as 'the man who saved my life', and I can still see and smell in my memory the big hampers of food and drink which Father sent to the General every Christmas until the old gentleman died.

As the Austrian army had no liking for anything simple, and its language a great liking for everything complicated, Ernst Klaar was not just a lieutenant, but a 'Military Administration Accessist', the equivalent rank in the Service Corps. When I was a teenager I found a photo of my father in uniform among Grandmother's old documents. I liked it so much and was so proud of it that I had it enlarged. It was one of my most treasured possessions, and it certainly was in my luggage when I fled Austria but somewhere or somehow to my regret it did get lost. It showed him as very slim. The military tunic with the one gold star on the high collar fitted him like the proverbial glove; he wore very well-tailored riding-breeches stuck into high, black riding-boots, and over his shoulders he had slung a short fur-trimmed military coat. All that, and the black shako, worn at a smart angle on his head, made him look, at least to my eyes, like a true Prince Charming. Father maintained, and I am sure he spoke the truth, that other eyes, of greater interest to him than those of his yet unborn son, also rested with great pleasure on the trim, young lieutenant. He was referring to the Italian girls of Udine, where he was stationed for a time, a town very near Fort Palmanova, where Herrmann Klaar lived through such a harrowing time. He said they called him their *bellissimo tenente*, a judgment his teenage son certainly agreed with.

Father always finished his Great War stories with the remark : 'Thank God, Georgerl, you at least will never see another war. We're a small country now, the Habsburgs have gone. This little republic will never get involved in such horrors again.' His interpretation of history made me unpopular with some of my school friends, when I insisted that the last war was entirely the fault of the Habsburgs – my father had said so – and that without a Kaiser we would grow up in a peaceful world. Actually what I said on his authority with such certainty in school was not quite what my father had said. He had not really blamed the Habsburgs entirely for the war. He was certainly no monarchist, but he had the usual nostalgic respect for old Franz-Josef and some pity for the unfortunate Karl I, the last Habsburg on the throne of the Dual Monarchy.

The Dual Monarchy had reached the end of the long road, it had fallen apart. The Czechs, Hungarians, Poles, Ruthenians, Italians, Bosnians and Croats had ceased being Austrians. Some of them, in the name of national unity and self-determination, founded their own states, others, also in the name of national unity and self-determination, were absorbed into these new states and promptly suppressed with a brutality unknown in the days of the Habsburgs. A suitable epitaph on the Austro-Hungarian monarchy was pronounced twenty years earlier by the founder and first leader of Austrian social-democracy, Viktor Adler. Speaking before the Congress of International Socialist Parties held in Paris in 1889, he said:

Freedom in Austria is a composite creature. It lives somewhere in the middle between freedom in Russia and freedom in Germany. In its form it is German, in its execution it is Russian. With the exception of France and England, Austria has probably the most liberal laws, so much so that it resembles much more a republic, which instead of a president has a Majesty at its head. Unfortunately, however, one does not practise what is laid down by law, but only what suits the police inspector concerned. He is entitled to confiscate all the legally guaranteed liberties, and one can well believe that he uses and abuses this right ... How strange, however: The government of Austria is as incapable of performing acts of justice as it is incapable of performing acts of oppression; it wavers this way and that — we have despotism mellowed by indolence.

As the men of the Czech legions, formerly soldiers of the Imperial army, who had changed sides and fought with the French, the Italians and the Russians against the Austrians, marched into jubilant Prague, Ernst Klaar left his last military post, the Prague military supply magazine, and made his way back to Vienna. He was released from military service on 27 November 1918.

The Viennese popular view of happiness and security was best expressed in a ditty which went something like this: 'No one is as well off as the chap with a secure job with a pension at the end, with a pension at the end.' That was the job Ernst had. The Länderbank had survived the war well. It merely shed the 'Imperially and Royally Privileged' from its name and became the Austrian Länderbank until a little later, being taken over by the French Banque des Pays de l'Europe Centrale, it became the Central European Länderbank. Ernst was not too greatly affected by the political and economic chaos around him, for the 'secure job with a pension at the end, with a pension at the end' was there waiting for him immediately after demobilisation. A bank memo, dated 2 December 1918, says: 'As Herr Klaar cannot, due to present circumstances, return to the Romanian bank, it is suggested that he should join the accountancy department because of his excellent qualifications for this position. It is also suggested that his income should be as generous as possible.'

Within less than a month of leaving the army Ernst was back in the fold, safe and sound, one of the fortunate few. But it was apparently not only good fortune that made the bank keen to have him back and offer him generous terms. He was also, now that war and age had matured him, at the age of twenty-nine, an extremely hard-working and efficient employee. Within three months he was promoted to 'Inspector' – they did and do like titles in Austria, be they ever so curious – and a month later the young Inspector was appointed Auditor to the People's Bank of Galicia in Lemberg, a city now in the new Polish Republic, as well as Auditor of the Länderbank's branch in Prague. This meant travel at a time when very few people anywhere could get outside the borders of their own countries.

At nearly thirty it is time for a man to take stock. The right partner had obviously so far eluded Ernst. In the olden days, back in the Bukovina or Galicia, finding a wife was no great problem. The traditional *shadchen*, the Jewish marriage-broker, was not used by the assimilated Viennese. They spurned the Yente, the match-maker in *Fiddler on the Roof*, but there were, to stay in the idiom of the popular musicals of our time, matchmakers like 'Dolly' of *Hello Dolly* fame. And so a 'Dolly' brought the Klaars together with the Schapiras.

A meeting was arranged at the Café Josefstadt between Ernst Klaar, bachelor aged twenty-nine, third son of Dr Ludwig Klaar and his wife Julie, and Ernestine, called Stella, Schapira, spinster aged thirty, eldest daughter of Bernhard Schapira and his wife Adele. This café was most conveniently situated in Florianigasse, about three hundred paces from Josefstädterstrasse 70, where Ernst lived with his parents, and only a hundred paces from the flat of Stella's younger sister Klara, who also lived in the Josefstadt at Bennogasse 8. This gave the excited young lady a base where she could refresh herself, while Ernst could spruce himself up at home after a day at the bank before the fateful evening *rendezvous à trois*, for 'Dolly' would, of course, be present too.

The Ernst who walked to the café was no longer quite so slim as the young officer on the photo, but he was still a handsome young man. His hair was very dark and with tight little waves; and he wore it rather long as an indication of the romantic poetic soul that dwelt in the young bank inspector's breast. The dark moustache, over the rather thin-lipped mouth inherited from Grandmother Julie, was of the bushy Austrian military kind; later it was most carefully trimmed, his brown eyes looked out from under strong eyebrows of somewhat mephistophelian shape, his nose was Julie's, but smaller, more finely wrought.

Stella, putting another dab of powder on her nose at sister Klara's flat, was tightly laced in a grey silk dress, to achieve a more shapely appearance than that with which nature had endowed her. She was a little on the chubby side, a bit *mollert*, as the Viennese say. Her very straight black hair, parted on the right, had been carefully marcelled and fell attractively over her oval forehead. Stella's best features – and she knew it – were her brown almond-shaped eyes, through which she viewed the world around her from within that eternal haze surrounding the short-sighted. Her small sensuous mouth had a smile of rare kindness and great sweetness, immediately reflected in her eyes. She was a woman to live with. And what was more, as events were to prove, she was a woman to die with.

My grandmother's flat – Grandmother Adele Schapira, that is – took up the entire top floor of a very grand house, Türkenschanzplatz 7, in Vienna's 18th district. The architect, who built it around the turn of the century, had followed the Ringstrasse style. After finishing the outer shell of the building he spattered all over it the caryatids, urns, garlands, figurines, the whole mock-Grecian, fake baroque and pseudo-gothic mixture so typical of all that was rich, but fake and false, in the Empire. Into the red-tiled roof with its copper facings with their green patina, he dipped mock-baroque attic windows. Over the huge green wrought-iron portal, flanked on either side by Grecian pillars, he put a stone ledge and on it generously proportioned classical gods and goddesses. Their stony gaze goes out to this day over the vast green expanse of the Türkenschanzpark just across the road, one of the city's largest and most beautiful.

When I stood before this architectural pot-pourri many, many years after the Schapiras had lived there, my feeling that nothing had changed was so strong that I should not have been at all surprised to see one of Grandfather Bernhard's two 'follies', huge German Adler automobiles, roll up the drive and stop before the green portal. Herr Klein, Grandfather's smartly-uniformed chauffeur, would get out of the car, stand by its open door and wait respectfully for Stock Exchange Councillor Bernhard Schapira to appear. Eventually Grandfather would come out, sniff the air, and then decide which car should be used, the open or the closed one. The whole setting suited Bernhard Schapira, seemed made for him. Wealth, or the appearance of it, rested easily on his six-foot frame. His grey eyes looked out at the world from behind gold-rimmed pince-nez with the masterful composure of the grand seigneur. His clean-shaven face was as smooth and unwrinkled as the skin on his bald pate. He wore a dark formal suit, the top of his waistcoat narrowly trimmed with white braid, and in his kid-gloved hands he held a gold-topped cane.

He was born Baruch Schapira in 1864 in Tarnów, a Galician town, but there was nothing of the East-European Jew about his appearance. He looked very much more like an American tycoon than a European businessman of his time. Wall Street would have fitted him like one of his own kid gloves. This was no coincidence. As a very young man Bernhard had emigrated to the United States and there laid the foundation of his future business career. Somehow this young Jew from Galicia established a connection with one of America's most 'waspish' firms, the Quaker Oats Company of Chicago, in those days already an important company, but not yet, by any means, the highly sophisticated food giant of today. Rolled oats for animal feed and porridge oats for human consumption were its two main products in the Eighties of the last century.

It took some conviction to believe that the people of Bismarck's Reich or Franz-Josef's Monarchy could be converted into porridge-eaters. Oats were fed to horses in those two countries, rarely to human beings. While sound of wind and limb, no good German or Austrian would as much as look at a bowl of good, rich porridge. But when their stomachs were a bit queasy their doctors often prescribed a diet of gruel. But Bernhard Schapira's astute mind must have seen a future in oats, and, even more surprising for someone of his *kosher* background, in bacon and lard. He returned to Austria and established himself as representative of Quaker Oats and Harrison Brand bacon and lard. His business having been established, the next step was to establish a family. He landed in the arms of twenty-two-year-old Udel-Leie (later 'Adele') Immerdauer in accordance with proper Jewish customs and rites.

Adele was the daughter of a well-to-do tobacco dealer. Father Immerdauer was supplier for the Austrian state tobacco monopoly. Adele came from a large family of seven sisters and seven brothers. A photo of this great-grandfather of mine and his wife, taken by one Blachkowski, a photographer in Lvov, about 1870, shows him in the timeless garb of the orthodox Jew. He wears a caftan reaching almost to the ground and a black velvet *yarmulke*, the little prayer-cap, on his head. My great-grandmother's fashionable clothes reflect the period. Her straight hair under a little bonnet is parted in the centre and looks natural. She apparently did not wear the traditional wig of the orthodox women. Although both the Klaars and the Schapiras were Jewish and belonged to the same social level, the marriage between Ernst and Stella united two different strands of Austrian Jewry. The Klaars were Austrians of the Jewish faith, while the Schapiras were Jews who lived in Austria. That Bernhard himself, Stock Exchange Councillor and member of the presidium of Vienna's Merchants' Guild, did not look Jewish, does not change the truth of this. Nor does the fact that he was almost as much of a Victorian family tyrant as Ludwig. The atmosphere in my grandmother Adele's flat bore the stamp of her personality, and that was Galician Jewish.

The difference is revealed in the old photos: of Immerdauer with his caftan and sidelocks, and Herrmann with his ramrod figure and imperial side-whiskers. Both men belonged to the same generation of Jews, both appeared to come from the eastern provinces of the Monarchy, but one had taken the road of assimilation, while the other remained in the world of the ghetto. Although both my greatgrandfathers appeared to come from the same regions of the Monarchy, their ancestors were subject to different historical experiences.

Galicia came to Austria from Poland after the second Polish partition. The Jews of Galicia were polonised and wore the caftan, the garb of the Polish aristocracy they adopted in the late middle ages when the Ashkenazy Jews arrived in Poland from Germany. Being eventually treated as outcasts by their Polish hosts they isolated themselves in their physical and intellectual ghettos.

The Bukovina, the land of the beech trees, had been under Turkish rule until 1774, when the Austrians acquired it from the Turks. Unlike the Ashkenazy Jews, who emigrated into Poland from the fourteenth century onwards, the Jews of the Bukovina had settled there much earlier, the first Jewish settlers probably arriving together with the legions of Imperial Rome. The Turks, much more cruel, but also much more indolent masters than the Poles, did not differentiate between the Jewish and non-Jewish inhabitants of the province. Between periodic outbursts of murder, pillage and rape, of which every section of the population suffered its share, they left the people alone. The Bukovina Jews did not wear clothing that made them look different from other people. They wore the colourful Moldavian costume, did not grow their sidelocks, were much more wordly and better educated in a secular sense than their brethren in Galicia.

Between the Galician Jews and the Poles there was a relationship, based not on love but on hatred – but nonetheless a relationship. Between the Turks and the Jews of the Bukovina there was no relationship whatsoever. The Austrian troops moving into the province were welcomed as liberators by the entire population, including the Jews, while to the Poles of Galicia the Austrians were an army of occupation. It is not surprising, then, that the process of Germanisation, the identification with the language and culture of the liberators was immediate with the Bukovina Jews, and the contact direct. In Galicia the Polish aristocrats remained the masters of their Jews, interpolating their own culture between the Jews and the Austrians, making Germanisation or Austrianisation, even for those Jews breaking with orthodoxy, a much slower and more difficult process. Historical and cultural factors thus combined to create a unique phenomenon in European Jewish history: an enclave of westernised Jews in the most eastern of the Imperial provinces, an oasis of western culture with the Jews both carriers and devotees of the Austro-German language, its art and literature.

This explains how Herrmann with his gold-tasselled sabre, three gold stars and spurs, came to stand in my lineage next to the caftaned tobacco-dealer Immerdauer; explains the different background from which the highly educated and musical Julie came as well as Adele with her slightly Yiddish-accented German. The Klaars and the Schapiras represented two different Jewish worlds which eventually became one again – behind the gates of Auschwitz.

Ernestine Schapira, my mother, was born in Lemberg, or to use the Polish name, Lwów, on 13 February 1889. Adele was still living with her parents, because Bernhard travelled virtually all the time, building up his business. All her adult life Adele was fat, but also very pretty. She had a certain inborn shrewdness, the inherited Jewish wit of old Immerdauer, but she lacked formal education. Orthodox Jews, like the Immerdauers, had the highest regard for learning in men; women had to know how to run a home, and, though they usually ran their men as well, books and knowledge were not for them.

Adele was a marvellous housewife. Everything was absolutely spotless; and she was an exquisite cook. She did not stand in front of the pots and pans herself, there was a cook to do all that; but by putting a bit of salt here, a tiny quantity of sugar there, Adele turned the good into the excellent. Altogether she possessed *tahm*, a Yiddish word meaning the ability to change without apparent effort the commonplace into the superb. Grandmother Julie did not have it, neither in the kitchen – which, in any case, was Annitschek's realm, and I do not think I ever saw Julie doing anything there – nor in most other things. But coming from an assimilated background Julie was highly educated. She continued to study even after her marriage, and the range of her intellectual interests was wide. She had much greater inner resources than Adele. After Ludwig's death Grandmother Julie continued her own life. Bernhard's death destroyed Adele. She never ceased grieving. She was a broken woman.

My mother was given the name Ernestine, presumably that of some long-departed Immerdauer or Schapira relative. Jews never give their children first names of relatives still living, but the memory of the dear departed is often honoured in this way. Whoever that deceased aunt, cousin, or great-grandmother might have been, her honour was very short-lived. 'Ernestine' was never used. My mother was known as 'Stella' from birth.

If Bernhard and Adele could have waited only another two years before having their first child they would not have upset my 'Austrian' susceptibilities. For years I resented the fact that my mother was born in Poland. They moved to Vienna in 1891, and there in 1893 Stella's sister Klara was born. Their first stay in the Austrian capital lasted only eight years, because the Quaker Oats Company had run into problems with their representative in Germany, and Grandfather Bernhard was asked to take over and sort things out. He established his office in Kaiser Wilhelm Strasse in Hamburg, the Reich's biggest port and centre of its import and export trade. When Stella was ten and Klara six, the family's new home was found in the Winterhude district by the Outer Alster, the bigger of the two lakes around which the city with its many green church spires is built.

It naturally took some time for Bernhard and Adele to adjust to their new surroundings, but the two girls, Stella and Klara, adapted, as children always do, very quickly. You could tell from the way both sisters always talked of their Hamburg years that it was a happy time for them. My mother never lost a certain nostalgia for that city, which to her also represented the last years of her childhood and the time of her growing-up. There the dreams of the young girl were dreamed and the fear, sadness, uncertainty and the hopes of puberty experienced. She often said how much she would like to

67

take me to Hamburg, show me the city, to which she only returned once, in 1929, when she and father spent a holiday travelling through Germany.

The family lived in Hamburg until 1906. Stella and Klara did not go to school there, but were sent to a boarding school for *höhere Töchter*, or 'higher daughters' that is to say young ladies from good families, near Hanover, where, so at least the Hanoverians claim, the best German is spoken – a claim which, where Mother was concerned, was certainly justified. She spoke neither with a Viennese accent, nor with the harsher, more Prussian sounds. She had a soft alto voice, which made her very pure German sound particularly mellifluous. The close friendships she made with many non-Jewish German girls at that school lasted for many years. Some kept in touch with her even after Hitler had become Chancellor of the Reich.

There are certain qualities in the North German character which corresponded to Stella's own. Though herself a warm – even an emotional – woman, she did not like to show her feelings except in her most intimate circle. She always tried to remain calm and controlled, to let her intellect and not her emotions determine her views and her actions. In that she was the ideal partner for my father, with his highly variable temperament, which often led to outbursts quite out of proportion to their causes. There is a certain similarity between North German and English attitudes. This affinity was also brought out in Stella's boarding school, which taught the girls to think clearly and objectively, to avoid mental flabbiness. Again this made her very different from my Viennese father, whose personal views and relationships were all too often determined by subjectivity, sometimes even by a not altogether healthy form of romanticism.

In school and also at home Stella earned herself a reputation for being a bit of a blue-stocking. Wherever one saw her she had her nose stuck in a book, her eyes, already short-sighted and bespectacled, flying over the pages. And she loved to tell stories. At the Hanover boarding school the younger girls flocked around her and listened to her gentle voice telling tales from Dickens, whom she loved above all other writers.

The point came when Stella told her parents that she wanted to continue her education at a university and eventually become a teacher. Adele sighed, she saw no harm in her daughters being better educated than she was herself, but their ultimate destiny was to be wives and mothers. Bernhard exploded. He was not going to stand for that sort of nonsense. He was perfectly capable of providing for his family. She, of course, accepted Papa's verdict.

During their whole childhood she and Klara, and the family's late arrival Louisa – called 'Lisa', born in Hamburg in 1902 – were taught to believe that the last word on everything was Papa's. If Papa felt slightly unwell, everyone had to be absolutely quiet, voices had to be hushed, movements subdued, no friends could come to the house to play, the whole world went dark behind drawn shutters : Papa had a headache. Even when she and Klara were grown-up young women, back in Vienna, and had tickets to the theatre or the opera, Adele would plead with her daughters not to go, because Papa was in one of his moods. Of course, they stayed at home.

My first experience of Judaism occurred in Grandmother Adele's flat. It was the Seder evening of the 1925 Passover celebrations. Mother and I had gone to Türkenschanzplatz in the early afternoon so that I could have a rest before the other guests came. They arrived at seven. Ernst Lamberg, Lisa's fiancé, came with his parents, a tiny little gentleman and a tiny little lady. They looked more like china figurines than real people. Aunt Klara and Alfred, her husband, came with their seven-year-old daughter Hedi. Adele's sister Netty, her grown-up son Oscar and my own father were the last to join us. We were fourteen sitting around the extended dining-room table with its gold-damask tablecloth, sparkling glasses, gold-rimmed plates and shining silver. The ladies wore long dresses and were adorned with their best jewellery, the men had dinner-jackets, and on their heads bowler hats instead of the traditional *yarmulkes*, the skull-caps of the orthodox Jews. At Stock Exchange Councillor Schapira's Seder evening city hats were *de rigueur*.

Grandfather Bernhard with his pince-nez was throned in majesty at the head of the table. Grandmother was on his left, and I sat next to her on a chair piled high with cushions. It is usual for the youngest male present to recite the *Mah Nishtane*, the introduction to the tale of Exodus, beginning with the question : 'Why is this night different from all other nights?' Those assembled reply, and thus, in question and answer, the story of the Jews' flight from Pharaoh's Egypt is told. While the recital goes on certain rites are performed, as each morsel of food that is taken during it symbolises the sufferings of our long-distant forefathers as they baked the bricks for the great pyramids in the hot Egyptian sun, the whips of the overseers lashing them, so the story goes, to ever greater effort. As I was too young to be able to read in any language, my seven-year-old cousin Hedi, strongly assisted by Aunt Lisa, had to stammer through the *Mah Nishtane*.

The dinner that followed was rich and long drawn-out, the two maids who were serving being commanded by meaningful glances from Grandmother Adele. Everything was perfection, and I was on my most angelic behaviour – not because the spirit of Judaism had entered into my soul, but because I saw before me a prospect of substantial personal gain. Grandmother had told me in the afternoon that she would hide a little piece of *mazzoth* in the course of the dinner, that this was called *affikomen*, and that it was always the youngest child at table who found it and could then claim a reward for its cleverness. So, as soon as Grandmother had hidden the *affikomen*, she bent down to me and whispered into my ear where I could find it. I could not but win and get my heart's greatest desire, a toy pedal car painted in the brightest of bright reds. My rich grandfather was going to give me that red four-wheeled heaven.

It took Moses some forty years to get his Jews into the Holy Land. To me, that dinner, merely commemorating the start of that journey, seemed to take a great deal longer. Course followed upon course. Eventually I began to get edgy. Grandmother noticed. She bent down and whispered that it would not take much longer till the great moment arrived. I knew exactly what it would be like. Grandfather would look up and ask if anyone had seen the *affikomen*. My hand would shoot up, my crumbly treasure in it. Bernhard's stern face would almost crack into a smile. I would state my wish. His hand would go to his breast pocket and he would take out his wallet. He would open it and take out the banknote with which I would buy the jazziest pedal-car in Vienna.

'Anyone seen the *affikomen*?' Grandfather's voice boomed at last. I held it up. 'So you've found it. How clever of you, dear child. You've earned a reward, you know. What would you like?' 'A toy car, grandpapa, please,' I replied. His right hand began to move – but not upward towards the wallet with the banknotes. It went down into his trousers pocket, and when it came out all there was in it was one lousy Austrian Schilling. You could not even buy a little model car with that.

I should have known, of course. For was there ever another grandfather who welcomed his grandchildren, when they came to visit, quite the way Bernhard Schapira did? When cousin Hedi and I arrived at Türkenschanzplatz (we were usually asked together so that we could play with each other and keep out of the grown-ups'

70

hair), Grandfather would eventually unfurl himself to his full height from his chair. Inviting us to follow him, he then strode into his study. There he would stop before the big bookcase, fetch his bunch of keys, secured by a gold chain to his braces, from his trousers pocket and unlock the right-hand bookcase door. This whole performance had the ceremonious air of a rabbi unlocking the door of the tabernacle in the synagogue before taking out the holiest of the holy, the scrolls of the Torah. What Grandfather Bernhard took out of his bookcase was a big bar of cooking chocolate. He broke off one rib for Hedi, one for me. Hedi curtseyed her thanks, I bowed from the waist. The cooking chocolate was put back in its drawer, the bookcase locked, the keys returned to the pocket. Grandfather's generosity towards his grandchildren, as well as his interest in them, was over.

The second Jewish experience of my early childhood was just as painful as the disappointment with the *affikomen*. It came on my sixth birthday. On that day Father announced that there would be no more Christmas tree and Christmas presents in future. I was old enough to do without it, we were Jews after all, and anyway my birthday was only three days before Christmas.

When I started to ask Mother how she and Father had met, she told me that there had been a lady, a mutual acquaintance, who had thought it a good idea for her to meet Father. That this enterprising 'mutual acquaintance' was actually a professional matchmaker I eventually learned from Annitschek. She, good soul, gave away the secret inadvertently. What she really wanted to tell me was how exciting and romantic my parents' first rendezvous had been; how father had returned from Café Josefstadt announcing jubilantly: 'I have found my love at last. Stella is the woman for me; she and no other!' And then Annitschek let the cat, or rather the 'Dolly' out of the bag. 'Who'd ever have thought,' she said, 'that such an arranged meeting could lead to love at first sight?'

Mother's reaction to Ernst was, so she said, slightly less enthusiastic. 'I didn't quite know,' she told me, 'what to make of that long-haired young man who wore his airy-fairy poetic soul for all to see. I'd imagined young bankers a bit different. Still, there was something about him I liked. We said we'd meet again.'

Ernst was a man for overstatements, Stella a woman for under-statements. But there must have been something in that soulful banker which captivated her. They met for the first time in the Café Josefstadt in October 1919, by the second week of November they were engaged, and six weeks later Inspector Ernst Klaar of the Länderbank wrote to his superiors:

The undersigned wishes to inform the esteemed Board that he and Miss Stella Schapira were married on 21 December 1919.
    The esteemed Board's faithful servant

                                                            Ernst Klaar

One notes that it is no longer the 'highly esteemed' Board. This august body is now merely 'esteemed' and Ernst is no more its 'humble', but merely its 'faithful' servant. One also notes that Staff Rule No. 19 – 'No employee can enter matrimony without the ex-plicit consent of the bank' – is ignored. The Board is only told after the event had taken place. Now that was good enough.
    Times had changed.
    Ernst and Stella had become citizens of 'The State Nobody Wanted', which was sketched into the map of Central Europe by the victors of the Great War. The men now running Austria were not the same who had ruled the Monarchy. They had not started the war. They were good Social-Democrats, not Habsburg imperialists, but as a non-Imperial Austria had never existed before they could not understand how one could possibly be viable now, and so they called it the 'German-Austrian' republic. That name had some mean-ing, for all that was left of 'Austria' were six million German speakers. More dangerously, 'German Austria' was not only a name, but also described political aim and programme of Austria's moder-ate Left. As they saw it, this rump Austria could not live on its own. They wanted to join the new democratic Germany, they wanted the *Anschluss* to the Reich. The Allies would not hear of it. They had not fought the German Reich for four years to make it now, in defeat, a power with borders reaching from Hungary and Italy right up to the Baltic Sea.
    Austria's moderate Right, the Christian-Socials, Dr Lueger's heirs, viewed the *Anschluss* policy with mixed feelings. They wanted a Danube Federation, geographically integrating most of the territories of the former Monarchy. But the successor states would not hear of it. A Danube Federation to them was nothing but the Habsburg

empire by another name. Both the Social-Democrats and the Christian-Socials agreed on one point only, the crucial one: an Austrian state of only six million people could never survive on its own.

The capital of this state condemned thus to spiritual death at the very moment of its birth, the once glittering Imperial city of Vienna, was destitute. It was reduced to chaos and misery. The city's chief medical officer reported that at least 20,000 children were close to starvation. 130,000 men, a high percentage of the working population, were unemployed. Every day money bought less and less. Every day, even with money, there was less and less to buy. One violent demonstration followed another. People died in the streets either of bullets or of hunger. Ill-clad they shuffled through the town, past rubbish heaped in its parks, through streets littered with refuse, looking for work, for scraps of food, for hope.

That was Vienna in the winter of the year 1919, when Ernst left Grandmother Julie's flat and Stella Grandmother Adele's, to begin their life together. In the last week of December 1919 they moved into their new home. My parents' flat was in Pichlergasse 1, in Vienna's 9th district.

Part Two

The woman opened the door of my parents' flat. She was over sixty, fat, slightly embarrassed. She asked me in, and for the first time in thirty-six years I stepped again over the threshold of my home. I had had many homes during those years I had slept in countless beds in many countries, but even after all this time whenever I said 'home' I still meant my parents' flat in Vienna, where I spent the first seventeen years of my life. No other home could be like my childhood home, could enfold me in that feeling of utter security, of all-embracing warmth and love and offer that utter certainty that no evil could reach me.

In my imagination I had revisited the flat often. Hand in hand with my father I walked through the rooms. He had liked to do this from time to time. He called it 'our museum round'. Together we looked at his pictures, at the bronzes and the beautifully carved and painted eighteenth-century wooden harlequin balancing a saw-blade clock on his forehead; at the furniture, the Louis XVI bedroom, the French writing-desk in father's study, the work of a Herr Gruber, one of the last true masters of the cabinet-maker's craft in Vienna; and, Father being Father, he proudly said what he had paid for his treasures, estimated present value, and always ended our 'museum round' with the words, 'and one day all this will belong to you, Georgerl'.

The flat where I walked with Father in my memory was big and spacious. It paired elegance with comfort, and, seen through the eyes of the child and growing boy, it encompassed within its walls everything that was beautiful and good and kind, everything that was my parents' life and my life, all that the word 'home' can mean.

Now, after so many years, I was in my parents' flat again. By my side was not my father, but that blowsy elderly blonde, sweet kittenish Viennese girl of yesteryear. And I had to accept that my parents had lived in two flats; the flat the eyes of the boy had seen and recorded, and the flat as it really was, the one the eyes of the man were looking at. For one moment as I stood in the hall, my lips forming words empty but polite, I thought I had made a mistake and gone to the wrong floor, but then, as I turned round I saw the protective steel strips my parents had fixed inside the entrance door to make it burglar-proof. I remembered the blue-overalled locksmith and his apprentice putting them up. I remembered my mother watching with scarf tied over her head and duster in her hand. It was dirty work, and Mother pounced on dirt like a snake at a rabbit. There they were still, these firmly fastened strips of steel no burglar could ever have broken through, but the criminals who eventually came to frighten and to steal did not have to use physical force to break in. The key of terror opens all doors, however well they may be protected.

I was in Flat 9, Pichlergasse 1. I was in my home.

I walked through all the rooms, and each was as it had been and at the same time each was different. I saw that our home had neither been as I had remembered it, nor had it been the place I now looked at. I felt resentful that strangers had imposed themselves on my memory of 'my' home. At the same time I felt ashamed of this re-action. I sat with the woman round the table in the middle of the dining-room, the very same spot where our dining-table had stood, I sipped at a glass of wine and made courteous noises.

Before leaving I asked her permission, readily and kindly granted, to walk alone round the flat once more. I went back into the hall. Through the door on the left I entered the kitchen where I had spent so many hours sitting on the coal-box dangling my legs and watching Poldi, our maid, one of the great influences of my childhood, busying herself in front of the kitchen stove, one of those old-fashioned iron ones fed with coal. I went into what had been Poldi's room through the door at the far end of the kitchen. It still had the knife-marks I made in it, when mad with jealousy on discovering that Poldi was engaged to be married, I, her eight-year-old lover, had taken the kitchen knife and stabbed the door again and again, screaming under my tears, 'That's for him, that's for him!' Other maids had slept there after Poldi, but to me that tiny, dark and dingy place, now used as a box-room, had always remained Poldi's.

Back through the kitchen into the hall, and a quick look into the tiny bathroom behind the second door on the left, scene of many battles between Mother and me about face-washing and teeth-cleaning, and all the greater and smaller principles of cleanliness and their importance for my present and future well-being. I fought hard against the fact of washing, I argued against its underlying philosophy. Of course, Mother had the better arguments, but I knew how to resist them and made important points, or so I felt, in favour of the unwashed state. Yet in the end brute force always won as Mother slapped the wet, soapy face-flannel on to my cheeks and started polishing away, ignoring my screams of protest that nothing of my face could possibly remain after this torture.

Our telephone was fixed on the wall in the corner next to the bathroom door and hidden by a heavy curtain. How old was I when it was installed? Three or four? I shall never forget the excitement when the black box with the white centre disc – it was a party line and when the other party spoke, the disc changed to black – was ready for use and we called father in his office. Nor shall I ever forget 'A–16–7–51', our Viennese telephone number, though I cannot recall the numbers of any of the telephones in my own past homes.

The small white door behind the telephone curtain opened into my parents' bedroom. I walked through it, ignoring the heavy, dark bedroom suite belonging to the woman, but recognised the green tile stove, our only source of warmth in the whole flat in the terribly hard winter of 1928, when cars drove over the frozen Danube, and coal became so scarce that only this one room could be heated.

Through the door on the right, next to where my parents' bed had stood, I went into my room, now that of the woman's thirty-year-old son, filled with jumble sale furniture. In the far corner my cot had stood. I was in it when Poldi came to apply for the job of nanny. According to my mother I had jumped up with outstretched arms and shouted 'Upuldi, Upuldi!' – undoubtedly my very earliest experience of love at first sight.

Later, my little bed had stood in the same corner, and on it I had performed my nightly 'good night' ceremony before the eyes of my adoring parents. I hopped up and down on the bed, lifted my little nightdress so that my naked bottom stuck out and yelled, 'The moon's coming out, the moon's coming out' and then collapsed giggling on to my sheets. Later, much later, my couch stood there and on it I dreamed my hot dreams of girls and women and sex, visualising how it would be again and again until, in theory, I had

77

performed every act and every contortion I had ever heard and read about, and in so doing created the most heavenly state of delight in myself and my partner.

And on this very couch I, the great theorist, the great know-all, did indeed have my very first sexual experience. But when it came to it, neither I nor the girl had the slightest idea what we were doing. It just happened. I did not knowingly enter her, but in the course of our petting I actually fell into her. It was all instinct, and none of it the gentle progress towards the great and final act of union I had read so much about. My disappointment and confusion were such, her tears of shame, surprise and fear flowed so profusely, that now that the great moment I had been longing for so much for so many years had come, I wished it had not happened.

Not surprisingly this scene, the most dramatic to have occurred in this room, came back into my mind as I looked at it. I turned to go back through the bedroom and its double door into the dining-room, banishing from my mind memories of how this had been the centre of our family life, not wanting to see my parents sitting there, not wanting to experience at that moment the pain indivisible from such remembering. The time to think and feel would come, but later, not now with that woman and her son by my side.

Finally, Father's study immediately adjoining the dining-room. It had a peculiar, rather elegant shape, trapeziform with one corner cut off. The room was in the corner of the building and its two windows offered different views. One looked out at the relative quiet of Pichlergasse, the other on the much busier Nussdorferstrasse, with its trams, cars and shops. Equidistant from both windows, exactly at the corner of the building, the cut-off corner of the trapezium in fact, a pair of French doors led on to the small wrought-iron balcony. The flat was on the first floor, but as all old Viennese houses have mezzanine floors, it was really the second and fairly high up. I rarely stood on our balcony. The feeling of vertigo which affected me made me fear that balcony and I could, at any second, tumble down on to the street below.

Their brief honeymoon over, Ernst and Stella established themselves in Pichlergasse, named after Caroline Pichler, poetess and foremost social chronicler of the Congress of Vienna.

Between Ernst and his new in-laws there was no honeymoon, however short. The problem was that Bernhard Schapira was not my father's type of person. The air of arrogance and tycoonery with which that tall gentleman looked down through his pince-nez on his son-in-law, grated on father's nerves, as did his unspoken, but implied, 'I suppose that young bank clerk had to do for Stella – after all, she was getting on a bit.'

Naturally it would have been difficult for Ernst to tell his bride right out, 'I don't like your father very much. The less I see of the old so-and-so the better.' He needed a good excuse for having as little to do with the Schapiras as possible. Grandfather Bernhard very obligingly provided it. On one of his early visits to Pichlergasse Father happened to point to the bare floors and mention that he had no money for carpets. Bernhard took this remark as the all too blatant hint it was. 'What d'you want carpets for,' he grumbled, 'cut up a few sacks if you need some floor covering. That'll do for a beginning.' Father loved this story. He told it again and again and always within my hearing. Mother protested that it had not been like that. It had been a joke, perhaps not a very good one, but a joke just the same. Father would have none of it. The story suited his purpose, and as he, like all the other members of the Klaar clan, had somewhat individual ideas about objective truth, he stuck to his view that Bernhard was a mean old miser. At best his relations with Mother's parents and her wider family were correct, at worst they supplied the raw material from which lovely scenes and rows could be created, an art at which Ernst was no dilettante.

The fourth member of our family, Poldi, our maid, was probably more important to me during my early years than either Father or Mother. A tough, resolute twenty-year-old Viennese working-class girl, she was unburdened by any but the most elementary education. She had never read a book on how to bring up children. But she knew. Poldi was the best and the wisest educator for a little boy like me. I loved her dearly. The way in which she dealt with me was simple and effective, though not always truthful. Until my parents went to sleep my father's bedside lamp was always left burning. One night, when I was four years old, I woke up. I called out, expecting to hear Father's grunted 'Go back to sleep, darling,' in reply. No answer came. No light either. I knew that something terrible must have happened. My parents lay murdered in their beds, their bodies bleeding from hundreds of stab wounds. I screamed. It must have been some scream for Poldi to hear it in her room behind the kitchen.

She came running, switched on the light and took me into her arms.

'Whatever's the matter, Georgerl?' Eventually I managed to control my sobs and told her. 'But you know that Mummy and Daddy are at a ball. It's only midnight. They won't be back till early morning,' she said. 'Why isn't the light on?' 'Oh,' she said, 'I was going to tell you in the morning. You see, a policeman saw the light from the street. He thought there must be a burglar in the flat. So he came up. When I told him that we kept the light on because you are afraid of the dark, he said we mustn't do that. It is very naughty to mislead the police. It's not allowed, he said. Angry he was, really. So, no more lights next door or we'll all get into trouble.'

And I actually believed every word of this cock-and-bull story. Dear Poldi had simply decided it was time I stopped being afraid of the dark. Once dear Poldi had decided something, that was that. And Poldi knew the psychology of a little Austrian boy. I would argue with my parents, I would even argue – sometimes – with Poldi, but never, never, never would I argue with a policeman. The green-uniformed guardian of the peace, armed to the teeth with long sabre, revolver and rubber truncheon, represented the ultimate in authority.

Poldi's 'applied psychology' worked, and from then on I went to sleep in the dark. Happily? Of course not! That fear of my poor parents lying butchered in their beds next door did not disappear for a long time. But that was something I had to deal with myself and silently. There was no other way. The fear of an angry Austrian policeman was the greater of the two.

Father was a first-class chartered accountant and an extremely hard worker. Many a Saturday afternoon and many a Sunday he spent behind his desk at home reading balance sheets, checking accounts, writing reports. On those occasions he was helped either by Fräulein Grossfeld, his own secretary, or by Fräulein Blankenberg. Hedwig Blankenberg worked in the secretariat of Herr Fischer, one of the Länderbank's two chief general managers, so Father could not just summon her. But he found a very Viennese way round this difficulty. He 'borrowed' her, as it were, under the pretence that 'My wife likes you so much, you know; why don't you come and have lunch with us this Sunday. Come about eleven and spend the day with us.'

Hedwig Blankenberg knew, of course, that Mother would be charming and kind, but that she felt no particular longing for her company at any time, and never on Sundays. Fräulein Blankenberg played her part in the game. She accepted the invitation 'with great pleasure; I look forward so much to meeting your wife again', but she also made sure of bringing her shorthand pads and lots of well-sharpened pencils for this 'social' occasion.

Of all the Viennese banks, the Länderbank was one of the most successful and most carefully managed. It survived all the storms and economic crises of the late Twenties and early Thirties, not merely because of its French connection. The two chief general managers, Fischer and Bergler, were highly astute bankers. They and their immediate chief, M. Reuter in Paris, kept the institute on an even keel.

The Länderbank, most likely because it was French-owned, had remained a substantial shareholder in leading Czech and Hungarian banks. As Father audited the books of most of these holdings, his work necessitated a considerable amount of travel and frequent, often rather long, absences from Vienna. An ability to speak languages would undoubtedly have been a great asset to his work, but though he was a genius at accountancy, when it came to languages, his was an absolute anti-talent. He was the only person I knew with the peculiar and highly individualistic trick of pronouncing English with a French accent, and of chewing French words round in his mouth as if they were English. What he might have done to such difficult languages as Czech or Hungarian, had he ever attempted to speak them, defies the imagination. In any case, the language spoken by the figures in the ledgers he examined was his *lingua franca*. He once had to go to Croatia to check the books of a firm which was in difficulties. The Croats spoke Croat, or Serbo-Croat – it did not matter which, he did not understand either – he spoke Viennese German which they could not follow, but even so, he very quickly found out that the books had been fiddled, and how the fiddling had been done.

Father loved the bank and his work and put his responsibilities there very high, if not at the highest point, on his scale of priorities. And yet, in spite of his devotion to the bank, in spite of his love for banking, he kept saying to me : 'You're not going to become a banker when you grow up.' Perhaps it was because of his disappointment at not having been allowed to follow an academic career. This must also have been his underlying motive for inventing a sort of 'What's my line?' game long before T.V. did. It was played with a panel of one – me – either in the street or in a park. Father would leave me standing at a street corner or sitting on a park bench; then he walked away a few yards, turned round and came towards me. It was my job to guess the profession of the 'strange' gentleman approaching me. He was most pleased if I put him into the academic intellectual bracket. Medical doctor or lawyer was good, university professor was better, famous writer was best. But filial popularity went right down to zero on the day when I felt either cheeky or angry or both and came up with 'a Jewish pedlar'.

Perhaps Herr Josef Lippert, father's personal barber, had something to do with Father inventing 'What's my line?' Lippert, whose barber's shop was round the corner from Pichlergasse, was awarded Father's 'by appointment' warrant in 1920, after Father had been promoted to *Oberinspektor* by the bank. Every morning, weekdays and Sundays, punctually at 8.15, Lippert entered the Pichlergasse flat with a breezy 'Good morning, *Herr Oberinspektor*. Good morning, madam.' Father had long since become a *Herr Prokurist*. In Vienna you were inevitably addressed by a title at least one grade higher than the one you actually had, so Father's barber, conforming to custom, should have called him '*Herr Direktor*' or even '*Herr Generaldirektor*' straight away.

There was a peculiar and also very Austrian reason why he did not do so. A *Herr Oberinspektor* was a sergeant in the Viennese police. Father often grumbled that he was 'no damn policeman', and that 'Herr Klaar' without a handle would do very nicely indeed, but Lippert took no notice of his protests. For him a police *Oberinspektor* was the most superior form of human being, more powerful and more important than any *Prokurist* or even *Generaldirektor*. So every morning the *Herr Oberinspektor* sat down before Mother's dressing-table, while Herr Lippert laid out his instruments, worked up a lovely lather in his soap bowl, still one of those shaped like Don Quixote's famous helmet, and began his operations. Shaving and lathering were only interrupted by Lippert snipping and clipping at Father's moustache as the ends of it emerged from the foaming shaving soap.

This daily morning ceremonial took place many years after King Gillette had invented and perfected his safety razor, an instrument father adamantly refused to touch or even have in the house. He was not really scared of the sharp razor blade, as he pretended. He simply enjoyed Lippert's services immensely. To emerge clean and smooth-cheeked from under the barber's lather, to have *eau de Cologne* sprayed onto your face, to have your jowls gently massaged by well-trained hands, to be dabbed and brushed and fussed over by

82

a true professional, makes you feel cleaner, smarter and also more prosperous and important than any 'do-it-yourself' shave ever will.

Budapest in the summer of 1926 was the capital of a country that was a kingdom without a king, ruled by an admiral without a fleet. Nikolaus Horthy de Nagybánya, fleetless ex-admiral of the Imperial Navy, self-appointed Regent of that kingdom from which he had kicked out the legitimate King of Hungary, the unfortunate Karl, the last of the Habsburgs, governed his country from the Royal Castle on Buda Hill. A man of limited intellect, but considerable determination, Horthy was one of the strangest figures among the makers of Europe's history after the Great War. He was a convinced antisemite, and his knowledge of the world was so limited that he assumed, in the Austrian tradition, that if the word 'Christian' appeared in the name of an organisation it must be anti-semitic; so he welcomed the visiting American Secretary of the Young Men's Christian Association (Y.M.C.A.) with the words, 'I am delighted to meet the head of such an important anti-semitic organisation.'

In 1926 Horthy was at the height of his power. To me he became a rather frightening figure. This had little to do with the man himself or his fierce Magyar expression in his photographs looking down everywhere on his people and on me. What frightened me were the big stone lions outside his castle on Buda Hill, and even more the soldiers who guarded it. Black-moustachioed giants, with big rifles and bayonets, they marched up and down their beat with the slow parade step of the Hungarian army, forward leg slightly bending at the knee as the foot touches the ground, creating an impression of slow, but relentless advance. I was certain that one of these giants would suddenly stop, swivel round, aim his rifle at Mother and fire. I could see her collapse to the ground next to me, the blood streaming from the wound over her heart. Crying and screaming I pulled her away. She, completely dumbfounded by this sudden outburst, tried to calm me, to find out what had happened. But I could not tell her. We never went there again.

Apart from this I loved our life in Budapest. We lived in one very big comfortable room on the top floor of a very elegant *pension*. Father liked to stay in nice places and to eat in the best restaurants. Two months in a top hotel would have cost too much. But our *pension* was first-class, it overlooked the 'Korso', where elegant Budapest displayed itself, and the Danube. which in Budapest on a fine day really was as blue as Johann Strauss describes it in his famous waltz. I loved this view. But then came the morning when I could have wished our windows had looked out over a back yard.

My parents were still asleep when I woke up. I heard music. I rushed to the open window, but the window-sill was too high for me to look out. I fetched one of the cane chairs and climbed on it. Now I could see. It was a glorious morning The sun sparkled out of a light blue sky painting silver-gilt freckles on the dark blue of the river. A big white paddle-steamer was floating on it. A boy scout band playing military marches stood on its open deck. It was such a lovely sight: golden trombones and trumpets, the flashing silver of the flutes, the big drums painted red-white-green, Hungary's national colours. I had never seen anything more beautiful. Wanting to see more I started to climb from the chair on to the window-sill. I was just about to bring up my second knee, when the back of my night-shirt was gripped by a strong fist. I was lifted off the sill. I fell. Father's big hands slapped down on my behind, my back, my head, just anywhere. He was quite beside himself with shock and rage. It was the most violent thrashing I ever had in all my life.

Father had woken up and seen how I was apparently about to throw myself off the sixth-floor window. Still half-asleep, the sight drove him berserk. It took Mother quite a while to calm him. He stopped, but he was trembling every bit as much as I was. This beating hurt my body – and how! But I knew that I had deserved it, and that Father, loving me as he did, could not have acted in any other way. I would never give him such a shock again. That was my first resolution of that day. The second was that I would become a boy scout as soon as I was old enough. I, too, would wear that big Mafeking hat, march smartly on parades, do a good deed a day, and altogether live up to the great Baden-Powell's motto: 'Be prepared.' But all that was in the future, and I certainly was not prepared for the further events of that Sunday.

Less than an hour after that drama at the window, when the last fumes of his rage had finally evaporated, Father was, as usual, very sorry for what he had done to me. He kissed my still flowing tears better and promised that we would go for a trip on a Danube steamer in the morning, lunch at a restaurant on Margaret's Island and then ride back to town in a horse-drawn hackney coach. My tears stopped quickly enough at the prospect of such a perfect day.

Father kept his promise. I was happily kneeling on the polished wooden bench of a river steamer a few hours later, looking out over the glittering water. Everything was lovely – until the moment when I turned round to ask Father a question. Then disaster – and Father – struck for the second time that day. I had begun my question with the words: 'Tate, what is ... ?' I felt a stinging slap on my right cheek. Father had hit me again. 'Don't you ever dare to call me Tate,' he hissed, 'never, you hear, never!' I have no idea what suddenly possessed me to call him Tate, to use the Yiddish word for 'Father', instead of the usual 'Daddy' or 'Papa'. I must have picked it up somewhere.

That brief and ugly scene, over in less than a minute, encapsulated the entire conflict dividing Central European Jewry. We, the Klaars, already belonged to the worldly Jews with Western European education and culture. We wore fine clothes, had access even to titles and dignities, possessed influence and wealth. But full equality, inner equality, still eluded us. It eluded not only those who like us had retained our Jewish faith, however spuriously we practised it, but even those who had gone the whole way and converted. We knew that the others, the Goyim, however polite or even servile, did not really differentiate between the caftaned Yiddish speaker with the long wobbling side-curls and the smoothly shaven elegant, à la Klaar, from the Viennese coffee-houses.

And perhaps we, the grandchildren and great-grandchildren, also subconsciously envied those strange alien creatures from the east for they possessed something that we, the coffee-house elegants steeped in German culture, had lost: a strong religious conviction with its belief in a divinely ordained future. This enabled them to bear lowly social status and prejudice with equanimity, while we trembled at the slightest sign of discrimination.

This bitter conflict, anchored deeply in the Jewish soul, affected every Jew in Austria, as it still affects every Jew living outside Israel today. The three principal aspects of this problem can be identified in the lives and works of three brilliant men, all Jews, all contemporaries, all Austrians: Karl Kraus, Moritz Benedikt, Theodor Herzl.

Benedikt, bullet-headed, coarse-featured, heavily moustached, a face of force and intelligence, was the powerful senior publisher and editor of the Neue Freie Presse, the only Austrian newspaper of world renown. He saw himself as an Austrian of the Jewish faith, as the completely assimilated Jew.

Herzl, aristocratically handsome, held one of the most influential positions in Austrian and German letters. As *feuilleton* editor of Benedikt's *Neue Freie Presse* he could make or break reputations in the arts. Born in Budapest, Herzl started life as a dedicated Austro-German, but in his short life he moved through many – often highly confused – phases until he found his true purpose and single-minded goal: Zionism.

The cleverest, the most scintillatingly brilliant of the three, was Karl Kraus. Irony glints in his myopic eyes, bitter sarcasm shapes the smile on his lips, vitriolic wit and passionate anger cut his sharp features, give them point and thrust. His is a face into which every line has been burned with the acid of a desperately unhappy soul. Kraus hated: himself, above all the Jew in himself, Benedikt as a lickspittle Jewish press-baron, Herzl as a vain visionary Jew. He hated and feared Zionism, longed for the disappearance of his race through assimilation and inter-marriage, and helped, to some extent unwittingly, to prepare the ground for the eventual destruction of millions of his fellow Jews. For, though his rapier-like pen denounced Gentiles as well, the poison of his venom flowed most freely when it portrayed, or rather caricatured, Jews.

Hating Jews like himself, who had arrived, who had achieved prominence and influence in society, he did feel an abstract, impersonal pity for the vast poverty-stricken Jewish ghetto proletariat of the east. Though not a socialist himself, he believed that socialism and not Zionism would eventually liberate the Jewish masses and lead them to the light. 'It is hardly conceivable,' Kraus wrote in a comment on Zionism, 'that this time the Jews will enter the promised land dry-shod. Another Red Sea – socialism – will block their way.'

The principal vehicle for Kraus's writings and ideas was his magazine *Die Fackel* (*The Torch*). For many years he wrote it all himself. My father, incidentally, read it for many years from cover to cover, but in spite of this was never a true *Krausianer*, one of those thousands, not only in Vienna, mostly Jewish, who adored this genius with near Messianic devotion. How many of them must have shared with Kraus that unquenchable hunger to be Austro-Germans, that unquenchable thirst to drink deeply of German culture and language, to belong wholly to a world that refused more and more vehemently to accept them as its own. They followed with blind adoration where Kraus led, and that was why Father never really joined the *Krausianer* community. He was too much of an individualist to join anything, be it a Freemasons' Lodge or a political party. What he admired in Karl Kraus was his exceptional mastery of the German language, his wonderful readings from the works of Shakespeare, Offenbach and Nestroy. When I was ten or so I was taken to one of Karl Kraus's readings. I remember the little man looking sternly at his audience. I think he was reading from Shakespeare's *Tempest*. Whatever it was, it was far above my head, and I sat there in polite but excruciating boredom, not appreciating that I was listening to a master of that art and was also privileged to see face to face the greatest living satirist in the German language.

That Kraus was a satirist is, of course, the defence used by his disciples to this day to excuse his viciousness. Kraus hated Vienna, hated Austria they claim, only because he loved Vienna and Austria so much. His hatred was merely the expression of his despair at the imperfections of the city and the state. But it is strange that not one past or present *Krausianer* has yet advanced the claim that, as hatred is well known to be the obverse of the coin of love, the great satirist's many denunciations of the Jews could only have been penned 'for their own good'. True greatness, even in a satirist, requires a sense of balance. Without it he is merely destructive, but the true purpose of satire is like acupuncture : the sharp needles of wit must prick the nerve endings controlling the sick parts of the body to heal, not to destroy.

Kraus's greatest work is *The Last Days of Mankind*, a savage satire on Imperial Austria and Imperial Germany in the Great War. The master's devotees understand this gargantuan play as the work of a great seer, as a prophetic overture to Auschwitz. It certainly is that, just as certainly as the bestialities of the Second War were the logical outcome of the brutalities of the First, but *The Last Days of Mankind* is more than just that. His attack on Imperial Austria and its army, administration and press, where Kraus saw only sham, lies and cruelty, is driven home with enormous power of language and perception, but when Jewish figures bestride Kraus's panoramic stage then the attack becomes really vicious, then he fills his pen not with the acid of satire but with the cyanide of deadly hatred.

Most of these Jews represent various facets of the character of Moritz Benedikt, the press-lord in whom Kraus saw the reincarnation of the devil in Jewish flesh and soul. There is the parasite Benedikt, the corrupt corrupter Benedikt, Benedikt the war-profiteer, Benedikt the lickspittle. He wears many names in *The Last Days of Mankind*, he bows and scrapes through its interminable pages, grovels before the mighty, stamps the weak into the ground. None of the Benedikt-Jews in Kraus's play speaks proper German. Some try, but inevitably they always fall back into their Jewish jargon.

Trying to rid himself of his Jewishness Kraus converted, first to the Catholic religion, then to the Lutheran belief. Searching for a non-Jewish identity, he did not, of course, find it. His own soul, his awareness of what he was, and the world around him, pulled and pushed him back again and again into the whirlpool of his own Jewishness, and he hit out at it like a drowning man being sucked into its vortex.

In Moritz Benedikt Kraus had a perfect target. Here was a Jew who stuck to his religion, but was also one of the pillars of Imperial Austria's establishment. Benedikt was one of Emperor Franz-Josef's few close confidants. In his *Neue Freie Presse* day by day he staunchly defended that whole system which appeared to stand so 'immovably in its place'. For Kraus Benedikt and the newspaper he controlled were the prime evil in Austria. Kraus came to see only wickedness in Austria-Hungary; Benedikt, with equal blindness, could only see good. Like many thousands of assimilated Jews Benedikt shrank from the Jews of the eastern ghettos, so uncouth with their Yiddish language, their beards, side-curls and strange garments. The westernised Jews regarded their mere existence as a threat to their own status, and when reminded by the single word, *Tate*, that they belonged to the same people as those others, those primitives, they hit out, like Father, in despair.

The only man who eventually recognised the dilemma, initially perhaps for the wrong reasons, was Theodor Herzl. Herzl gradually came to realise that Jews are a people, and not merely a religious sect. This realisation did not come, as is often said, virtually overnight when he was reporting the Dreyfus case for the *Neue Freie Presse* from Paris. It came much more from the fact that he was an Austrian living in Austria at a time when all the many nationalities in the Dual Monarchy started to clamour ever more loudly for their own national independence, and when – at the same time – anti-semitism became more strident, more open. If Czechs and Poles and all the other nations of the empire could claim to be oppressed minorities, if they, who all had national homes of their own, were fighting with ever-increasing vehemence for their liberty, were they not pointing the way for the one people that was a perpetual minority everywhere; the only nation without even one square mile of land anywhere in the world to call its own? Living in the era of nationalism Herzl came to believe that Jewish nationalism, Zionism, a Jewish state, were the only guarantee for his people's future. Herzl was not the creator of the Zionist idea. The importance of Herzl to the cause was that he was the first assimilated and influential Jew to make Zionism his life's mission. He was the first Zionist leader to hold a highly respected and important position in the outside, the non-Jewish, world. He had the looks, the personality and above all the dynamic will to turn Eastern Jewry's dream into reality.

Herzl's driving force was not only pure love for the Jewish millions who lived in misery. His personal vanity, his failure as a dramatist, a strong feeling that he was special, different, chosen, all these played their part in his fight for recognition as the one and only leader, as the prince, the king, of the Jews. A certain temperamental instability made him at times even favour proposals and ideas which were nothing short of ridiculous. Very much a man of his period – he could not have read Machiavelli – he put his trust all too often in princes. At one time he proposed to 'do a deal' with the Pope. If the Pope would agree to become Herzl's ally in the fight against anti-semitism, then Herzl in return would start a great movement among the Jews for conversion to Catholicism. One Sunday, to the pealing of the bells of St Stephen's cathedral, Herzl would lead a great procession of Jews to Vienna's principal church. While Herzl and other Zionist leaders would wait outside the cathedral's huge gothic portals, the Jews would enter and be received into the Church of Rome by the Cardinal Archbishop.

Even a convinced assimilationist like Benedikt, Herzl's chief, thought that this hare-brained scheme went too far. 'For a hundred generations,' Benedikt told Herzl, 'your line has preserved itself within the fold of Judaism. Now you are proposing to set yourself up as the terminal point in the process. This you cannot do and have no right to do.' That Herzl could even think of such a plan may seem incredible, but it is not so incredible if one knows how completely Austrian his own background and early family life were.

Occasionally, when I visited Grandmother Julie, there was a little old lady sitting with her in the music- and living-room. Lina Marmorek was a friend of Grandmother's from the days when they had both been young. She was also the sister of Oskar Marmorek, one of Herzl's closest collaborators and had been a frequent visitor to the Zionist leader's home. She told me how Christmas had been celebrated at the Herzls'. There was the big candle-lit Christmas tree with the family, including Herzl, standing round it and singing

'Silent night, holy night' with the same fervour it was sung in millions of Austrian Catholic households. All this ended as Herzl became more and more aware of his Jewishness and of his mission, as his conviction grew that Jews could never be safe as long as they remained alien corn in foreign fields.

Benedikt, not surprisingly, would not have anything to do with Zionism. According to Karl Kraus, Benedikt had one standard phrase, which, once he had said it, could finish or ruin a political or artistic career. It was 'Not shall his name be mentioned in our columns!' And indeed for a name not to be mentioned in the *Neue Freie Presse* was virtually a death sentence for the ambitions of its owner, such was then the power of this newspaper and its publisher. That Moritz Benedikt should, as Kraus claimed, have said this in the Jewish jargon instead of using the proper German sentence construction, 'His name shall not be mentioned in our columns', is probably just another one of the libels the great satirist liked to write into the record. Kraus, who possessed almost unrivalled mastery of the German language, fought against its misuses all his life, but is it likely that Benedikt, the owner of the best German-language newspaper in Austria, a man with contacts in the very highest circles, did not know how to construct his sentences in proper German? However Benedikt may actually have put it, he undoubtedly kept the names of people of whom he did not approve out of his newspaper. He certainly did not approve of Zionism, yet he could hardly keep the name of its leader, his own literary editor, Dr Herzl, out of his columns. But Zionism was not mentioned in the *Neue Freie Presse*. For Benedikt it did not exist. His newspaper did not report Herzl's journeys to the mighty, the princes of the world, it did not mention with as much as even one word one of the greatest events in Jewish history, and one not insignificant in world history, the first World Zionist Congress in Zurich.

Benedikt relaxed this iron rule only once – in Theodor Herzl's obituary. Then he allowed the inclusion of the sentence: 'The deceased devoted much time and energy to the Zionist cause.' And to be fair it must be said that Benedikt allowed Herzl 'to devote much time and energy to the Zionist cause', while Herzl was still in his employ.

Like many assimilated Jews, not only in Austria and Germany, but also in France and Britain, Benedikt was afraid of Zionism. Rich and prominent Jews in all these countries saw Zionism and anti-semitism as a 'chicken and egg' dilemma. Which came first? To the myopic,

Zionism was a Jewish movement which proved the anti-semites right: if the Jews saw themselves as a nation, if they themselves claimed to be different by descent and not merely by religion from their host populations, were they not confirming the anti-semites' view that Jews were aliens usurping positions of wealth and prominence? Only the far-sighted understood that the 'chicken and egg' conundrum was not a true analogy, that Zionism was not furthering anti-semitism, but foreseeing its inevitable 'final' logic.

One aspect of Zionism, hardly understood by any assimilated Jew, but seen very clearly by Herzl, was that Zionism was not just a nationalist movement like any other. It did hold out to the Jewish millions the hope of a free life in their own country, but over and above that it also held the promise of the rise of a new and different type of Jew, different from the insecure assimilants and different from the ghetto-created perversions of Jewry. The Jews who killed themselves rather than surrender at Massada, the warrior Jews described by Flavius Josephus, or more recently in history, the Jews of Spain before Ferdinand and Isabella, or those of Italy, France and Germany before the Crusades and persecution began, were proud men and women, different from the downtrodden, cringing ghetto-Jews. The return of a whole people to its true nature, that was the ultimate aim of Herzl's Zionism, that was and is the true greatness of his vision.

Another famous Austrian Jew, Arthur Schnitzler, physician, playwright, contemporary of Kraus and Benedikt, like them had intellectual brilliance, but he also possessed a quality less highly esteemed by intellectuals, but more important – instinct. This gave him a prescience which all those other highly gifted men lacked. In his novel *The Road to Freedom*, written before the First War, Schnitzler touches the very core of the problem. Baron Georg von Wergenthin, the hero of this book, accuses his friend, the Jew Bermann, of suffering like most Jews from an eternal persecution complex. 'No,' replies Bermann, 'the Viennese Jews, you know, do not suffer from persecution, but from security mania. Compared to that a persecution complex is harmless. You are aware of danger, real or imagined, so your very animal instincts rise to your defence. A security complex lures you to destruction.'

Within a few days of the *Tate* incident Mother and I sat in the Budapest-Vienna Express on our way home. Father had not exiled us because of my 'impossible' behaviour, nor had he hastened our return so that I could get back to speaking again the proper 'Schönbrunner' German of our family, instead of with an almost Hungarian accent, and (God forbid – which God, I wonder?) occasional Yiddish expressions. No, it was time to go back. Father had only another two weeks to work in the Hungarian bank before rejoining us.

The summer before Budapest we had spent our holidays in Lovrana in Italy. It was a real family holiday. Mother's sister Klara, her husband, Uncle Alfred, their baby son Fritzl and his sister Hedi, closest friend, confidant, almost sister, of my childhood, all stayed at the same hotel. It was the Klaars' and the Bartmanns' last family holiday together.

During the twelve months between Lovrana and Budapest, Grandfather Bernhard had died. In consequence the two brothers-in-law started to fight over the inheritance. But in Lovrana Alfred had still been simply 'Uncle Alfred', good-looking in a somewhat severe way, rather strict, rather determined. At this Italian seaside resort Mother did take an occasional dip in the water, but Father kept well away from the sea. Getting him to come to the beach at all was an effort. He was not keen on the sun, but that was only one reason. The other was that he hated himself in his swimsuit. Swimming trunks for men were already quite usual, but for Ernst Klaar to run about half-naked in public was unthinkable. On the beach he wore a black one-piece bathing garment, its coy little skirt at the bottom end covering his maleness. Father's figure had, by that time, become rather portly. Under the black swimsuit his 'spare tyres' were very much in evidence, and with his pale, white thighs and legs emerging from under that rather ridiculous little skirt, Father was no bathing beauty, and he knew it. Dressed in too short white flannel trousers and a none too smartly cut light summer jacket, he still looked impressive and handsome. Though certainly not without vanity, Father was never very concerned about his clothes. Mother had to use all sorts of wiles to get him to his tailor and order a new suit. Unlike Uncle Alfred, who only went to the very best tailors in Vienna, Father made do quite happily with some more or less adequate little chap in a back street. Lovrana was father's final farewell appearance in a bathing suit. Although we later spent holidays at Austrian lake resorts, I never saw him in a bathing suit again.

I joined the second form of the Währingerstrasse elementary school in September 1927. Our form master, Herr Lehrer Schneider, tall, good-looking, friendly, strict, but not a typical Austrian school disciplinarian, was a first-rate teacher. He gave one the feeling, rare indeed, that he actually liked little boys and had not forgotten that he had once been one himself. When he was present we were a very well behaved lot, but God help the poor candidate teacher who had to take over our form when Schneider was ill or away at a conference. Then the classroom became a hell filled with seven-year-old devils roasting the poor young substitute alive, until the head, Oberlehrer Sobotka, hearing the fiendish noise, rushed in and restored order. We were a very mixed bunch. Potential, in some cases already actual, juvenile delinquents, rubbed shoulders with little middle-class Lord Fauntleroys, mummy's darlings, in neat suits, with short pants and long woollen stockings, while the majority came from *petit bourgeois* backgrounds, the sons of shopkeepers and minor employees. A fair number, perhaps twenty-five per cent, were Jewish, by no means all from well-to-do homes, but none of them joining the roughs and toughs. All the boys had all their lessons, except religious instruction, together.

The first time we split up for religious instruction, the Catholic boys remained in the classroom and the Jews filed out to the chorus of 'Yid, Yid, spit in your hood, tell your mummy that is good!' As I was leaving I noticed that Fredl Resch, the quiet round-faced, chubby boy at the desk next to mine sat silently staring into space. For many years Fredl Resch was to be my closest friend. We never talked about these incidents, but his silence, while most of the other Catholics yelled at us Jews, might well have had something to do with the beginning of our friendship. In any case, we Jews did not accept the others' behaviour meekly. The next time they started their 'Yid, Yid . . .' we shouted back at them *'Christ, Christ, g'hörst am Mist!'* Whether one of us had actually invented that charming line: 'Christian, Christian, thy place is on the dungheap!' or whether both, the anti-semitic litany and our responses, were part of an old Austrian school tradition, I cannot say. As far as we were concerned, the score was even. We played and worked happily enough together, Jews and Christians, and whenever there was, thanks to Lehrer Schneider's temporary absence, an opportunity of creating havoc in class, the little Jewish and Catholic devils formed a firmly united front.

My performance in school was at best mediocre, and when Mother went to see Lehrer Schneider (Father would not have dreamt of going), to ask about my progress, he told her: 'Your son is a bright and intelligent boy, but he just won't bother to work. He won't concentrate. His mind flits from one thing to the next. If he understands something immediately, well and good, but if it means thinking things out, it's too much trouble. Anything that requires an effort, he doesn't want to know.'

Herr Schneider was a shrewd and experienced teacher.

After that interview Mother gave me a serious talking-to. It made no impression whatsoever. Had Father said something, that might have been different. But he, probably remembering his own school-days, did not see that I was heading for eventual scholastic disaster. The only conversation about school I had with him whilst I was at Währingerstrasse Elementary did not spur me to greater efforts. He was at home, suffering from boils and lying on the chaise-longue in the bedroom, when I marched in with my school report. It was yet another one of the 'Could do better, if only he tried' variety. Father looked at it, smiled and said: 'Oh well, I suppose I don't really want you to be a teacher's pet. School isn't all that important. Lots of famous men were pretty lousy pupils. You have your wits about you, you'll do all right in life, that's what matters, but do try a bit harder.'

He was right, of course, but quite wrong to tell me. His words reinforced my conviction that I, his darling boy, could hardly do wrong. I knew that I was the apple of his eye. At times he would go to quite ridiculous extremes in his love for me. When I had the measles and ran a fairly high temperature, Father went into one of his rages, shouting at Mother that it was all her fault. How could she allow me to catch the measles?

The main problem at school was that I would not do my home-work. I read a great deal, but not school books. I read, sitting at my table, lying in bed, often with a torch under the blanket, on the lavatory, in the tram going to visit Grandmother Julie. My favourite reading apart from books was *Der Gute Kamerad*, a German maga-zine for boys. The annual subscription to the *Gute Kamerad* was Grandmother Julie's standard birthday present for me. The maga-zine was full of stories about German discoveries, inventions, achievements, inevitably better than any other nation's. Avidly I followed each instalment of its serialised novels. How I identified with their heroes, always blue-eyed, clean-limbed, fair-haired

German boys, and how I booed, at least mentally, the villains, always dark, swarthy, with Slav, French or Italian sounding names. Sitting on the lavatory one day, reading in Father's newspaper that a French passenger plane had crashed killing all eight people on board, I thought: 'Jolly good. Another eight of the enemy dead.' I gloried in everything German, and also, of course, in Austria's great past.

My favourite book was the *Kaiser Book*, also a present from Grandmother Julie. It was a heavy tome published in 1908 for the sixtieth jubilee of Franz-Josef's coronation. On its thick brown cover was a gold-embossed portrait of 'our Kaiser' surrounded by a laurel wreath. Underneath it, in a flowing scroll, stood his Imperial motto *Viribus Unitis*, 'Strength in Unity' – an unintentionally ironic choice for an empire that was to collapse is disunity.

The Austria of the First Republic had no nationality problems, and yet was no more united than the old empire had been. The two leading political parties, the Social-Democrats and the Christian-Socials, viewed each other across class and social barriers with the same deep-seated suspicions, mistrust and hatred that had formerly divided the nations of the empire. After seven hundred years of absolute, or near-absolute, rule, a nation like Austria, one totally confused about its own identity, could not develop into a functioning democracy virtually overnight. The trappings of democracy were there, but the content was missing. The leaders of the Social-Democrats, moderate men on the whole, leading a party of the moderate Left, felt obliged to use the language of the barricades. Class struggle, capitalist exploiters, fight, battle, smash – those slogans flowed all too readily from their lips. In truth they were highly intelligent, civilised men, largely middle-class, largely Jewish, anything but fanatics. Indeed, these same men, after 1918, defeated a Communist attempt to turn Austria into a Soviet republic.

Nor were their Christian-Social opponents fascist beasts. But to them there seemed little difference between Social-Democracy and Bolshevism. They felt their bourgeois existence threatened. They too used strong language on public platforms, ranting on eternally about the need to defend Western Civilisation and German Christian values. By that they meant anything that was not 'Jewish-Bolshevik'. Their speeches were liberally sprinkled with anti-semitic remarks, always popular with the Austrian electorate since the days of Lueger and indeed before, and always effective.

Each side began to pay increasing attention to its private armies. The Social-Democrats had their *Schutzbund*. It was mostly composed of war veterans and commanded by some officers of the Imperial Army including even one former major-general. He, General Koerner, decades later became a much-loved President of the Second Republic.

Whilst the Social-Democrats had control of their party soldiers in the *Schutzbund*, the Christian-Socials did not really control the private army closest to them, Prince Starhemberg's *Heimwehr*. Like them it was against the 'reds', but it followed its own policies, which were never clearly defined because they depended on the Prince's whims of the moment or on those of his provincial satraps. There was a lot of in-fighting among the leadership of these green-uniformed troops with cocks' feathers on their hats. They were united only in their admiration for Benito Mussolini and his fascist militia. It was the model for most of the *Heimwehr*, except for one splinter group which was more impressed by Hitler's storm troopers and eventually joined his Nazis. This prevalence of private armies, in Austria as in Germany, their marching and counter-marching, their street battles with whips, beer bottles, knuckle-dusters and occasionally even fire-arms, proved not their strength, but the weakness of the state.

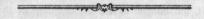

The summer of 1927 began hot, and was going to get hotter. Father had decided to save money. We would, therefore, not go on holiday, but stay in Vienna. For a little boy it promised to be a pretty dull time in the hot city. Not having been to school yet I had no friends to play with. It was dull, very dull and very hot.

But then, one morning, it was still hot, there was excitement in the air. I was wiping the sleep out of my eyes when Poldi came rushing into my room. 'Come on, you've got to get dressed quickly. Mummy and Daddy have gone to find a taxi. Mummy is going to take you to Grandmother Adele. You'll stay there overnight. You'll have the big flat to play in and also the lovely garden.'

Poldi should not have mentioned the garden, for in that garden at Türkenschanzplatz there lived a bald-headed ogre, Colonel Besser, late of the Imperial army, brother of the lady who owned the house. This martial giant was in charge of the garden, and whenever I was playing in it and my ball or my foot touched one of his precious flower-beds, he let out an almighty roar, loud enough to frighten a regiment of Imperial troopers out of their wits, never mind a six-and-a-half-year-old little boy. I was scared stiff of the old Colonel, whose bark in truth was infinitely worse than his bite.

Having been reminded of his existence – Poldi for once being most inept – I howled that I would not go, but by that time my parents had come back, the taxi was waiting with its engine running, and I was bundled off downstairs in double-quick time. Once we were in the taxi I shut up very quickly about not wanting to go to Türkenschanzplatz. That we were to have a taxi ride all the way out there had not really sunk in when Poldi had mentioned it. Taxis were a very rare and very special treat. Ordinarily one went everywhere by tram and did not waste money on this highly luxurious form of transport in Vienna in the Twenties. And going to Grandmother Adele's flat was a long and, therefore. doubly enjoyable ride, twenty minutes at least. In normal traffic conditions – the cars having to wait behind the trams in the narrow roads whenever they stopped to let people off and on – it took that time, but on the morning of 15 July 1927 traffic conditions were anything but normal. There were no trams; very few cars and people were on the roads and in the streets; but lots of policemen seemed to be about; and as we drove out of the city we met a number of the wide-bodied police emergency coaches driving in the opposite direction towards the city. Mother explained that there was trouble in town, she did not really give me any details, nor would I have been particularly interested, and that it was better for me to stay with Grandmother. Daddy would probably come out next day if it was all over, and fetch me back home. We reached Türkenschanzplatz much too quickly for my liking, I was handed over to Grandmother and mother took the taxi straight back to Pichlergasse.

Had it not been for the night at Grandmother Adele's flat, I would not have any personal memories of 15 July 1927 at all. For me the day, spent playing and enjoying myself in the garden – the ogre-colonel was blissfully absent – was quite uneventful. It was not the first time I had slept in Adele's flat. I had spent two nights there in the autumn of 1926. We had had to get out of Pichlergasse after Father woke up one morning to find to his horror a couple of bed-bugs on the war-path on his sheet. In spite of Mother's super-cleanliness, bedbugs invaded these old houses from time to time. A specialist firm of vermin destroyers was called in, and the flat was fumigated with poisonous prussic acid fumes. It killed off the bugs, but made Pichlergasse uninhabitable for three days.

My happy play-day in Grandmother Adele's garden was a water-shed in Austria's history. Before 15 July there was a chance, how-ever slight, that Austria's Left and Right might still find a formula for co-existence. After it there was no hope. The ostensible cause of this catastrophe was the acquittal by a Viennese jury of three *Heimwehr* youths who had shot one member of the *Schutzbund* and injured five others. They had also accidentally killed an eight-year-old boy who happened to be on the scene when the shooting started.

This crime had been committed in a little village in the Burgen-land, most backwoods and backward of all the Austrian provinces. At their trial in Vienna the *Heimwehr* men admitted the shooting, but pleaded self-defence. The jury accepted this, and the judge had no option but to let them off. When the verdict was announced on 14 July there were angry demonstrations in the court. By the even-ing a feeling of tension and general unrest had spread throughout the city. Vienna's police chief contacted Social-Democrat leaders to ask whether they intended to organise protest demonstrations for the next day. He was assured, quite truthfully, that no demonstrations were planned and that the *Schutzbund* would not be called out.

But when the leaders gave their assurances they were unaware that some members of the party were already taking matters into their own hands. The city electricity workers met during the night and decided to strike. The editor of the party paper *Arbeiter Zeitung* wrote a leader denouncing the acquittal of the *Heimwehr* men in words of incendiary violence. He may have wanted his articles to act as a safety valve, but if so, then the result was the opposite of what he had intended. The political situation had reached com-bustion point in any case, the acquittal and the *Arbeiter Zeitung* leader were the sparks that set off the explosion.

From early morning on 15 July groups of outraged workers came marching down the arterial roads leading from the suburbs to the 'Ring'. No rifles or guns were aimed at them as they began to fill the open squares so carefully mapped out by the generals of the old army. The government could not trust either its soldiers or some of its officers. They were believed to be in sympathy with the socialists. Keeping order was left to the police, who were unprepared, thin on the ground, and armed only with long cavalry sabres. They were quickly overrun. By mid-morning the few hundred demonstrators of the early hours had grown into a raging mob, and thousands more were still streaming towards the city.

It was a very Austrian shambles. Official reaction, as usual at first too little and too late, became eventually, also as usual, too brutal and too violent. And, also as always, the sensible men trying to avoid disaster failed to make their voices heard in time. By mid-morning the Social-Democrat leaders called out the *Schutzbund* to help control the fury, but when the party leaders and their soldiers went into action at last, the fevered hate of the crowd had become so infectious that half the *Schutzbund* went over to the demonstrators. Leaders pleading for reason were shouted down and even physically threatened.

Whether the crowds followed a pre-arranged plan or whether it just happened, no one knows to this day, but they converged on the Justizpalast. For them this building symbolised the hateful class-justice which had let off the *Heimwehr* murderers. The police on the spot could only look on as the mob's leaders stormed into the building and set it alight. But by now police reinforcements armed with rifles taken from the army's arsenals were on the move.

They were closing in just as the Social Democrat leaders and the loyal *Schutzbund* men were beginning to get control over the crowds. With flames rising high above the roof of the Justizpalast the revolt had reached its climax. The tornado of mob fury was about to blow itself out. Realising that the worst was over, police-president Schober and Julius Deutsch, the senior Social-Democrat leader, agreed that no further force was needed. Emissaries were sent out to the police detachment with orders for them to stop where they were and stand by for further instructions. But by now neither Schober nor Deutsch were in command. Austria's nemesis had taken over. Her tragedy had to be played out to the final curtain.

Schober's and Deutsch's messengers failed to get through the dense crowds in time. Embittered by the knowledge that some of their comrades had been battered to death by the mob, the armed policemen fired at the demonstrators. The salvos rang out the death-knell for eighty workers – and for Austria. The bodies of these dead men were from now on an unsurmountable obstacle in the path of reason.

Neither the Right nor the Left had wanted this slaughter. But both were equally guilty of poisoning the political atmosphere. 15 July

1927 was not a civil war. It was only a one-day revolt, but the events of that one desperate day made the civil war of 1934 inevitable.

In our own family, however, 'civil war' had broken out one year earlier, in April 1926, and in 1927 it was still raging. Bernhard, who had never known a day's illness in his life, died on 8 April 1926 at 11 a.m., as he was about to address the Presidium of the Vienna Chamber of Commerce. He was only sixty-two. His death had hardly any meaning for me. But the death of 'rich' Bernhard, or rather his inheritance, had a great deal of meaning for my father, Uncle Alfred and Ernst Lamberg, fiancé of Aunt Lisa, my mother's youngest sister.

Bernhard Schapira wrote his last will and testament on 1 July 1917. It read:

Having considered the matter most carefully and being free from all pressures and fears I set down my last will as follows: As the sole heir to my entire fortune under whatever name and whatever heading I appoint my wife Udel-Leie (Adele) Schapira *née* Immerdauer. As witness of this I have written this testament in my own hand and signed it in my own hand.

Adele was nobody's fool, but she knew nothing about business affairs, neither her own husband's nor anybody else's. Her role had always been that of wife and mother. But after his death she became the sole heiress of all Bernhard owned, including his firm, which, as it turned out, had not been nearly so successful as the family had assumed. When everything was added up, and when the firm's outstanding debts were deducted, the net value of Bernhard's assets came to 36,034 Austrian Schillings. Austrian banks have worked out a rule of thumb based on purchasing power, according to which one pre-war Schilling bought as much as fifteen Schillings do now. Bernhard, therefore, left something like 540,510 Austrian Schillings in present-day value, roughly £18,000 – not much of a fortune.

There is, however, a mystery suggesting that there could have been more to Bernhard's wealth than was allowed to meet the eyes of the Austrian officials valuing his estate. The mystery is that of the two missing cars. They are not listed in any of the documents. But they existed. I saw them, and I rode in them when Bernhard was alive and after his death. And Father, who, as we know, was not too fond of his father-in-law, pointed out from time to time how stupid Grandfather had been to spend so much money on luxury cars, bound to be wasting assets, when he could have bought that magnificent house in Türkenschanzplatz for the same money. In balance-sheet terms Father was certainly right, but Bernhard must have got a great deal of fun and satisfaction out of owning these cars, so important for his grand-seigneurial life-style. His heirs, Father amongst them, would have derived greater eventual benefit from the ownership of that prestigious villa and, of course, lots of fun and excitement from fighting over their shares.

The purchase of the two cars might well have been a much shrewder business move on Bernhard's part than my father suspected. Many people owned houses in Vienna, but very, very few owned cars. And to be the owner not of one, but of two cars, enhanced Bernhard's reputation and also that of his business. Cars were then the most impressive status symbol anyone could possess.

Whatever Bernhard's motives may have been when he bought those two Adler cars in 1922 or 1923, they were not shown among his possessions, but they were there, and they became Grandmother's property. Eventually they were used as taxis, and when the taxi business turned out a failure the cars were sold. The coupé disappeared from sight; the limousine was sold to Grandfather's driver, Herr Klein and continued to work as a taxi. I last saw it in the early Thirties when it drew up outside Pichlergasse 1 and Herr Klein gallantly helped Poldi's successor, Otti to mount – no other word will do – his vehicle, which by then would have looked much better in the hall of a motor museum than on the streets of Vienna. It went all right, and Otti proudly drove off to her wedding in what used to be Grandfather Bernhard's number one folly.

The black granite stone was not yet in place on Bernhard's grave at Vienna's Central Cemetery (Gate IV – Jewish Section) when the two sons-in-law Ernst and Alfred, and also Aunt Lisa's fiancé, the lawyer Ernst Lamberg, began to put pressure on his widow. Adele had suffered a slight heart attack after the funeral and was confined to bed when the family drama began. It was not of classical proportions, had no Othello or Desdemona, but it did have, in my father's very strongly held view, an Iago to out-Iago even Shakespeare's evil intriguer. Father cast Alfred in that role. His name was never to be mentioned again in our house. 'Never, d'you hear!' Father had shouted at Mother. That was how it was to be for ever and ever, amen. Mother and I, of course, obeyed. It was Father who did not stick to his own commands. Well, not quite. He did not actually mention Alfred by name, but he returned to the subject of the family feud again and again, using a rich, choice and varied selection of uncomplimentary names for the one uncle I really liked. When Father spoke of the 'rogue, ruffian, dog, swine, blackguard, scoundrel, villain', as he frequently did, Mother and I had no difficulty in guessing what particular gentleman he was referring to.

What happened according to Father was this : shortly after Grandfather's funeral and before everything could be settled concerning the future running of Grandfather's firm, he had to go to Budapest. He did not even have time to study the books with his trained chartered accountant's eye and to make recommendations. He asked Grandmother not to sign any documents or make any binding arrangements until his return, and this advice she agreed to follow. But the very moment Father sat in his train to Budapest, Iago-Alfred appeared at Grandmother's bedside and, using every wile in the intriguer's armoury, he cast aspersions against Father all over Grandmother's duvet.

Alfred Bartmann was 'appointed until further notice joint managing director, together with Mrs Adele Schapira, of the firm Bernhard Schapira, each of the two joint managing directors being entitled to represent the firm and sign on its behalf independently of each other'. This entry appears in the Vienna Companies Register dated 24 April 1926, two weeks and two days after Bernhard's death and about one week after Father's departure from Vienna.

The explosion, when Father heard what had been done, can be imagined. Shock waves and fall-out spread from Budapest all the way to Türkenschanzplatz. This family war delayed the granting of probate for Grandfather's will for a long time. Dr Rumpler, the family lawyer, first asked for a postponement to 1 May 1927 'as the negotiations between the heirs concerning the future of the family firm have not yet been settled', but when that date finally approached he had to appeal for a further delay until 15 June, 'as in spite of strenuous efforts to achieve complete agreement between the interested parties and in spite of various contractual arrangements having been considered there is still a lack of unity. Although Mrs Adele Schapira, as sole heir, would have every right to have the firm registered in her name only, she does not wish as yet to do so in order to ensure the peace within her family.

Poor Grandmother obviously tried her best to deal with the family fragmentation caused by the time-bomb her husband set ticking on 1 July 1917. But the family peace was beyond repair. She finally acted. The appointment of Alfred Bartmann was cancelled on 8 July 1927 and Adele took over as sole owner of the firm. After that Father was on speaking terms with his mother-in-law again. I can only guess at the reasons why Grandmother finally decided to remove Alfred from the firm altogether. She may have hoped to reconcile her two sons-in-law by having neither of them in the firm.

Two years later Klara was allowed to visit Pichlergasse again. It was a sensation, and I stood on our balcony impatiently hopping from one leg to the other to be the first to catch a glimpse of her. It was a warm, sunny spring day. At last I saw her slim little figure walking towards our house, clad in an elegant navy blue suit and a matching hat, trimmed with white. A short while later Aunt Lisa arrived, and then Mother's best friend Käthe Mautner, their friend Hannerl Herlinger, and finally, from the other side of Pichlergasse came Selma Ornstein. Mother was giving her first 'at home', to be followed by many others, attended nearly always by her two sisters, their closest friends, sometimes by the wives of some of Father's colleagues at the bank, and occasionally special visitors, of whom I remember particularly a very elegant lady dressed in a flowing pearl grey robe with matching cloche hat – all the ladies wore hats for tea. She was Mother's English teacher at the Hanover boarding school, who had come from London.

Mother adored her 'at homes'. Only for them did she bring out the Japanese tea service, blue-grey wafer-thin china decorated with hand-painted geishas. Tiny croissants, crisp poppy-seed and crystallised salt rolls had been bought that very morning from Vienna's most select bakery, Herr Fritz's in the Naglergasse. They were cut, buttered and spread with delicate *Teewurst*. The second course was a rich cream cake, nut, orange or chocolate, and home-made.

The dinner-parties my parents gave from time to time were much more fun than Mother's 'at homes' They normally started with a selection of cold *hors d'oeuvres*, followed by Chateaubriand, home-made potato crisps – the ones made of salted plastic had not yet been invented – rice, salads and finally our own *Sachertorte*, at least as good as that from the famous Café Sacher, although its chocolate icing did not have quite that elegantly polished look.

Once the guests arrived – the Mautners, the Herlingers, very often Uncle Paul and Aunt Alice, some of Father's closer colleagues from the Länderbank and their wives, occasionally Aunt Sally and her strange musician husband Robert, who played the piano after dinner, and inevitably Dr Maurer, an apparently professional bachelor, who was the parents' 'house friend' and entitled to pop in whenever it suited him – I disappeared into my room to escape having to shake hands, bow politely from the waist and murmur well-brought-up thank you's to those guests who had remembered to bring me little presents. This worked well enough when I was smaller, but after my tenth birthday escaping the grown-ups became more difficult. Father loved to have me come in and say good night after dinner, to show me off to his friends, make me tell a joke, focus everybody's attention on his child, who would have liked nothing better than for the floor under his feet to open and swallow him up.

Later, when I had reached my teens, Father and I had some furious rows about these guest appearances of mine. I felt shy, hated being talked down to by my parents' friends, had nothing to say to them and wanted to live in my own world in my own room, immersed in my books. The battle-honours in these fights were pretty evenly distributed. Sometimes I surrendered, sometimes Father did. When he did, his disappointment was so obvious that I gave way at the next dinner-party and joined the grown-ups for half an hour or so. And in the end I found that I did not mind so much any more. I actually began to enjoy listening to their talk and particularly to Father's sometimes slightly sarcastic but often very witty sallies, which made the guests laugh aloud and created a relaxed atmosphere in which I no longer felt Father's polite boy show-piece, but almost a grown-up taking a part in the conversation, however modest. I see him before me laughing and happy and so real that I can hear his very breath and touch the warmth of his body.

Of all my parents' friends it was Dr Maurer, the bachelor, who impressed me most. He had the reputation of being an intellectual, but if he was, he was one of the painless kind. He had a way of talking to me that I found fascinating and enjoyable. He could talk about politics, history, about virtually any subject, without ever appearing to lecture, always choosing simple, straightforward words, even when explaining complicated issues.

I must have been ten or eleven, when, with some of my school chums, I marched in the traditional Social-Democrat demonstration on 1 May, Labour Day. When I came home Dr Maurer was sitting by Father's bedside. Father was recovering from 'flu, or something very minor, and the 'house friend' had just popped in to see how he was. I was flushed and excited from marching to the music of the bands, from all the shouting, the hundreds of red flags, the clenched fist salutes. Never again in my life was I to be so much of a political radical as at that moment, and in my buttonhole I proudly wore the Social-Democratic party badge, a red carnation on a black enamel background.

Dr Maurer took one look at me and said: 'Georg, I have been a Social-Democrat all my life, but let me tell you: one never wears one's political convictions in one's buttonhole.'

We were, of course, all Social-Democrats. What other party could a Jew vote for? The Social-Democrats were, at least officially, not anti-semitic, and many of their leaders were Jews. Viktor Adler, the founder of Austria's Socialist party, had been a baptised Jew. In the Twenties and early Thirties, the party was led by Otto Bauer, a Jew, as was Julius Deutsch, his deputy, who was also the top commander of the *Schutzbund*. Jews were prominent throughout the leadership of the party and its many subsidiary organisations, few of them of working-class background. Most of them came from well-to-do middle-class homes. They were idealists, do-gooders many of them, who devoted their lives to improving the lot of the working classes. Their conscious motives were absolutely sincere, their subconscious ones were guilt and fear. The guilt that drove them was the same that motivates so many middle-class people today, who, ashamed of their inherited educational and social privileges, turn to 'progressive' causes, so long as they can form an élite of the Left and enjoy more equality than the others. Their fear was of the anti-semite mob. A party that stood first and foremost for equality obviously could not allow inequality between Austrians who were Jewish and those who were not. Hence every Jewish Social-Democrat sensed a protective wall of non-Jewish Social-Democrats around him. And an added attraction was the intellectually fascinating challenge of the human engineering needed to create the egalitarian society of the socialist dream.

Most of the Klaars were merely Social-Democrat voters. Their socialist convictions could easily have been knocked down with the feather of liberalism, had a worthwhile Liberal Party still been in existence. The one exception was Anni Klaar, a distant cousin of my father's, nearly twenty years his junior, who became very friendly with my parents. A dark, attractive Jewess, she remained a convinced Social-Democrat all her life. No one could have been more typical of the Jewish bourgeois Social-Democrat party worker than our Anni.

One day Anni, by then a lady in her seventies, told me the story of how she had gone for a long walk in the country during a holiday and lost her way. She did not know which way to turn to get back to her parents. She was twenty when this happened. At last, a lone motor-cyclist came down the road. He stopped, took off his dust goggles, and Anni saw that he was a very good-looking young man. 'Jump on the back of my bike and I'll run you home, my girl,' he said. Socialist Anni hesitated. To ride on the *Pupperlhutschen*, the 'dollybird-swing', as the pillion of a motor-bike was called in the Viennese idiom, was all right for a girl from a working-class suburb, but not at all the thing to do for a young university lady. She had no choice. It was getting dark. So she climbed on to the seat, careful not to show too much leg and gingerly put her arms around the young man's waist. 'If you don't hug me tighter I don't mind,' he said, 'but you'll fall off at the first bend.'

He took her safely back to her parents. As she gave him her hand to say good-bye and thank him, he quickly pulled her towards him trying to give her a kiss. Anni, shocked, refused and ran away. 'I could not possibly have allowed that chap to kiss me. He was a carpenter or plumber, I can't remember which – a proletarian, you know.'

One of the advantages of Socialism in Vienna which we enjoyed was that rents were frozen. The rent Father paid for Pichlergasse was a mere 125 Austrian Schillings per quarter. It was ridiculously cheap, and was the main reason why my parents never thought of moving to a bigger flat, though we really could have done with one. Not because Pichlergasse was too small for the family, not at all, but we were running out of wall-space to hang the pictures Father kept buying. Art objects and paintings were his great passion.

The first indication Mother had of this passion was the famous white elephant. It arrived one morning – my parents had only been married a short time – from one of Vienna's best-known china shops. Mother stood speechless before this unwanted and unexpected animal. The flat was not yet properly furnished, neither Bernhard's cut open sacking nor real carpets covered the floors, but there she was looking into the raised trunk of a porcelain elephant. Adoring young wife though Mother was, she had a very sound sense for essentials, and, however lustrous the white sheen on the elephant's flanks, however satisfying the smoothness of its texture, however cool and sensuous to the touch, the thing had to go. And it actually did go right back to the shop where Father had bought it. Was it young love that made him give in so easily, or had he actually been a bit doubtful about this purchase himself and the money he had spent somewhat recklessly? Had Mother not taken such a determined stand, would the flat have housed a china menagerie eventually? I rather think that Father really was none too certain about this first 'art' find of his. Never again did he buy china, neither animals nor figurines. His true love was for paintings and painters. At one time he had a friendship with a painter called Schindler. He often took me to that man's studio, where he could spend a happy hour silently watching him at work. Eventually he bought one of Schindler's still-lifes, a rather large painting showing a table covered with a damask cloth, with a medieval cuirass, helmet and sword lying on to it.

Later Herr Schindler was replaced in Father's affections by the painter Oncken. Tiny Herr Oncken, who must then have been in his seventies, was frequently invited to our dinner-parties, looking very neat and dapper with his beautifully barbered white beard and moustache, and enveloped by his enormous Valkyrie of a wife, who could easily have picked up her little artist husband and cradled him within her arms like a baby. That indeed appeared to be their true and happy relationship. In the course of time Father bought quite a number of Onckens. In my memory these paintings were very beautiful, particularly one of a tree, but in the Vienna art market of today Oncken is considered to be somewhat mediocre. In the early Thirties father met and helped to find a job for the son of Egger-Lienz, the highly esteemed Austrian peasant painter. The young man showed his gratitude by presenting father with Egger-Lienz's sketches for his famous painting of Pater Haspinger, the catholic priest and spiritual guide of the Tyrolean leader Andreas Hofer.

As more and more paintings kept arriving Mother announced in mock despair that she would soon have to nail them to the ceiling, as there was not one inch of wall-space left. Still, even without moving to a larger flat or using ceiling space, our hanging committee somehow always managed to find that little bit of extra space for Father's most recent acquisition – not altogether surprising considering that that committee had only one member – Father.

Mother did not really disapprove. On the contrary. She wanted a beautiful home, she wanted the Pichlergasse flat to have some of that air of luxury which had permeated her own father's spacious establishment, but she would much rather have spent money on lovely furniture than on relatively useless works of art. She also wanted useful modern household equipment, one of the new-fangled vacuum-cleaners and most of all a refrigerator to keep food cool and fresh during the hot summer months.

She got her vacuum-cleaner. The fridge remained a dream all her life. What was wrong with a simple ice-box like the one his mother had used for the last forty years? Father wanted to know. Not much, Mother replied, except that forty years ago was 1891 and now was 1931. In any case, his question seemed to her somewhat irrelevant as we did not even possess an old-fashioned ice-box. All we had was the kitchen larder with two ventilation grilles into the back court-yard. In summer she had to put a basin with two ice blocks into it so that the food would not spoil.

Re-furnishing the flat was a different matter. Mother wanted to live in surroundings as beautiful and luxurious as Türkenschanzplatz and with that Father had every sympathy. By now he had two in-comes, his salary from the bank and a substantial regular fee from the Austrian branch of the French cigarette-paper manufacturer Abadie. He audited that firm's books and prepared its annual com-pany report.

Gradually the old furniture disappeared. First to go was my parents' bedroom suite. The new one, whether genuine antique or reproduction I do not know, was in the Louis XVI style, white wood with carved scrolls, flowers and bows, the head and foot of the big double-bed and the backs of the two chairs made of wickerwork, giving lightness and grace. Then Herr Gruber, the bearded cabinet-maker, made Father's writing-desk, very French, with inlaid wood and ormolu-decorated drawers and corners, as well as a big repro-duction side-board for the dining-room. Finally Herr Leonhardts-berger turned up, an interior designer, very smooth in looks and manner, and no respecter of other people's money, as Father sighed more than once. He removed the big double-door, dividing dining-room and study, so that the two rooms were one, making the flat look much more spacious than it was. A soft blue curtain with em-broidered gold leaves was hung in the door opening, and the dining-room chairs were upholstered in the same material, creating a pleas-ing unity.

But for my money, or rather for Father's, Leonhardtsberger's masterpiece was my own room. All my childhood furniture was thrown out. My new big wardrobe, desk, couch and chairs were made of dark brown-red mahogany, smooth and shiny, and – triumph of interior design – a scarlet lacquer bedside table was put next to my couch, matching the scarlet wood framing the chest-high jute covering on the wall next to the couch.

I sat the grammar school entrance examination together with Fredl Resch and a number of my other elementary-school friends. They all sailed through; I scraped in by the skin of my teeth. Studying in the Wasagymnasium was not all swot and sweat. There were the intervals between lessons, and there was the tuck-shop in the main hall run by the wife of the caretaker, who – this being an Austrian school – had to have a title: he was addressed as Herr Pedell, and naturally the tuck-shop lady was Frau Pedell. There one got delicious open sandwiches and a wide selection of chocolates and sweets. But, all in all, the years in the Wasagymnasium loom as gloomily in my memory as the corridors and classrooms of that school.

The happiest moment of my day was when I ran out of the school portal after the lessons were over, and moments of supreme happiness were when I raced down the steps and saw my father waiting for me on the opposite side of the street. This did not happen very often, although his office was less than ten minutes' walk from the school, but when it did happen and I saw my father there I felt immensely proud and elated and ran straight into his arms, although this was ridiculously childish behaviour for a student at one of Vienna's top gymnasia, one who actually had visiting cards printed saying 'Georg Klaar, stud. gym., Vienna IX, Pichlergasse 1'.

My second year at the Wasagymnasium was a year of disaster. By the end of that year I had achieved the lowest marks in both Latin and Mathematics, and this meant that one could not pass to the next higher class, but had to repeat the whole year.

This calamity was not taken too seriously either by my parents or myself. As I had done my first school year at home in order not to lose time and entered school by special exam, I was younger than most of my colleagues, so that lost year only put me into the age-bracket in which I would have been had my school entry not been advanced by a full year. So the family excuse was that I had not yet reached the level of maturity of the other boys; that was bound to come second time round. I was far more intelligent than most; what I lacked was concentration and dedication, but without any doubt that experience of failure, that shock, would prove a salutary lesson.

I was bound to soar to the top from now on. My parents believed this, though Mother perhaps was a little more doubtful than Father, but I certainly believed it. Repeating the second form was going to be as easy as snapping my fingers.

We spent a glorious holiday at Seeboden in Carinthia on the shores of Lake Millstatt. Father only joined us later, but the Bartmanns were there, and so was Uncle Paul, Aunt Alice and their two boys – plenty of company for me. It was a very hot summer, the swimming was marvellous, and as even the wider family readily agreed that my dismal performance at school was not to be taken too seriously and appeared to have every confidence in my future, I was not worrying. Once again we drew up a list of lousy scholars who had become great men – Bernard Shaw, Albert Einstein and lots and lots of others. Perhaps I had really only taken the first step on the road to later greatness.

Mother's unhappiness, at least during the early weeks in Seeboden before Father joined us, had nothing to do with my performance. She cried a good deal, and said she could not explain why. She suffered from the intense heat, and suddenly something like a fine hair seemed to rotate before her left eye making her bad eyesight even worse. She went to see a specialist, who gave her eye drops and all sorts of lotions, but nothing helped. There was nothing in her eye, and the specialist she later consulted in Vienna could not find an explanation either. That thin line, like the fine hair-line cross in the viewfinder of a camera, was there for many years, the speed at which it rotated varying with the state of her nerves.

Once Father arrived she brightened up, but she got no joy out of the high-comedy put on at Seeboden by those two low comedians, Ernst Klaar and Alfred Bartmann. How those two brothers-in-law ignored each other in that small village, where they came face to face at least twice a day, was a truly magnificent performance. When one spied the other coming round a corner, he smartly gave himself the command 'Eyes right' or 'Eyes left', whichever was appropriate, and thus they passed one another like two ostriches stalking around with their heads in the quicksands. Only their shadows touched occasionally. By this time their antipathy for each other had reached an all-time peak. As the years passed, the battle over Grandfather Bernhard's firm, which they had both lost in the end, rankled less. But the beginning of an awareness of how much better it might have been for everyone, most of all for Grandfather's firm itself, if instead of fighting they had put their heads together, made them dislike one another even more. Who knows, with their joint experience of business and accountancy, Bernhard Schapira Import might have done quite well.

Adele died on 21 June 1931. The grief of the three Schapira daughters for their mother was much more intense than it had been for their father. Between him and them there had always been a distance, a sort of glass wall through which one could see but not really feel – a 'respectful affection'. But between Adele and her daughters there was a very strong bond. Many aspects of her personality were to repeat themselves in each of these three women. They all shared the emotional character that had ruled Adele's existence. But Mother also had an intellectual detachment and a calm objectivity, which her sisters did not possess to the same degree. These two traits came out very strongly when Adele's valuable jewellery had to be divided between the three daughters. It was a wonderful opportunity for the three husbands to try and revive the battles of yesteryear: how to distribute the diamond tiara, the brooches, earrings and rings, so that each sister got the same as the other two, was not easy.

It was Mother, my gentle Ernst-adoring mother, who cut the Gordian knot. Taking absolutely no notice of my father's view that she was entitled to a major share – was she not the eldest? – she summoned her sisters, and the three of them decided among themselves what each one was to have there and then, leaving their husbands feeling impotent and ignored.

Another Gordian knot my mother cut was one I had tied for myself. My performance in the second form of Wasagymnasium the first time round was brilliant compared to my results when I repeated that class. On the last day of every term the reports were handed out. This time there was none for me. 'You will find your report at home,' the form master said. 'It has been sent by post.' Next morning it arrived in the blue official envelope. First time round I had failed in Latin and Mathematics. Now, having repeated that same class, I had failed not only in those two subjects, but in History and Geography as well.

The Austrian government forced the issue. Worried by the number of out-of-work graduates, the government wanted to reduce the student population at grammar schools and at the universities. A new law was passed, laying down among other things that a grammar school pupil could only repeat a class once. If he failed a second time then he was thrown out of the higher education stream and automatically relegated to an ordinary secondary school.

When Mother and I opened that blue envelope we were of course prepared for the worst in Latin and Mathematics, but not for the additional catastrophes in History and Geography. We both burst into tears. My sobbing became almost hysterical. Mother took me into her arms and kissed me and kept saying, 'We'll get this straightened out, Georgerl. It'll be all right, it really will.' Not one word of reproach from her, no accusations, only love and understanding. 'You can't stay on at that school, of course,' she said, 'I know the school for you to go to.' And she showed me the prospectus of the Landerziehungsheim Grinzing. The Grinzing Country Educational Home. In spite of its curious name, this was not a Borstal institution, but a private boarding-school I had heard a lot about, and which was said to be for idiots from well-to-do homes. The photos on the prospectus showed that it was very different from the state schools I was used to. The main building with the offices, the dormitories for the boarders and the dining-hall looked ordinary enough, but the pupils were taught in bright little wooden huts connected by a central corridor, much airier and freer than the dark, dank classrooms I knew. What impressed me most when I looked at a photo of the interior of a classroom was that the boys sat behind proper little tables on ordinary chairs, instead of being strait-jacketed into those narrow bench-desks used in the state schools for over a century. Tears still flowing, I sobbed that I wanted to go to that school.

'I'll talk to Daddy about it now,' Mother said, and she went to the telephone and booked a call to the Czech National Bank in Prague, where Father was spending four weeks auditing its accounts. When the call came through an hour or so later, Mother gave me the second little ear-piece attached to our telephone, so that I could take part in the conversation. 'Ernst,' she said, 'Georgerl's school report has arrived, and it is very bad.'

'How bad?'

Mother told him and added: 'He cannot go on in the Wasagymnasium. We've got to take him out. He must go out of the state sector. There's that new law, and in any case he needs a private school where they have smaller classes and teachers who have more time for the individual pupil. Above all he needs a school where homework is supervised, and that's exactly the school I have found.'

'What school is that?' Father asked, and you could hear from his voice that he was getting a bit tetchy.

'I think the private boarding school in Grinzing would be the best for him,' Mother said, 'as a day-boy only, of course.'

'And how much do they charge?'

Mother dropped her bomb-shell: 'The fee is 250 Schillings per month, that includes tuition in the afternoon, second breakfast, lunch and tea. It is a lot of money, I know, but it's got to be done.'

When Mother said 'It is a lot of money' she somewhat understated the facts. 250 Schillings a month was the average income of an Austrian worker. A full-time maid like Poldi or her successor, Otti, was paid 60 Schillings a month. It was by the standards of that time a great deal of money, indeed it was no less than ten per cent of Father's salary from the bank before tax.

Not altogether surprisingly at this point Father lost his temper. 'But that's impossible!' he shouted. It was a very good line to Prague, and Father's voice came over loud and clear. 'All that money for that lazy ne'er-do-well. Let that boy become a cobbler or a road-sweeper. That's apparently what he wants and what he's good for. Never! Where am I supposed to get that money from? Steal it, or what? This is out of the question! He'll stay where he is, and if they kick him out in the end he can look after himself. I don't care what becomes of that little rotter. It's his own fault. He's cooked his own goose. No, no, no!'

When Father shouted, Mother easily burst into tears. That was a fairly regular monthly event. At the end of every month Father 'audited' her household book, and there nearly always was a row. Not that Mother had overspent recklessly. Not at all. Knowing the consequences perfectly well, Mother nevertheless gave small monthly donations, never more than twenty-five or thirty Schillings, to some of her Immerdauer aunts, cousins, great-aunts – they were not in short supply – who had fallen on hard times. She could easily have fiddled her accounts. Father might know the prices of all industrial raw materials, but he had no idea what meat, fruit or vegetables cost, but she would not have dreamt of doing so.

But now, talking to Father about my future, she remained totally unmoved by his anger and quietly but with complete determination in her voice she said: 'All right, Ernst, if that's how you feel about it, there is very little I can say to change your mind. But what I want you to know is that George is going to that school. As you cannot afford it, I shall sell the jewellery I inherited from my mother.

That will be enough to pay his school fees for the next few years.' Again Mother had left nothing to chance. She had been prepared for Father's reaction. She had had her jewels valued and knew exactly what they were worth.

A moment's silence. Then Father said: 'I suppose you better get him registered for that school. The sooner he changes over the better. We'll talk about the rest when I'm back. How soon do you think he can start in Grinzing?'

'Very quickly, I believe,' Mother replied, and then they spoke briefly about other things before finishing the call. Mother turned to me and said: 'You are starting in Grinzing next Monday. I have already spoken to the headmaster. He wants to have a short talk with you, but that'll be all right. We'll have some lunch now, and then I'll take you to the cinema.'

I was stunned and deeply moved. My tears started and rolled down my face into the soup. Now that the battle with Father was over, Mother also was near tears again. Neither of us had much of an appetite.

One hour later we sat in the cinema. Mother had taken a whole box for the two of us, again something that had never happened before, and through a wet veil of tears, embracing each other from time to time, we watched *Audienz in Bad Ischl* with Paul Hörbiger playing Emperor Franz-Josef, not the real one, but one made of sugar-icing by court confectioner Demel. That sticky kitsch, aeons away from our reality, was just right for Mother and myself.

In everything she did on that day my mother showed a profound understanding of her twelve-year-old son. Trying to make a child understand that what he learns at school is ultimately for his own benefit and not for the good of his parents, never works. What can a concept like 'ultimately' mean to a child? It concerns a future that is years – and therefore an infinity – away from what he can conceive as reality. It means something vaguely important at some remote period of time, intellectually just conceivable but emotionally meaningless, because no child can possibly identify with the man or woman he or she is going to be ten or twenty years hence. But a child can identify emotionally with his parents. What they feel about him, that to him is reality. And my reality, my identification, on that day was Mother. The mother who had wept with me, had shared my guilt, was prepared to sacrifice her jewellery for me, doubly dear to her because it was her own mother's, and finally had taken me to the cinema instead of punishing me.

On that day I swore a silent oath that I would work in that new school as I had never worked before, not for my own sake, that of the stranger that would be me in twenty, thirty years' time, but for my mother.

———— ❦ ————

Landerziehungsheim Grinzing was an excellent school. It attempted, on the whole successfully, to blend the high academic standards of the state's higher education system with the more liberal ideals of some of the best English public schools. Hermann Lietz, the founder of the Landerziehungsheim movement, had adapted some of the ideas of the famous Dr Reddie, the highly eccentric educational thinker, who, as headmaster of Abbotsholme produced many new ideas, some good, some cranky. After leaving Abbotsholme, where he had been an assistant master, Lietz returned to Germany and founded a number of Landerziehungsheime, the most famous of them Salem.

Grinzing, the only Landerziehungsheim in Austria, never had more than twenty-five boys, boarders and day-boys, in one form. Most important for me was its tutorial system. Instead of going home after lunch, as one did at the state schools, to do or not do one's home-work on one's own, one had lunch in school and then stayed on until the tutor was satisfied that one had completed and understood one's homework.

By the standards of the time educational liberalism at Grinzing was taken to extremes. One of the best teachers at the school, Pro-fessor Kollmann – we had him in Geography – even allowed the boys in his form to address him with the familiar '*du*' instead of the prescribed formal 'Herr Professor' and '*Sie*'. He had been with these boys since they had joined the school aged ten. According to Austrian regulations, once you were in the fifth form and fifteen years old, you had to be addressed as '*Sie*' by the teachers. Kollmann thought this nonsense. He got round the rules in the simplest possible way. On the day his boys started in the fifth form he told them, 'From now on you and I are going to be on first name terms. I'll go on calling you "*du*" and you call me "*du*" as well.' He never lost the respect of his pupils. On the contrary, even the worst louts adored him. The discipline in his class was the best in the school.

This element of unorthodoxy at Grinzing, combined with the

tutorial system, immediately improved my performance. I became one of the best in my class. Mother was happy, Father was happy, and I was happy. And not one word more was said of Mother having to hock her jewels to keep me at that expensive school.

I had no problems with my teachers. The only problem I had was the class bully, a boy called Jessner; he was tall, wiry and very strong, and at fourteen two years older than the class average. He lived in the same house as the Bartmann family. My misfortune was that I was told to sit at the desk next to his, and so I quickly became his nearest and dearest victim.

Jessner was a master at inventing exquisite little tortures, particularly during lessons, distracting my attention and worrying me no end as I was so desperately trying to live up to my silent oath to be a good pupil. When no teacher was around he often went for me quite brutally. For a long time I tried to placate him, to buy him off with little presents, but peace never lasted for long. And then one day something snapped in me. Much smaller and much weaker, I threw myself at him with berserk fury. We had a vicious fight until the other boys got worried we might really hurt each other and separated us. From that day on I had a much easier life with Jessner.

After I had left Grinzing I only saw him one more time. It was in the street where the Bartmanns lived. He did not see me. That was a stroke of good luck. It was 1938, a few weeks after the *Anschluss*, and Jessner was in the black and silver uniform of Himmler's S.S.

The years I spent at Grinzing – I was there from the age of twelve to fourteen and a half – were the most harmonious and the most tranquil my parents and I had together. Of course there were also rows, the worst when Mother's 'past' suddenly caught up with her and infuriated Father.

One day the telephone rang. It was a Herr Ingenieur Wolf phoning from Budapest. He was coming to visit Vienna and could he see Mother? She was thrilled to bits to hear from this admirer from her past, not that Herr Wolf meant anything to her, she said, but that he wanted to see her again, that she was going to have a 'rendez-vous', simply that another man still showed an interest in her after fifteen or twenty years, all this pleased her no end.

Of course, she made no secret out of it. That would have been dishonest, but also only half the fun. She told Father she was going to meet this old friend at a café, just to talk over old times. No doubt she enormously enjoyed seeing Father's face. He looked as if he had chewed and swallowed a whole lemon. But he had to accept it; after all, he was not Ludwig, but Ernst Klaar. Next afternoon a smiling Mother, her hair freshly shingled and wearing her smartest dress under the Persian lamb coat she had inherited from Grandmother, sailed forth from Pichlergasse to meet the man of her past.

At about six in the afternoon Mother returned. Herr Wolf was with her. He was tall, about as richly proportioned as Father, had thick, black hair, and on his upper lip was a very neatly trimmed, narrow moustache of the style fancied by Hungarian Don Juans. I was proudly introduced and then joined him and Mother in the study. He stayed only a few minutes. He had not come to visit, but merely to see Mother home. Complimenting her on her beautiful flat and delightful boy, he thanked her for a charming afternoon and took his leave.

An hour or so later – he usually came home from the bank between seven and eight in the evening – Father arrived. He only grunted an acknowledgment of some sort when Mother told him that the flowers in the vase were a little present from the attentive Herr Wolf, but then, when it came out that Mother had actually brought the oily Hungarian back with her, had let him enter our home, had been shameless enough to let him meet me, Father's son, all hell broke loose. Oh, the fuss! The louder he shouted, the more Mother lapped it up. Eventually things reached such a pitch that she simply left the study and dining-room where Father was pacing to and fro roaring like a stage lion. When she joined me in my room, Mother was not actually giggling, but amused and far from unhappy. So there they were : Father scowling in his study, Mother sewing in my room. Deadly silence in the whole flat.

Something had to be done. I took a big, white napkin and tied it like a brassard round my right arm. I had seen officers do this in films when negotiating an armistice.

Opening the door to the sitting-room I walked towards Father. He stood, or rather posed, looking very fierce, by the fireplace in the sitting-room, another one of Herr Leonhardtsberger's innovations. When he saw the white napkin round my arm the wrinkles of determined fierceness on his forehead began to smooth out. He was not yet ready to smile, but I could see that the worst was over.

'Has your mother sent you?' he asked.

'No, Daddy. She didn't. I'm chief negotiator. I've appointed myself.'

'Well, tell your mother then that I expect her to understand that she behaved very badly. I don't bring former girl-friends up here, do I?'

I went back to my room and told Mother what he had said.

'Tell your father he's ridiculous and making a mountain out of a molehill,' she said. 'I didn't meet Herr Wolf in secret. Can I help it if he insists on taking me home?'

Back to Father, back to Mother. I shuttled back and forth between the two parties for quite a while, but at last they were reunited in Father's study, and I – tactful for once – withdrew and left them to sort out on their own the events of that afternoon and evening.

How secure and established in its routine everything was at home. Father went to his office, came home for lunch, had his little snooze in the big armchair in his study, returned to the office, came home for dinner, religiously took his Waldheim pills, harmless laxatives his ideal digestion did not need at all. Supposedly helping one to slim, they were a wonderful excuse for overeating. Mother was devoting herself to the household, doing the shopping early in the morning, and then, a scarf tied over her head, an arsenal of dusters in her hands, her daily battle against her principal enemy dirt, commenced. No maid could ever do that job to her satisfaction. For finding hidden dust behind ledges and on picture-frames her right forefinger was what the rod is for the water-diviner. She always struck – dirt. She dusted and cleaned, washed and polished, the maid following in her wake, an expression of utter defeat on her face. Of course she had done the dusting, but it was never good enough. Round and round went the dust-chase; short-sighted as she was, Mother missed no crevice, overlooked no crack, routed dirt, was the most thorough detergent ever invented. Cousin Hedi called Mother her 'Wash-auntie'. That summed her up.

After dinner, usually a cold meal with tea to drink, and after Father had devoted a fair while to his newspaper and the effects of his Waldheim pills – always a joint activity – my parents settled down in the study, which doubled as a lounge, and talked about the events of the day. At least once every week Father visited the Josef-stadt, and Grandmother's and Aunt Sally's latest shenanigans – he did not actually use that Irish word, but the rather similar-sounding Yiddish one *sheegans* – were then reported to Mother. I do not think she was vitally interested, but she listened patiently enough, well knowing that these two women played a big role in Father's emotional life and that, though he might sometimes be critical himself, he would resent disparaging remarks about his mother and sister even from her.

My parents read a great deal. Sometimes they read aloud to each other. Father never could resist this temptation when he held a volume by his favourite poet Rainer Maria Rilke in his hand. Then the banker gave way to the romantic, and he lost himself in Rilke's lyric verse and imagery, tasting the beauty of the language on his tongue as he recited it. Not that he was a master of that art. Far from it. He got too carried away himself, over-emphasised passages where emotional distance was needed to retain clarity and purity, raised his voice too excitedly – in short, gave a bit of a ham performance, but enjoyed himself hugely just the same. Mother sometimes retaliated with passages from Dickens or John Galsworthy, another of her favourites, but her reading aloud was always a pleasure to listen to. She had that rare gift of reading dialogue in such a way that one always knew which character was speaking. Unlike Father she kept her distance from the work she was reading, and because of this detachment the author himself seemed to be speaking. Father reading Rilke felt himself to be Rilke, Mother remained Mother and so never superimposed herself on an author. She just lent him her voice and tongue.

Then there was the radio. The early earphone models with the crystal, their tinny sound all too often interrupted by wailing banshees when some neighbour twiddled with his set, had been replaced by a proper loudspeaker, and Radio Vienna's evening programmes were often very good. Although my parents rarely went to concerts, they liked to listen to them on the radio, usually sitting next to each other on the settee holding hands.

On the whole they preferred to spend their evenings at home, but there were, of course, evenings when they went to the theatre, the cinema, met friends at a café, and very occasionally Mother managed to drag Father to the opera with her. He, having absorbed all the classical drama at the Burgtheater in his youth, was more a man for the lighter muse. He adored the comedies of Franz Molnar, always amusing, yet never shallow, but was not too keen on operettas, the favourite entertainment of the Viennese. Franz Lehár was perhaps the most popular and admired composer of the time, closely followed by Benatzky, Oscar Strauss and Robert Stolz. Indeed, the deeper the country plunged into economic and political crisis, the greater became the popularity of the operetta, the most escapist of all art forms, conjuring on to the stage the world of the imaginary 'good old days'. In many of them the man who had come to personify the happy times of yesteryear, Franz-Josef, appeared, usually as a minor part. But that did not matter, even if he only stood 'immovably in his place' for a couple of minutes or so on the stage, the applause was thunderous. Max Reinhardt was the great wizard of the contemporary theatre, much admired by Father ever since he and Mother had seen some of his major productions in the Berlin of 1929.

That tour of Germany had made a deep impression on my parents. They spent four weeks travelling through the Reich, went to Munich, Frankfurt and Berlin, where they visited Alfred Bartmann's two brothers and their families – first cousins of my mother's, of course – and from there they went to Hamburg, Mother's favourite city. They came back full of admiration. Father told the most mouth-watering stories about the breakfast buffet at the Excelsior Hotel in Berlin where they had stayed. You carved your own roast beef, ham, or sausages, had a choice of eggs fried, boiled, scrambled, took as much as you wanted for an all-inclusive price. Even the dear old Waldheim pills failed before this assault, and his weight, around 95 kilos most of the time, shot up to 105 kilos during that trip. Mother, as always was eating 'hardly anything', but fate, as usual, mocked her, and she returned five kilos heavier than her normal eighty.

But an impression that my parents had been on a glutton's 'bummel' through the Reich, and had nothing else to report on but food, would be quite wrong. They admired how Germany was overcoming the effects of the lost war, the speed with which things got done there, the Germans' determined efficiency and the grandiose scale of everything, particularly when compared with tiny, provincial slothful Austria.

When my parents visited Germany in the early summer of 1929, the Wall Street crash and world economic crisis were yet to come. It was the happiest period of the Weimar Republic. A sense of purpose and optimism was in the air. Germany appeared to have found a new identity for herself in the republic, while Austria remained not merely a country without identity, but also one that knew not where or how to search for one.

But within a mere four years after my parents' journey through Germany – their second honeymoon coinciding with the brief one of the Weimar Republic – the masters of the country which had so enthused them, where the arts had flourished and Berlin had become Europe's cultural capital, were the brown columns of Hitler's storm troopers and his black-uniformed S.S.

A unique combination of historical, political and economic factors had fated Adolf Hitler into power in January 1933, just when his political popularity and fortunes were beginning to decline.

Father, himself a veteran of the Great War, could not help admiring in some ways this former lance-corporal, who had risen so high, and I, the boy nurtured on the *Gute Kamerad*, on so many stories of German valour, on the stab-in-the-back legend, on endless talk about the iniquities of the Treaties of Versailles and St Germain, read with fascination the speeches of this man, who promised to make Germany great again.

We knew about his anti-semitic tirades, of course; we knew about the 1933 anti-Jewish boycott, but, strange as it may seem – it was really a form of self-protection, foolish certainly, but very human – we looked for, and found, excuses for these excesses. Having used anti-semitism to help him achieve power, like so many demagogues before him, did Hitler have any choice but to allow his storm troopers their field-day? Had we not been there before? What about Lueger's anti-semitic speeches? They had sounded just like Hitler's. And when, at last, he was Burgomaster of Vienna had he not wined and dined with his wealthy Jewish friends? When reproached for this inconsistency, he replied: 'I am no enemy of our Viennese Jews; they are not so bad, and we cannot do without them. My Viennese always want to have a good rest, the Jews are the ones who always want to be active.'

True, Grandfather Ludwig's career in the municipal service had suffered, but followers of Lueger had finally spoken up for him and got him his promotion. Had one single Jew ever been physically harmed under Lueger? Hitler was a rabble rouser, just like the young Lueger. Would he, now that he had achieved his ambition, behave any differently? In any case, Germany's powerful traditional and conservative forces were bound to make him toe the line. Look at that photo of the new chancellor shaking hands with President von Hindenburg. How servilely Hitler bows before the ramrod old field marshal. How disdainfully that old soldier looks down on that little man – the Bohemian lance-corporal, he calls him privately – so ridiculously turned out in white tie and tails; like a head-waiter from Sacher's except that head-waiters at Sacher's had better-fitting clothes.

Oranienburg, Sachsenhausen, Dachau! The Austrian newspapers wrote a good deal about the new concentration camps, but surely these too were only the first excesses of a new regime. The sound and fury of the early days could not last for ever. Even Hitler would have to mellow in the end. Political realities, last but not least the great powers, would see to it. That was more or less how people in Vienna talked, at home, in offices, in coffee-houses. A dark, but far-away cloud had appeared on the political horizon. They hoped the winds of time would chase it from the skies. The few who saw the danger were dismissed as professional pessimists.

One Sunday afternoon in the autumn of 1933, when Hitler had been in power for about ten months, we visited the Herlingers, Mother's cheerful, blonde friend with that pleasing hard Russian accent and her husband Ernst. With them was Ernst Herlinger's brother who had arrived the day before from Berlin, or to be more exact, from Oranienburg concentration camp where he had been imprisoned for six months. An active Social-Democrat, he was arrested after the Reichstag fire. He had lived in Germany for many years, but had retained Austrian nationality. That had saved him. He spoke freely about his experiences. That was a courageous thing to do for, the Nazis had forced him to sign a document stating he would say nothing about Oranienburg, and had described in considerable detail what they would do to him if he ever spoke out. They need not have bothered. The burn marks on his nose and cheeks, where the S.A. camp guards had stubbed out their cigarette-ends, told the truth.

I have never forgotten that afternoon at the Herlingers. Obviously this man's story had made a deep impression on me, but, looking back, there is another reason why I shall always remember it: our reaction to his tale. We listened with rapt attention, we took it all in, everything he said. We pitied him, but, genuine as our feelings were, they stopped short of true emotional understanding. The sheer terror of the hunted, tortured human being, which Ernst Herlinger's brother described, cannot be shared by the intellect alone.

I became aware of this later, when, after my escape from Nazi Germany, I told friends in England and in Ireland what it had felt like for a Jew to live in Vienna after the *Anschluss* or to witness the *Reichskristallnacht* in Berlin, when the synagogues were burnt, Jewish shops smashed and plundered, and Jews, young and old, arrested indiscriminately.

How shocked those kind English and Irish friends of mine were as they listened, and how it reminded me of that Sunday afternoon in Vienna with Ernst Herlinger's brother! They also listened attentively whilst chewing tiny cucumber sandwiches and tiny cakes with sickly pink icing on them. 'It must have been quite, quite terrible for you,' they said. 'Do have another piece of cake, George, please do. And some more tea?' It flowed readily, the strong English and the even thicker Irish tea of human kindness. But it was rare to be asked a second time. By December 1938 there were so many refugees, so many harrowing stories in the newspapers. It was only a few weeks after Munich, and 'Peace in our time', and these cruelties were happening in a world which for most of them, emotionally, was on the other side of the moon.

The understanding and comprehension of most people in spite of all the stories in the newspapers was on a par with that of those lovely elderly English Women's Voluntary Services ladies, who gave me lifts in their cars when I served in the British Army during the war. After a few minutes they spotted my accent.

'Where d'you come from? . . . Oh, Vienna in Austria. How lovely! I've always wanted to go there.'

Then a moment's silence. You could hear the penny drop.

'But aren't the Austrians fighting with the Germans?'

'Yes,' said I, 'they are.'

You could see confusion clouding their grey-blue little eyes. 'But you're fighting against your own country then?'

I said I was a Jew.

That meant nothing. However much the dear creatures strained their imperial Victorian brains, even that statement did nothing to click things into place.

'Yes, quite,' they said, 'but the Austrians are your own people, aren't they?' And they drove on more puzzled than before.

Our reactions to events in Germany during Hitler's early years were, naturally, never quite as remote as that. But then his Brown-shirts were much closer to our Jewish skins than ever they were, even in the darkest days of the war, to those of my English friends. And yet this was only a question of degree, the glass wall, thinner in our case than in theirs, was there just the same. We did not close our eyes to what was going on in the Third Reich, but we did not open them too wide either.

And even had we looked with wide-open eyes we would not have seen much, for the writing on the wall for the Jews was still in virtually invisible ink. Looking back, the road leading from that first official boycott of Jewish shops in Germany in 1933 to Auschwitz appears short and straight. It has been said that Germany's Jews went to their doom like sheep to their slaughter. Such a view is entirely based on hindsight and betrays a very poor understanding of human nature. One must judge these things with the contemporary circumstances of the time in mind. The Nazis moved very cautiously at first. After each step they carefully tested the response of public opinion before they took the next one. Each area office of the Gestapo had to report reactions immediately.

Very few German Jews actually emigrated as early as 1933 or 1934. Those who did were usually people not only blessed with exceptional foresight, but also with substantial means and good international connections. Many German Jews, not yet middle-aged in 1933, grew up firmly believing in Prussian virtues. They had fought for Germany in the Great War and saw themselves as Germans. Thousands had abandoned the religion of their forefathers. There were tragically many whose minds worked like those of my little English ladies, the only difference being that their mental world was not Victoria's but Wilhelm's. Loving Germany as they did, how could they foresee the bestialities that were to be committed in the name of the country so dear to them? How could anyone?

And if the German Jews could not understand what was to come, how could an Austrian Jew like my father discern the threat to himself and his family? Particularly as the new head of the Austrian government, the forty-year-old Engelbert Dollfuss, was fighting the Nazis in Austria with more determination than his predecessors.

The new chancellor, a tiny man of five-foot-nothing, promptly nicknamed the 'Millimetternich' after Austria's most famous statesman, strongly believed in his small country's special mission in history, one it could only perform if it remained independent : defending the values of western Christian civilisation. Dollfuss certainly did not mean western liberalism by this. His ideology was a German-Austrian near-mystical concoction containing a good deal of the Holy Roman Empire of the German Nation, a fair sprinkling of the Holy Grail and a large dose of the spirit of the Crusades. He chose the Crusaders' crutched cross as his political symbol. And by 'Christianity' he understood the political catholicism of the C.V., the *Cartell Verband*, the Catholic students' fraternity, whose 'old boys' held all the important levers of the state machinery in their hands. Millimetternich's programme also contained some elements of the great Metternich's policies, a strong belief in legitimacy and historical continuity, and also a very scant regard for political freedom and democracy. But Dollfuss really believed in Austria. He did not see his country as just another German province. On the contrary, he was totally convinced that Austria's long history, its position at the crossroads of east and west, north and south, had fashioned a nation, which though of the German tongue, was not German, one, which by combining through the centuries the highest cultural attainments of the Romance, Slavonic and Germanic peoples, had not only the right but the duty to continue its own independent existence.

Dollfuss's views were quite unacceptable to the two political parties diametrically opposed to each other on every other issue: the Austrian Social-Democrats and the Austrian National-Socialists. The majority of the Nazis wanted the *Anschluss* and wanted Greater Germany; the Social-Democrats wanted it too, but not while Hitler ruled the Reich.

This conviction of the Social-Democrats was so strongly held that even after the Nazi *Anschluss* in April 1938 Otto Bauer, the Socialist leader, wrote in the Paris émigré journal *Der Sozialistische Kampf*:

The watchword with which we oppose foreign rule over Austria by satraps of the Reich cannot be the reactionary slogan of Austrian independence, but rather only the revolutionary watchword of the all-German revolution, which alone can free the Austrian tribe of the nation from the fascist tyrants along with the other German tribes.

Dollfuss's and his successor's, Kurt von Schuschnigg's, attempts to imbue the Austrians with a strong sense of patriotism were to Bauer vain efforts to bring alive a reactionary mirage. Dollfuss and Schuschnigg failed. The satire written by history being so much more sardonic and sharper than anything the human brain can produce, it was left to Adolf Hitler to accomplish what the two Austrian chancellors could not: to give the Austrians a strong sense of their national and independent identity.

11 September 1933 was a crucial day for Austria. Dollfuss had ordered a mass rally of his political supporters on Vienna's Trotting Racecourse. There, in a major speech, he announced the end of parliamentary democracy in Austria and its replacement by an authoritarian corporate state. One of the witnesses of that rally, G. E. R. Gedye, the Vienna correspondent of the London *Daily Telegraph*, wrote:

It was all very picturesque and depressing at the same time. The Heimwehr Regiments in their green uniforms were flanked by Tyrolean defence volunteers in their colourful traditional native garb. Hundreds of thousands screamed 'Heil' as the diminutive chancellor in his grey-green uniform of the Kaiserjäger, the Imperial Alpine Regiment, a military cape over his shoulder and a white feather on his cap, traipsed up the speaker's dais.

Another witness of that occasion, one of the hundreds of thousands who screamed 'Heil Dollfuss!', was I. I had kept my resolution, made in Budapest at the age of five, to become a boy scout, wear that big Mafeking hat, march smartly on parades. And here I was 'Heil-ing' away at that little man up there whenever the others 'Heil-ed'. Not yet thirteen years old, I looked in my enormous scout hat like a bloated mushroom, for at this, the fattest period of my life, I seemed, at least to myself, as wide as I was tall. Joining the scouts, quite apart from being misused in this way for political purposes, had not been a very wise decision. I should have listened to Father. He was against it. For all the wrong reasons. He thought that all this scouting, what with climbing mountains, sleeping in tents, crawling all over the countryside, handling sharp knives and axes and all the other adventurous things these boys did, was far too dangerous for his son.

I had believed that scouts treated each other with brotherly love. But the boys in my troop were merciless, and a kick up your backside if you moved too slowly at your chores in camp was one of the milder forms of encouragement. No matter, little boys will always be beasts to each other. What mattered to me was the ideal of scouting, one for all and all for one, the togetherness in a good and just cause. But that was not how things worked out in Austria, not by a long shot. Even the boy scouts were divided into Jewish and 'Aryan' troops. To make this less obvious each Jewish troop had one or two 'show-goys'. The 'Aryan' lot managed quite happily without show-Jews.

One side of scouting I did enjoy was parades and marching. I was very proud therefore when we were detailed to march to the Trotting Racecourse to act as extras – 'Austria's youth, her future, is with the Chancellor', that sort of thing – at Millimetternich's mini-Nuremberg party rally.

Our column stood next to a *Heimwehr* battalion. I had plenty of time to look at them. Poldi's husband, a life-long Social-Democrat, had always described them as a motley crowd of rowdies, peasant toughs, fascists, near-Nazis, and a few genuine patriots commanded by playboy officers. That was exactly what our neighbours from Prince Starhemberg's private army looked like.

It was, as Gedye describes it, a picturesque scene. Not only because of the Tyrolean lads. I was more impressed by the Austrian army contingent and their officers. For the first time they wore their new old uniforms. The Dollfuss government, regardless of cost, had dressed its soldiers in the old Imperial uniforms. After the Great War the *Anschluss*-hungry Socialist government had put the Austrian army in uniforms almost identical to those worn by Weimar Germany's *Reichswehr*. It was an astute if expensive move to bring back the uniforms of the old army as a visual reminder of Austria's continuity. Retired colonels and generals dusted down their old outfits, polished their spurs, sabres and medals, and clanked proudly through the streets of Vienna – colourful, but somewhat decrepit advertisements for past glories.

A sudden wave of nostalgia inundated the land. Even real-life archdukes, surprisingly many, came back. Looking as if they had stepped straight off some operetta stage, they could be seen tottering from balls to bazaars, from memorial services to regimental reunions and patriotic rallies. Otto von Habsburg, eldest son of the last emperor and pretender to the throne, was back as well – not in person, the Czechs, Hungarians and Yugoslavs would not have stood for that, but on picture postcards showing him in full regimentals or in Tyrolean national costume. Virtually overnight they appeared in all the newsagents' shop-windows. But in a country politically as sick as Austria, nostalgia was at best no more than a placebo. More than that, a wonder drug, was needed to heal the festering wounds which suspicion and hatred, inflammatory speeches and actions, and above all the bullets of July 1927 had inflicted on Austria's body politic. Such a miracle drug Dollfuss did not possess, nor did his opponents. What the peasants' son Dollfuss did possess was a much clearer and simpler relationship to power than the complex intellectuals who led the Social-Democrats. Unlike the socialist Bauer, Dollfuss, not being a follower of Karl Marx, did not have his hands tied behind his back by a belief in historical inevitability and the irreversible logic of events. Acting while his opponents pondered, he performed major surgery, by cutting parliamentary democracy from the Austrian constitution. And he tried to heal the country's wounds old and new by applying his own panacea – the authoritarian corporate state, the 'new' Austria.

At that Racecourse monster rally Dollfuss announced what he had done and what he was yet going to do. And the thousands cheered and *Heil*-ed Millimetternich's new era.

Father had a somewhat ambivalent attitude to Dollfuss's Austria. Although he had voted for the Social-Democrats at every election, Dollfuss struck him as a man who had the courage of his convictions, believed in Austria and the country's independence, and wanted to create a state which at least in its outward manifestations had similarities with the Habsburg Austria in which Father had grown up. Above all the tiny chancellor, unlike his predecessors, had had the courage to ban the Nazi party.

Unless you were a political activist, you could go on leading your own life under the Millimetternich. You had to join his 'Fatherland-Front', but that was such an amorphous political entity, that becoming a member did not involve great issues of conscience. Father joined. And like millions of others who were anything but fanatical followers of Dollfuss he wore the 'Fatherland-Front's' little red-white-red ribbon in his buttonhole.

On 12 February 1934 I was still limping as a result of a ski-ing injury. It was a dark winter's morning. In the classrooms at the Landerziehungsheim the electric lights were on. Suddenly, shortly after 11.30, the rooms went dark. We reacted as schoolboys always do to any unexpected break in their dreary rountine – with cheers. By now it was light enough to see, so the teacher carried on. Not for long, though. After another few minutes the senior housemaster came storming down the corridor, yelling, 'Out into the main courtyard, everybody out!'

When we were all assembled, headmaster Lohan addressed us: 'A general strike has been declared. Go back to your classrooms now and collect your things. Boarders will go to the main building. Dayboys will go home by the quickest possible route. I believe the trams have stopped. You may have to walk But, as I said, straight home, please. No loitering about! Be as quick about it as you can.'

With that we were dismissed. We raced down the road to the tram-stop. The trams were there with their crews standing in the street next to them. 'Don't bother to wait, boys,' one of the conductors told us, 'there's no electricity, we don't know ourselves what's going on.'

In spite of the headmaster's instructions we were in no particular hurry. Leisurely we sauntered along the main road from Grinzing to the city, passing more and more stationary tram trains, some still with their crews, others without them. There was hardly any traffic about. The few pedestrians one saw all seemed in a hurry. Lorry-loads of armed steel-hatted police passed us. We felt that heady mixture of fear and excitement, prelude, not only for boys, to all sorts of follies. I was together with two other boys who lived near me, and we decided to walk right on to the Inner City. The route we wanted to follow was down Währingerstrasse, one of the main arterial roads, then cross the Ring at Schottentor and go from there to the Chancellery on the Ballhausplatz.

We made it as far as the first major road intersection where Nussdorferstrasse crosses Währingerstrasse, just about two hundred yards, no more, from Pichlergasse. A barbed-wire barrier blocking off the whole Währingerstrasse stopped us. From behind it three heavy machine-guns manned by soldiers in full war-paint were pointing at us. 'Get back, you!' an officer shouted.

As I did so I trod right on the toes of my very pale and very angry Father: 'Where the hell have you been? Mother phoned the school. You should have been home at least half an hour ago! I've been standing here for the last twenty minutes waiting. Not a word. You're coming with me this very minute. And you boys get home immediately.'

Back home we stood for a long time by the window in Father's study and looked down on Nussdorferstrasse. It was an eerie picture. The shops had let down their steel shutters. Not a soul was to be seen on that road always so full of traffic and people. No sound came from it. Dead and ghostly, the street lay there in the gloomy early dark of winter. No lights anywhere. From somewhere in the distance one heard the rattle of machine-guns. All Father knew was what he had heard at the bank. In the early morning police, looking for hidden *Schutzbund* weapons at a working-men's club in Linz, had been fired on. The police had stormed the building. After that the Social-Democrats had called out the workers on general strike.

The clerico-fascist forces had been preparing for just such a 'show-down'. On 11 February Major Fey, commander of the Vienna *Heimwehr* had told his men: 'Discussions we have had with the

Chancellor yesterday and the day before have shown that he is on our side. I can tell you still more, but only briefly : we'll have work to do tomorrow.'

Fey knew what he was talking about. There was not going to be a repetition of 15 July 1927, with angry demonstrators marching in their thousands down the main roads towards the city, overwhelming easily a few badly armed and confused policemen. This time Dollfuss's forces were fully prepared and well organised. The army, the police, and the *Heimwehr* militia were controlling Vienna's arterial roads. Instead of the workers marching into the city, the Government's soldiers were moving out into the working-class suburbs surrounding the big blocks of flats the Social-Democrats had built for their supporters. For years the Right had mocked these buildings, called them shoddily-built playing-card houses bound to collapse, but now suddenly these very same buildings were denounced as veritable fortifications, civil-war bastions holding Vienna in their grip, sited upon a carefully prepared strategic plan.

We sat at home in the falling dusk. Mother had put out some candles, but we had not lit them yet. We had enough food for two or three days. Our coal – it was bitterly cold – would last for a week at most. At about four in the afternoon we heard a booming noise in the distance. Then again and again. We could hardly believe it, but they were using artillery. Heavy guns were firing at the workers' blocks of flats with women and children still in them. That was murder! Had Dollfuss gone mad? In contemporary reports and books the picture of the mad 'pocket dictator', of a murderous little man killing working-class women and children, was drawn again and again, till Dollfuss looked like one of Hieronymus Bosch's man-eating monsters. He committed a political blunder of some magnitude when he had himself photographed, stupidly wearing his wartime officer's unifom for the occasion, together with the army commanders watching the shelling of the council flats.

In fact, Dollfuss was not a bloodthirsty demon. The use of artillery was not his idea. He had wanted to use tear gas, but under the peace treaty of St Germain Austria was forbidden any gas weapons, and all Austrian governments of whatever complexion observed the terms of the treaty rigorously as they were economically so totally dependent on international goodwill.

However, army commanders will always find humanitarian reasons for escalating destruction, and Austrian generals were no exception to this rule. Proposing the use of heavy artillery, they argued that the shock of gunfire would force the speedy capitulation of the *Schutzbund*, while infantry operations being too slow would ultimately cause greater loss of life on both sides. From a tactical point of view the officers may even have had a point, but politically their advice was disastrous. No European government up to then had ever aimed its artillery at buildings with women and children in them. But *Heimwehr* Fey, vain, ambitious, aggressive and just then at the peak of his power supported the army, and Dollfuss gave way.

Individual *Schutzbund* men performed feats of heroism, but their leaders had allowed themselves to be surprised by events. After twenty-four hours of fighting they realised that the situation was hopeless and that the state was the stronger. They fled. Small units kept on fighting for two more days until they too were forced to surrender. But the victorious Dollfuss only had little more than another five months to live.

On 25 July 1934 I had been out cycling all afternoon. It was a hot day. I felt doubly hot and sweaty after carrying my bike up the two flights of stairs when I came home for dinner. I propped my bike against the white wooden bench under the hall mirror, its usual parking place, but such was the fascination it still held for me that I swung myself into the saddle again, just for another taste of it, to wait there till Father came home and we could eat. It was only six-thirty, so there was still about half an hour to go. The dining-room door suddenly opened and much to my surprise there was Father with Mother standing behind him.

'There you are at last,' he said. 'Dollfuss has been murdered. Where were you? We were worried.'

'I don't believe it,' I replied. 'Who killed him? It can't be, everything is perfectly normal outside. Not at all like February.'

'There's been a Nazi *Putsch*. They shot him. It's gone wrong, thank God. They've all been arrested. Come in, we're listening to the radio.'

The July 1934 *Putsch* and Dollfuss's assassination could have been prevented. Since 29 May of that year clear evidence of the planned Nazi conspiracy was available to the Austrian authorities. It came from a number of highly reliable sources. The warnings were passed to the senior security officials who were charged with the protection of the state, the government and the Chancellor. Without doubt some of them collaborated with the Nazi conspirators. Also without doubt some of the others acted with typical Austrian *Schlamperei*. They did not take the warnings seriously.

The murder of the little Chancellor should have been a sort of *Mene Tekel*. But for us this writing on the wall was still invisible. We were no better at seeing it than were the Jews of Germany in reading the first signs pointing to their destiny. A genius of foresight, an Arthur Schnitzler perhaps, would have understood. Father was no Schnitzler.

The government propaganda machine raved about Mussolini, our country's powerful ally, whose troops would bar Hitler from our frontiers forever. It also went on and on about how much stronger the Dollfuss state was now, how much more firmly established and more deeply engraved after this tragedy into the hearts of its people.

Benito Mussolini did indeed despatch some of his divisions to the Brenner border.

Poor Dollfuss was turned into a sort of Austrian Horst Wessel. What that murdered pimp from the gutters of Berlin was to the Nazi movement, its martyr-in-chief, Dollfuss now became for Austria's patriotic authoritarian movement. The Nazis howled their Horst Wessel song, always played after the German national anthem, we strained our vocal cords in the Dollfuss song, also always played after our national anthem. It was called the 'Song of Youth'. Its opening lines were: 'We, the young ones stand prepared to march with Dollfuss into grand new times . . .'

Dollfuss, the martyr Chancellor, was given the most pompous, and yet somehow moving, funeral in Austria's history. Dollfuss pictures and busts appeared everywhere. Every morning we now had to greet our teachers with a resounding '*Heil* Austria'. We had to listen to or read tales about how Dollfuss had always been the best pupil in his school, how everybody who knew him as a boy had adored him, and how his leadership qualities had already been obvious to one and all when he was only a youth. The little man's sanctification followed very quickly. They were in such a rush, they missed the beatification stage. He was our 'heroic Chancellor', the heart-blood of Austria; and within one year an entire Dollfuss mythology had been created and his near-deification accomplished. To the Dollfuss squares and streets in every city, town and village, they added Dollfuss chapels, altar pictures and eternal flames. The crucified Christ still remained over the altars, but Dollfuss's effigy stood nearby.

This was not entirely the artificial creation of the government's propaganda machine. Dollfuss had been a man of the people. He did speak their language, did possess warmth and great courage, even his diminutive stature had helped his popularity. He could and did establish a direct contact with the Catholic and conservative masses because he so patently held his beliefs with much greater sincerity than did the run-of-the-mill politicians whose petty jealousies and squabbles had done quite as much to destroy parliamentary democracy in Austria as Dollfuss had done himself.

Kurt von Schuschnigg succeeded Dollfuss as Chancellor of Austria. A thirty-four-year-old lawyer from Innsbruck, the Tyrolean capital, the Minister of Justice in the last Dollfuss cabinet, Schuschnigg was as different from his predecessor as chalk from cheese. Dollfuss came from peasant stock, Schuschnigg from an officer's family. His father was a retired general. Dollfuss left few people indifferent, one either hated or loved him. No one loved Schuschnigg. Dollfuss was human, could relax in the company of his friends. The studious Tyrolean lawyer rarely smiled and appeared cold and distant. That intelligent and perceptive Habsburg, the pretender Otto, called Schuschnigg's spectacles 'the glass wall dividing him from other people'. Schuschnigg, though a man of great honesty and absolute integrity, unlike Dollfuss, the man of the people, was every inch an elitist.

Wilhelm Miklas, the Federal President, accepted Dollfuss's testamentary choice and appointed Schuschnigg, but not because he believed in that young lawyer or even in the Dollfuss-created authoritarian state over which he found himself presiding. The only alternative to Schuschnigg, such was the power structure in the state, would have been Prince Starhemberg, or another senior *Heimwehr* leader, and Miklas could not abide that fascist militia or any of the men who commanded it. The democratically elected president of the corporate Austrian state actually deplored it. Only a strong sense of duty and the hope, vain as this was and always must be, that his presence might prevent some of the more blatant abuses of power, kept the conservative democrat Miklas from resigning.

In this whole tale of the first Austrian Republic, the one unsung hero is this former provincial headmaster, who was elected Federal President of Austria in 1928 because he was the only candidate all political parties could agree on. Never a prominent leader of the Christian-Social party, he was no 'progressive', but a firm believer in parliamentary democracy and in Austria. In 1918, on 11 November, when the Austrian Republic was born, Wilhelm Miklas was the only member of its first provisional parliament to vote against paragraph 2 of the law establishing the new state which began: 'German Austria is a part of the German Republic.'

In an article written in 1929, the Austrian poet Anton Wildgans wrote this definition of *Homo austriacus*, the Austrian man:

By his language and by his original descent Austrian man is German, and as such he has performed many valuable services in all areas of human activity for German culture and for the German folk; but his German-ness, loyal and faithful as he feels towards it, has, through the mixture of many bloods in his veins and through historical experiences, become less single-minded, less harsh, more conciliatory, more cosmopolitan, more European.

Wilhelm Miklas was a true *Homo austriacus*. One point on which he agreed with Dollfuss was that Austrian man, though of German kind, was not a German.

Most Sunday mornings Father and I took a No. 5 tram to our usual Sunday morning destination, that empire which stood even more 'immovably in its place' than that of the Habsburgs had done – Grandmother Julie's flat.

Father's weekday visits to his mother varied, but the Sunday routine was as invariable as the opening ceremony of the British Parliament. Father's relationship with his mother was also cast in historically immutable concepts. To the outside world, possibly to Father himself, these frequent visits to his mother proved that there was a warm filial contact between him and Grandmother, but the formalism in which it was clothed was merely a cover, not only for a deep mutual concern, but also for a high degree of mutual dependence.

When I was smaller I had to accompany Father every Sunday and suffer Grandmother's wet kisses like a good little boy. After this ex-change of endearments I was left in peace, and while Father was with his mother and sister, I spent the morning with Annitschek mixing my fantasy medicines and eating endless slices of bread and butter thickly smeared with anchovy paste. Occasionally another visitor turned up on these Sunday mornings, an elderly Herr Hofrat, probably one of Grandmother's beaux of yore. He was a most im-pressive gentleman, bald, but with an artistic fringe of long grey hair and a thick black moustache. Always clad in an impeccable black suit, he wore light-grey spats over his highly polished black shoes. His gold-topped cane, left in the hall stand, was one of my favourite toys.

Mother never came with us. I did not ask her why she did not come as well; I could guess. Father's intense involvement with the two women in Josefstädterstrasse was probably quite enough for her at one remove. She heard more than she wanted about their doings, their thoughts, their latest stomach upsets and headaches within her own four walls. She did not have to go there to listen to it all over again. Second-hand information in this case was as good as a feast for her. There may, however, have been another reason why Father never tried to make her join us. Grandmother Julie herself. She accepted, albeit somewhat reluctantly, that her sons were men and had to have wives. But this did not mean that she had to have sons' wives around her twice weekly as well.

Julie was not a religious Jewess, but the tradition that women worship separately from men in the synagogue was one she liked to extend to her own home where her sons and their wives were concerned. Her sons' wives were received, of course, but never, if avoidable, together with their husbands. They were formally invited to call for tea once a month or so. If she had a favourite daughter-in-law it was probably my quiet restrained mother. Crazy Gisi and grandiloquent Hanna were beyond the pale in any case – though I have actually seen Hanna in Grandmother's flat once or twice, Gisi of course never; and Alice, Uncle Paul's wife, probably fussed her. Mother was quiet and polite and never argued about her husband's monthly contribution to the Josefstädterstrasse household. It was his money and his family – not quite Alice's attitude.

As I grew older Father no longer insisted that I come with him every Sunday. He let me decide whether I wanted to come or not, and very often I did. I enjoyed being alone with Father, even if it was only for the tram ride to Josefstädterstrasse and back.

During such a Sunday morning tram ride in late August 1934 Father told me that the school year 1934–5 was to be my last at Grinzing. I was doing well at school, and there was no need for him to go on paying those high school fees. He did not lay down the law, but explained his position kindly, flattering me about my achievements and pointing out how much it would mean to him and to his mother if he could give her more money. I did not particularly look forward to changing schools yet again, but I knew well enough that sending me to Grinzing had been a real sacrifice on his part. I felt confident that I could do just as well at another school.

At fourteen one considers oneself an adult, of course. A point of view my parents did not share completely, but they went along with it to some extent. My pocket-money was increased, enabling me to replace the Sunday morning walk with Fredl Resch with a night out on the town every Saturday with my new boon companion Fritzl Pollack. Nothing too gay, nothing outrageous, you understand. We were two young blades of very decent and firmly established habits. We met at five, saw a thriller at the movies at six and dined at eight. Our meeting-place was the Sirk-Corner opposite the opera, once the starting-post of the gallant Corso of lost Imperial Vienna. From there we walked the few steps towards Krugerstrasse, a small side road, much frequented by prostitutes, leading into Kärntnerstrasse. The girls were not the reason why we went there, though we were more than aware of them and viewed them with what we hoped were hardly noticeable sidelong glances. To tell the truth, we were rather scared of them – though very, very interested – for two reasons. We were afraid that one of them, resenting too obvious stares from two callow boys, might box our ears, but even more we dreaded one approaching us to ask whether the two sweetie boys would like to have a bit of fun.

Our destination was the Kruger-Kino, the one cinema in Vienna specialising in the very latest Hollywood gangster films, often with James Cagney in the lead, either as a G-man, as F.B.I. agents were called then, or as a homicidal maniac. The film finished, we marched back in the same direction from which we had come past the new German State Railway travel office with a bigger plate-glass window than any shop in the whole of Vienna, so that you were sure to get a good view of the larger-than-life Hitler portrait on the far wall opposite its corner entrance. We crossed the Ring at Opernplatz and on the other side, almost exactly facing Opernring 3 where Grandmother Julie had lived before her marriage to Grandfather, there was the O.K. restaurant. It was really two eating-houses in one. One was the big self-service snack section, the other the much more elegant O.K. Stüberl, where we went, with proper waiters, neatly laid tables and very good food.

Fritzl Pollack and I wasted no time on studying the menu. We knew what we wanted, and every Saturday we wanted the same : two big steaks, fresh potato chips and a bottle of that queen of all table condiments, Worcestershire Sauce.

Father, very involved professionally with the Czech branch of the Länderbank that year, spent much time in Prague, and Mother and I joined him there for Christmas. We all loved Prague, the marvellous food, the unique atmosphere of that beautiful old city.

I got drunk in Prague for the first time in my life. At lunch Father had introduced me to the joys of the original and genuine Pilsner beer. I drank three glasses, for boys will try hard to prove that they are men. One cannot argue with three glasses of Pilsner beer. I certainly could not. Having thus quenched my thirst I was in no fit state for anyone's company. I was drunk. Mother took me back to the hotel, and the longest afternoon sleep of my life put me, so to speak, on my feet again.

Christmas that year was marvellous. Father took us to the best and most elegant restaurants. Observing one evening how I wetted my forefinger and then circled it over my bread plate so that the crisp crumbs from my rolls stuck to it and I could lick them off, father said that he knew another person with the same habit, his 'God', Herr Direktor Fischer, one of the two chief managers of the Länderbank. Perhaps I was destined to become a banker too, Father joked.

That trip to Prague did not start me on a career in finance, but it did teach me something about the intricacies of international currency controls and the highly intimate sins of transgression in this tightly packed yet nationally and politically fragmented and separated European family of nations. When I helped Father to unpack on our return to Pichlergasse, I noted that he took out of his case a dozen of the freshly laundered and starched stiff collars he always wore, and from inside each collar's upper fold he took a tightly rolled high-denomination Czech banknote. It was the salary he had earned in Prague, which 'legally' he was not allowed to take out of Czechoslovakia.

During the early months of 1935 I came across Hitler's *Mein Kampf* on the shelves of my lending library. I took the book home and read it thoroughly. It certainly did not bore me. The one passage which particularly affected me was Hitler's description of the Jew-boy lurking spider-like at street corners for innocent 'Aryan' maidens to be vilely seduced by him. That I thought absolutely ridiculous. After all, I was a 'Jew-boy' and one very interested in girls, but I could not have cared less whether they were blonde maidens, Jewesses dark or fair, rosy cheeked Slavs or high-boned Hungarians. What mattered was that they were attractive girls. In any case, what was so irresistible about a Jew-boy? The girls I ogled were far from swooning into my ready arms. They did not even notice me. He did not give me an inferiority complex though, because I knew that other 'Jew-boys' of my age had the same problem. Hitler was talking nonsense.

And even without that racial sex-appeal with which the Führer's imagination had endowed me, I did, soon after reading *Mein Kampf*, meet the first girl who cared for me. It was the summer of 1935 in Jevany. In this lake-side resort, less than an hour's bus ride from Prague, we spent three weeks in July, Father again auditing the books of the Czech bank. Father went into town every morning from the very pleasant modern hotel with its own lake-side beach where we stayed and came back in the evening. Our most prominent fellow-guest, and as Father said the most interesting one, a veritable mummy of a man with heavily rouged cheeks, dyed hair and eyebrows, very old, very brittle, was Professor Stocklasa, one of Masaryk's closest collaborators and fellow-founders of the Czechoslovak Republic.

Personally I found two other hotel guests of much greater interest than this ancient politician : two girls, daughters of a Jewish jeweller from Prague, who spent their holidays in Jevany. The older was about my age, her sister, one year younger, was the prettier of the two, but I preferred 'maturity' to looks. In any case the older sister did notice me, was more obviously interested in me than the younger. She became my first girl-friend. We actually did kiss a few times, held hands more often and finally parted, having sworn each other eternal love.

Mother was very good about it all. She did not say much and was nice to the two girls. Father showed much too openly how amused he was by his young son's first 'adventure'. Saying he thought the younger sister the more attractive playmate, he added jokingly that the older sister would do very well for his future daughter-in-law, because, gentleman in the jewellery trade being well supplied with gold and silver and precious stones, her father should be able to provide a substantial dowry.

Father also made remarks of that sort when my girl-friend and her sister were with us, well knowing that they, though being Czech nationals, were also Jewesses and therefore *Deutsche Kulturträger* and spoke our language just as well as we did. I often wished they had no German when he made his embarrassing jokes.

What hurt me much more than Father's leg-pulls was that he so

138

obviously did not take me seriously. Suddenly I had become a very serious young man involved in a very serious emotional experience. All his nonsense about calf-love! Did he not know that his son's feelings were much more mature than that, that I took myself seriously? Very! No, my love was real. The girl was the 'woman of my life'. I wanted to share my life with her. Voluntary separation was unthinkable, unavoidable separation, tragic.

The trouble with Father's jokes, though some like the one about the dowry were more than a bit off, was that they were often also very funny, and such was my lack of single-mindedness that I hated and loved them at the same time. Or maybe I hated the jokes, but loved Father.

When we left Jevany it was with a sad heart in my body, noble thoughts in my mind and lyrical stirrings in my soul. I remained in this state during the whole ensuing fortnight in Vienna. The following four weeks I spent in a lake-side holiday camp in Lower Austria, while my parents took the waters again, this time in Marienbad instead of Karlsbad. My heart stayed sad, my thoughts noble and my stirrings lyrical in that holiday camp. But it was a different young lady who inspired these feelings now.

Her name was Lisl. I was attracted by her, she by my pyjamas. I spotted her immediately upon arrival, she saw them while unpacking my luggage. She was captivated by their green silken elegance, the most exquisite, striking and widely discussed night apparel ever seen in that holiday camp.

Those four weeks were heaven when she looked at me and hell when she did not. Lisl was nine months younger than I, just a little over thirteen and a half, but her kisses, the few I did get, were much sweeter than those I had been given by whatever her name was, in Jevany.

After the Schopenhauergymnasium debacle I continued and ended my school education at the Privatrealgymnasium Juranek, an independent grammar school in the Josefstadt. It was a curious school. The headmaster, Egid von Filek, was a well-known author. Brilliant teacher at one moment, he could behave like a lunatic the next. Highly-strung, highly eccentric, you never knew where you were with him. Our form master, Professor Frey, was a very good teacher, but most of his colleagues were pretty hopeless.

Juranek's was not a boarding school and much cheaper than Grinzing. It therefore did not have the reputation of being a school for well-heeled idiots — just for idiots. The pupils were about one-third Jewish, one-third out and out Nazis, one-third politically indifferent. Most of our Nazi colleagues were older than I, proof that they were unable to cope with the state schools, because they were either too dim or spent all their free time working for the cause. The strangest thing was that they behaved decently towards us Jews. After the *Anschluss* a fair number of them turned up at school in Hitler Youth, S.A. and S.S. uniforms, but not one of them ever did or said anything against the Jews at school. This was very different from the events at a number of state schools where Jewish students were badly beaten up, and occasionally even stopped by force from entering their schools immediately after the Nazi takeover.

Our school Hitler Youth leader sat next to me. A few days after the *Anschluss* he wanted to make an announcement to the other Hitler Youth members in the class, but instead of shouting 'Jews out!' or even worse, he just said: 'If our Jewish colleagues wouldn't mind leaving the classroom for a few minutes I should be grateful. I have a confidential message for the other Hitler Youth boys.'

In 1936, as I ended my first year at Juranek's, Herr von Papen, Hitler's delegate in Austria, achieved a major diplomatic success. The first two years of his mission had not been easy for him. He arrived in Vienna after the murder of Chancellor Dollfuss in 1934 without any illusions. He knew how difficult it would be to break the ice. But he hoped that his Catholic conservative background would enable him to establish personal contacts with some members of the Austrian government. He quickly learned otherwise when presenting his credentials at Ballhausplatz. His reception was truly glacial. He was shown into the very room in the Chancellery where Dollfuss had been murdered. There, in front of a marble plinth from which the martyred Chancellor's death-mask looked down at him as he entered, the assembled Austrian government awaited Germany's new ambassador. None of the Austrians spoke one word more than was absolutely essential during the accreditation ceremony. Everything was strictly protocol, no personal remarks were made, no word of welcome, not even in the most formal sense, were extended.

But von Papen knew how to wait, how not to rush matters, to allow time and the constantly changing international scene to work for him. Hitler and Mussolini, Austria's chief protector, began to draw closer to each other during the following two years. One did not have to be a diplomat to understand how this development worried the Austrian government. Another factor at least as important in helping von Papen to break through eventually was the confused state of the Austrian mind without the psychological anchor of Habsburg loyalty. The Chancellor, Kurt von Schuschnigg, was himself a perfect example of this. An Austrian patriot and general's son, he viewed the vulgar demagogue and upstart Hitler with dislike and disdain, and yet, feeling himself to be also German, he could not but admire the Führer, who had made Germany great and feared again.

Ignaz Seipel, Austria's chancellor during the Twenties, coined the phrase 'One nation, two states' to describe Germany and Austria. The formula was used again fifty years later by West German chancellor Willy Brandt to define the relationship created by his Ostpolitik between the democratic Federal Republic and communist East Germany. Such a formula can be highly dangerous, if one of these 'states' not only proclaims its ardour for unification, but is determined and possesses the strength to impose its will on the wary and recalcitrant other 'state', using the 'one nation' concept as justification for aggression.

Von Papen argued that the two German states ought to be able to live side by side in close amity; that two countries which had fought shoulder to shoulder in history's most terrible war could not and should not differ on basic German issues. Had Germany and Austria not shared the shame of unjust defeat? Had not the two German states both been stabbed in the back by Bolshevism? Had they not both been treated as pariahs and lepers by the victorious powers, had they not both been labelled and libelled with the war guilt lie? Surely so much joint suffering should create a bond of unity stronger than the issues that divided them. Why not let bygones be bygones? The Führer was ready to do this. As a first step he had authorised von Papen to negotiate an Austro-German friendship treaty, one that would not merely respect Austria's independence, but explicitly confirm, even guarantee, it.

Schuschnigg did not for long resist the song of Hitler's suave, elegant siren, nor Mussolini's pressure that he should accept a treaty which apparently offered a solution to all Austro-German problems. He did not dwell too long on the idea that 'he who giveth' also possesses the power to take away. Hitler's guarantee implied that

Nazi Germany was basically the only danger to Austrian independence; that although Germany had the desire and will to effect an *Anschluss*, it decided to restrain itself. Neither the Kaiser's nor Weimar Germany had ever offered Austria such guarantees. But then neither of those two German states had ever threatened Austria's independence. That Hitler should offer such a guarantee was surely proof that the adherence to the 'One nation, two states' concept depended solely on Nazi Germany's willingness to behave itself. There was no provision for what might happen if Austrian independence were to be smothered by its ardent lover, Nazi Germany itself.

The treaty for the 'Normalisation of Relations between Austria and Germany' was released to the press late at night of Saturday, 11 July 1936. Its two crucial paragraphs said : 'Germany has neither the intention nor the desire to interfere in Austrian internal affairs, to annex Austria or to make it part of the German Reich [*oder es anzuschliessen*]' and 'The Austrian Federal Government will base its policies in general and those concerning Germany in particular on the fundamental fact that Austria acknowledges itself to be a German State.'

For the next few days Vienna's newspapers were full of the treaty. Not to discuss it – that was not really possible – but to praise it and the Chancellor, whose great statesmanship had ensured this 'great success' for Austria. Hidden among all the columns expressing Austria's joy, the approval of foreign governments and newspapers, there was a tiny item in the *Neue Freie Presse* on 14 July which we ought not to have overlooked. It said : 'The Austrian Consul-General in Jerusalem, Dr Ivo Jorda, will be available to members of the public requiring information from 10 a.m. to 1 p.m. at the Federal Chancellery, 1 Ballhausplatz, 2nd Floor, room 63.'

The Klaars, loyal Austrians that they were, did not avail themselves of this opportunity.

Benito Mussolini, although for his own ends he had pressed Schuschnigg to accept the treaty, nevertheless warned the Austrian Chancellor about the value of a Nazi guarantee. One month after the signing of the July agreement he received Colonel Liebitzky, the Austrian military attaché, at the Palazzo Venezia and told him that Hitler was determined to settle the Czechoslovak problem in 1938. 'Tell the Chancellor again that Austria only has another twenty months' time!' he added.

Stefan Zweig, living in Salzburg, very close to the German border, aptly summed up our attitude and that of the overwhelming majority of Viennese Jews, when he wrote:

They behave as if the putting beyond the pale of doctors, lawyers, scientists and actors were happening somewhere in China as if this and their becoming pariahs outside the law were not taking place in a country a mere three hours' journey away and one where they speak the same tongue we do. No, they still sit comfortably in their homes and drive around in their cars. And every one of them consoles himself with that foolish phrase: 'Hitler cannot last long'

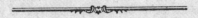

For us, my parents and me, life continued as usual. We were packing for our summer holidays: Bad Ischl again.

Oh ye travellers of today, trussed, packaged and despatched to Mallorca, Tenerife, battened down and sardined in your charter jets, flying round the globe, what do you know about the joy and excitement of journeying from Vienna to Bad Ischl in 1936? Six hours in the train. One change at that marvellously named onomatopoeic railway station 'Attnang-Puchheim'. Say it in German quickly with ever-increasing speed and you hear the sound of the train's wheels rumbling over the rails as it brings you nearer to your holiday destination.

That railway junction was where the Klaar travellers who only had a picnic hamper with cold chicken, ham, sausages, bread, butter and cheese to sustain them during the first hours of the journey, could fortify themselves for the rest of it with fresh, hot coffee and freshly cooked frankfurters.

The actual travel was the least of the fun. The joy, the spice, was in the preparations. Two weeks before the red-capped stationmaster blew his whistle, and we were off, the trunks and suitcases were brought up from the cellar into the flat. You stumbled over them everywhere. They were packed and unpacked, something that should have been at the bottom suddenly turned up at the top, the dress in this one ought to go in that one, the table-linen – we had rented a flat in Bad Ischl and had to bring our own things – had got mixed up with the bed-linen, and that again, for some totally inexplicable reason, had hidden itself under the bath-towels. What excitement, what confusion! What was still needed had been packed, what was not needed and should have been packed was ready to hand. Stumbling over and groaning under things Mother and the maid shuffled from one room to the next, from one suitcase to another and then on the day, miraculously, every trunk was closed, the inner resistance of some of the too full ones overcome by Father or Mother sitting on them. The items had been counted and recounted and we were really on our way.

Something, of course, was always forgotten, but never Father's holiday notebook. He did not keep a diary, but on holiday he recorded every item of expenditure. Why, I do not know, but he drew up a daily balance sheet so that he always knew what we had spent on our holiday. Whether he did this only in order to keep his hand in or to find an excuse for not going on holiday next year, must remain an unanswered question.

As a small boy I had always hated Bad Ischl. Now, at fifteen-and-a-half, I had a new feeling for Ischl. I joined a group of young people, we went on long walks, we flirted and intrigued a bit, we danced, we strolled along the Esplanade, we wore the costumes of the natives, were very Austrian, and I began to sense the unique atmosphere Bad Ischl had in those days.

All the great names were there. On the other side of the river Franz Lehár was in his residence, you rubbed shoulders with Emmerich Kalman, you giggled when you saw the twin brothers Goltz, the operetta librettists, looking as alike as one egg from a Jewish mother hen looks to another, both rather incongruously disguised in the local dress, as we were, as genuine Austrian hill-billies. You saw most of the great names in Austrian literature, journalism and medicine, as well as the country's most famous actors and actresses eating their breakfast eggs at the Café Zauner on the Esplanade, or later drinking coffee and munching delicious cakes at Herr Zauner's famous patisserie. You knew every one of the waitresses there, but did not flirt with them, they all appeared to be in their sixties and seventies and immortal. On my first return visit to Bad Ischl, a few years after the war, they were still all there, now presumably close to their eighties and nineties, and at least one of them recognised me immediately, remembered Father and Mother and Grandmother and Aunt Sally. Mixing with the crowd in Zauner's tea-room as if they were just perfectly ordinary human beings, you saw princes and even Habsburg archdukes, and you felt sure that from somewhere up above the rain clouds, always plentiful over Ischl, the man who had made the spa so famous, had so loved its mountains, where he had stalked stag and chamois, Franz-Josef himself, no less, looked down benevolently on his people, Jews and non-Jews alike. The Kaiser and his mementoes were everywhere.

Perhaps it is even more true of Ischl than of the rest of Austria to say that the monarchy died only in 1938.

We had four weeks in Bad Ischl in the summer of 1936, my parents and I. Then Father's holiday was over. He and Mother returned to Vienna, while I spent the rest of that summer at a holiday camp in a village in the Upper Austrian mountains. It was managed by the same young couple who had run that lake-side place, where, the summer before, I had fallen out of my first and into my second love. This summer that second love of mine, Lisl, was not coming. She had told me so herself. During the year we had met in Vienna several times. For me these meetings had not been happy. Whether I wanted to or not I soon realised that my role was that of stand-by boy-friend very much playing second fiddle. I had got on the nerves of my young lady-love, making big eyes at her and following her around with a hang-dog look on my face, sighing and moping, groping in the cinema for hands which did not want to be caressed, an insecure nuisance of a boy. She, quite rightly, preferred older boys, more sure of themselves and less immature.

Imagine my surprise when Lisl suddenly turned up at that holiday camp three days after I had arrived. It made me very happy, but also quite indescribably conceited. I must have been unbearable. If they are petted, hang-dogs, however small, begin to see themselves suddenly as St Bernards and trot about as if they owned the world and all the girls in it. Our relationship did not develop any too well.

Austro-German relations made much more rapid progress. It was autumn, and, if one believed our government propaganda, the fruits of the July agreement with the Reich fell, a joyous harvest, right into our Chancellor's lap. As one of his 'great' concessions Hitler had ended the one thousand Reichsmark barrier keeping the much needed German tourists from Austrian resorts, which none other than he himself had imposed three years earlier. Citizens of the Reich wanting to visit Austria had to pay the then enormous sum of one thousand Reichsmarks for a German exit permit. Now German holiday makers could come again. And they came in their thousands, bringing not only their much needed money, but also word-of-mouth propaganda, the most effective of all. Far more affluent than the Austrians, which the Germans had always been, they talked about all the wonderful things happening in the Reich, lavished praise on Hitler and the miracle he had performed in a few short years. The

Austrians accepted these tales as avidly as they did their visitors' cash.

Trade relations between the two countries were also 'normalised', thus correcting a state of affairs which had only been 'abnormal' thanks to Hitler.

Of course, we did not know that a secret protocol had been attached to the July treaty, but eventually one began to see the results. Certain German newspapers were again on sale in Vienna and other cities. Not National-Socialist party newspapers – they were still banned. But all newspapers from Germany were controlled by Goebbels's Propaganda Ministry anyway. That they painted a rosy picture of Hitler's Germany and National-Socialist achievements goes without saying. As a *quid pro quo* Austrian newspapers were also allowed into Germany, now that Austrian censorship prevented them from writing anything unpleasant about Hitler's Reich.

Far more effective as propaganda than any newspapers, magazines or books from Germany were German films, particularly their war films. Over the Colosseum Cinema in Nussdorferstrasse, which I could see from Father's study window, appeared the huge cardboard figure of a steel-helmeted German soldier, his wide-open mouth screaming in fury at the enemy, his raised right arm about to throw a grenade. These films reminded the Austrians, particularly the younger generation, of our gallant war-time German blood-brothers, all of them appealed to pan-German solidarity, all of them showed how German and Austrian front-line fighters had been stabbed in the back, betrayed and, of course, never defeated in fair and honest battle. But the German film industry under Goebbels also made propaganda for the Nazis in more subtle ways. Well made and lavishly produced historical dramas and romances pulled the crowds into the cinemas where they could see valiant German heroes defeating square-faced Slavs who were about to ravage the German countryside and its maidens. And there were those witty, light comedies and musicals, quite harmless and without any political content, showing how joyfully, elegantly and well one lived in the Führer's Reich.

Schuschnigg had to tolerate other things which proved to be even more dangerous. We suddenly learned that we also had, in addition to the Nazis, something called the 'Nationalist Opposition'. Nazis were nasty, noisy plebs, the rough, tough mob. The 'Nationalist Opposition' were gentlemen with academic degrees, pan-German souls, but, we were told, with good, honest red-white-red Austrian hearts. One of their leading lights, a member of the same student fraternity to which our martyred Engelbert Dollfuss had belonged, ex-army officer comrade and personal friend of Chancellor Schuschnigg, was Dr Arthur Seyss-Inquart, a well-known lawyer.

That tall, bespectacled gentleman with a somewhat shy and hesitant personality was put in charge of a newly-created section within the 'Fatherland Front'. the 'Nationalist Political Chapter' of the 'Front'; and the 'Nationalist Opposition' was to gather around it to play its part in Austria's political future.

This 'opening to the Right' resulting from the July agreement opened even the doors of Schuschnigg's cabinet to a senior member of the 'Nationalists'. General Glaise-Horstenau, director of the Austrian army archives, became Minister without Portfolio. Schuschnigg knew that this was the most dangerous of all his concessions to Hitler, but he also believed that it was a way of tethering these nationalist war-horses with a red-white-red ribbon to the stable-post of his 'Fatherland Front'.

I was preparing my things for my Christmas ski-ing holiday when Father, in a sort of aside, asked whether Lisl was coming too. He did it so conversationally that I did not smell trouble, and replied 'yes', she was coming.

'I wonder whether you should be going then,' he said. 'You are seeing far too much of that young lady. At your age one does not get too stuck on one girl, one has many girl-friends. You would do better not to go.'

Father was being reasonable, did not put his foot down, just sort of pondered aloud whether what I was doing was wise. There was no row, nor was there a determined attempt to stop me from going.

But after my return from that holiday, during which Lisl and I had got closer than we had been before, though not nearly so close as Father thought we were, the Klaar family suddenly started to make remarks. When the Klaars 'made remarks' it was an indication of imminent danger. Annitschek made the first one. Apparently engrossed in stirring whatever was in the pot on her stove, she said : 'Well, I never! There I was always thinking your cousin Hedi was your only love and that you'd marry her one day, and now there's someone else.'

After that first diplomatic sally from the family premier, the sovereign herself, Grandmother Julie, looking me up and down, came right out with it. 'Your father is worried about you,' she said. I asked what she meant, but only got an oracular 'Oh, you know all right what I am talking about. Your father is upset and you better know it!'

Aunt Sally's remark was somewhat coy. Apropos of nothing she declared that love must be wonderful, while Uncle Paul, flitting out of his surgery to have a quick snack in Annitschek's kitchen, more mindful of physiology than psychology, that subject apparently having been assigned to Aunt Sally, mumbled something like 'If you can't be good, at least be careful,' which was totally inappropriate because most decidedly, and much to my regret, there was nothing I had to be careful about.

By now it was more than obvious, even to me, that Father was discussing my affairs with his mother, sister and brother and Annichek. Mother and he had met Lisl only once in a cinema and by accident. She and I were leaving after the afternoon performance when I spotted my parents in the cinema lounge waiting for the evening show. There was no escape. I practically ran straight into Father's arms. I introduced her. Mother was polite, Father very cool, very distant. From then on Father's remarks became personal, they were also unfair and naturally achieved the exact opposite of what he intended. The more abusive he became about Lisl the more he aroused my chivalrous instincts. The more he thundered that I was a bloody fool and ought to have a whole string of girls, the more determined I became that she was the only one for me. And the more he carried on, the less I told him. For all he knew I was still following my old Saturday routine of Fritzl Pollack, beefsteaks and Worcestershire sauce at the O.K. Stüberl, while in truth Fritzl had become less of a friend and more of an alibi. Sometimes he was allowed to join us, but most Saturday evenings were spent dancing with Lisl, alone and unchaperoned by any third party. More and more I began to lead my own life, my confidant being neither friend nor Father or Mother, but only my diary in which I recorded my feelings and my longings.

I was away somewhere up in the clouds, hardly noticing, or if noticing, not really aware, of what was going on around me. The more Father increased his pressure, the more I turned away from him. I could not turn to Mother; I sensed that she was basically on his side, though she never said so, and often tried to calm Father down and restrain him when he became too vehement.

One Sunday morning in February 1937, a few days after Herr von Neurath, the German Foreign Minister, had been on a state visit to Vienna, the big bust-up between Father and me finally came. Herr von Neurath was supposed to be one of those legendary men who would keep Hitler on a tight rein. A minor aristocrat, he was a man of the old school, a conservative and a German traditionalist. Tall and distinguished, silver-haired, every inch a gentleman, one would have thought him light-years removed from the brash, loud-mouthed partisans of the Führer. The shock was, therefore, all the greater when Herr von Neurath, stepping off his train, greeted the waiting Austrian diplomats with his right arm raised in the Nazi salute and a resounding 'Heil Hitler'. He 'Heil-Hitler-ed' his way through Vienna, frenetically welcomed wherever he went by thousands of Austrian Nazis 'Heil-Hitler-ing' back at him with hysterical joy. Perhaps even more disturbing than this was the behaviour of our police. They seemed to think their job was to safeguard Austria's world-famous reputation for Gemütlichkeit. 'Gentlemen, gentlemen, please,' the police exhorted the cheering Nazis, 'you really shouldn't do this. Please calm down.' But had the crowds shouted a socialist slogan instead, our gemütliche police would have cracked their heads with their truncheons.

This general atmosphere of tension and fear helped to cause Father's outburst on the following Sunday morning. After breakfast he suddenly began to lay down the law.

'And what are you doing today?' he asked.

'I'm going to Grandmother with you in the morning.'

'Right. And after lunch?'

From the way he said it and from the way he looked at me I saw he was angry. I might have lied, but I did not want to. Perhaps I too wanted a confrontation.

'I'll be going out.'

'Where, doing what?'

'If you must know, I'm going to the five-o'clock tea at the Café Splendide.'

'With her?' The question was almost spat into my face.

'Yes, of course I am.'

'You're not, you know. This has to end. It's gone far enough. I forbid you to see that girl again. I'm not having my son making an ass of himself.'

He began to shout: 'You are much too young. However conceited you may be, you don't know what you're doing. I absolutely forbid you to continue this affair.'

There it was, my first grown-up row with Father. There was to be only one other. Grown-up in the sense that, however he might see me, I did not see myself as a child any more. He could no longer rule me, decide for me, tell me to do this and to stop doing that. I was my own master, I could love whom I wanted to love. I was over sixteen. I was his little boy no more.

'It's none of your business,' I shouted back at him. 'You can't imprison me. I'll do as I jolly well please!'

Our exchange became more and more heated. Not only our voices, also the words we used became harsher, culminating in my furious 'If you're like that then I don't want you for my father any more.'

The moment I had said this I saw on his face how deeply I had hurt him. That I was capable of saying a thing like that frightened him, because it made him understand how much I was head over heels in love. Perhaps it also made him see that Lisl was the one person who, merely by being, gave me the strength to break away from him. I knew that I had given my father great pain, and in spite of the fury in my heart I also knew how much I loved him and how much hurting can hurt.

After that last sentence of mine Father did not say another word. He left the dining-room. I did not go to Grandmother with him. But I did go dancing in the afternoon.

Cousin Hedi and her brother Fritz had spent several happy summers at a children's holiday camp in Cesenatico on Italy's Adriatic coast. The people who ran it – a real Frau Doktor was in charge – had an excellent reputation, and when I asked my parents whether I could go there for my 1937 holidays they agreed immediately. I was to have four weeks in Italy, then join my parents for one week in Schruns in the Tyrol, and from there we would go on to Bad Ischl for three weeks. I was happy, my parents were happy, particularly as I had not asked to go again to that other holiday camp in Upper Austria. In Father's mind the young couple who ran that place were no better than procurers. It was their fault that his son had fallen in love with 'that girl'. They ought to have stopped it. Why or how were matters on which he was less than precise.

Cesenatico was a different matter. The holiday camp there was much bigger, supposed to be fairly strict, the Frau Doctor was a well-known educator, and her staff had the reputation of being properly trained. I knew all this as well, but it did not put me off for one very good reason. Lisl was coming too. That was our great and extremely well-kept secret. It had to be. Although her parents were always very kind to me, and she never had any problems with them even remotely similar to mine, they also felt that our relationship was too close and should not be encouraged. As far as I can remember neither Lisl nor I actually had to lie. The two sets of parents just assumed that we were each going our separate ways that summer. But we both had a mutual problem: how to stop our parents from seeing us off at the railway station. If we tried to talk them out of it they would grow suspicious, if we said nothing they were bound to come. In the end Lisl and I agreed to let matters take their course. Her parents would not make too much fuss, and once I was on the train, the whole holiday having been paid for in advance, my father was not likely to storm the railway coach, grab me and yank me out again.

The departure day arrived. My parents were standing on the station platform talking to me through the open coach window, saying all those inane last-minute things one says on these occasions. They took no notice whatever of my repeated hints that they need not wait around, that I was safely installed in my compartment and that the train would leave in a few minutes anyway.

I desperately tried to hide my nervousness. It was very near departure time. Where was she? At last, only a couple of minutes before the train was due to pull out, Lisl came down the platform, accompanied by her mother, father and big sister. The moment I saw her my whole inside started to shake and tremble, and not for love either. The way Lisl looked, she had done everything, but everything, she could possibly have done, to provoke my father. She wore a bright red hat, of a red so bright it even subdued the stationmaster's red cap. Much worse, she was made up heavily, had too much lipstick on and, something Father hated like poison, had over-rouged her cheeks.

Why, I thought, why, oh why, does she do it? Much as I loved her I knew it was wrong for a girl not yet sixteen to put on so much war-paint. Maybe I was particularly sensitive on this point, because Father had hammered away at it ever since he had first met her in the cinema lounge? While all these thoughts were shooting through my brain and numbing it, Father saw her. He went pale. But the look he gave me had no anger in it. It was one of sadness. He took Mother's arm, both stepped back from the window, just acknowledged the greetings of her parents, convinced that they, poor innocents that they were, were deeply involved in our plot. Mercifully everything then went quickly. The train started to move, we waved and the moment of danger I had feared so much had passed without the volcanic eruption I had expected. Perhaps we were only spared because Father was so stunned. Possibly he consoled himself with the thought that we would be under strict supervision.

How or why Frau Doktor and her staff had acquired their great reputation will always remain a puzzle. If they had ever deserved it, how was it made to stretch over the years? The holiday camp in Cesenatico was an utter shambles. We older ones were 'looked after' by amateurs only two or three years older than ourselves. The male 'supervisors' were randier than the boys they were supposed to control, and their female colleagues were no angels either. That Cesenatico was going to be a paradise for us, but not remotely what our parents expected, became clear during the night journey to Italy.

The older boys and girls shared one train compartment and enjoyed a very happy and busy night together. So actively were we engaged with each other that we hardly had a free hand to hold out our passports to the Austrian and Italian border control officials. The Italians must have told each other about the interesting things going on in our compartment, for, once we had crossed their border, a differently uniformed comic-opera general opened our compartment door every half-hour or so, looked at the peep-show within with a broad grin on his face and disappeared again, leaving us to our own devices until the next chap was due for his peep. To tell the truth, nothing worse than kissing and petting went on in there. But for fifteen and sixteen-year-olds it was an exciting, sleepless night.

We were more than a bit the worse for wear when we stumbled on to the station platform in Venice at five next morning after an indigestible breakfast of one hard-boiled egg and one hard pear each.

To walk through Venice during the early morning hours can be a delight, but not after a sleepless eleven-hour train journey. Our organisers could not have cared less. The whole troop – and there were small children too – was dragged first to a park where we were supposed to rest, and then, from eight onwards we roamed the streets like lost sheep getting more miserable and more hungry all the time. It was hot already and was to get much hotter. The little ones started to cry and to fight. Tired out, they refused to walk and kept falling down. Eventually we were allowed to rest in St Mark's Square. At one o'clock, overtired and sick with hunger, they took us to a smelly eating-house, where we were served with polenta and a mess of greasy, oily fish. It made one sick just to look at it. No one ate much, and those who tried, like myself, were really sick after a few bites.

We lived on ice cream for the rest of the day, and when evening came the older ones had a great time pairing off into gondolas. How the little ones managed to survive until we finally trotted back to the railway station to catch the midnight train to Cesenatico, where we arrived at seven the following morning, can only be explained as yet another one of St Mark's many miracles.

Cesenatico in 1937 was still mainly a fishing village. It did have one Grand Hotel, some streets with elegant villas owned by rich Italians, a few boarding houses, but it was far, far removed from the mass tourism 'paradise' of our time.

That one summer holiday was the only taste I ever had of what it means to be young and carefree and in love with love. There was my one special girl, but there were others to flirt with as well. Maria, a lovely dark-haired Italian of good family, who was not nearly as closely chaperoned as Italian girls from good families were supposed to be. There was also one of the young female supervisors, a little older than I, and therefore that much more fascinating. There were moonlight trips on fishing smacks, singing Italian sailors, genuine ones, bottles of Asti Spumante and Làcrima Christi, and Lisl in my arms. It was still all fairly innocent, but full of romance, much of it kitsch maybe, but at sixteen and a half, kitsch can be very beautiful. I took Italian lessons from an Italian medical student, Mario Finzi, a stout fascist. How his eyes lit up in pride whenever Italian air force planes bumbled overhead! Marshal Balbo, the bearded chief of the Italian air force, was his hero. No man could have been a prouder, more patriotic Italian, none could have looked more like a darkly handsome Italian renaissance prince. I did not know then that Finzi is a Jewish name, nor did Mario know that the fascists he so admired were so soon to become his deadly enemies. He survived and became one of Italy's foremost surgeons.

This, the last holiday of my youth, when the future seemed to offer increasing independence, a carefree life at university, and also one whole year of waltzing through Vienna in the glamorous uniform of an Austrian officer cadet, did not end with the four weeks in Italy. From Cesenatico, for the first time alone, I travelled back to Austria, to Schruns in the Tyrol, where I joined my parents for one week before we continued to Ischl together.

Father and Mother were now treating me as almost an adult. My final accolade came in a talk Father had with me in a little inn. For the first time he told me with pride what he had earned that year, how much of his income had come from the bank and how much from the French cigarette manufacturer Abadie. We discussed the future, his and mine, carefully avoiding one subject only – Lisl.

Less than eight months later we were proscribed, hunted, despised. But in August 1937 we sat cosily in that little inn chatting time away as if it were stretching ahead of us endlessly and happily.

Ischl meant my old crowd. By that I mean the young crowd I joined the year before. They were all there again, a little more mature, quite a little more flirtatious – and two new passions. One was a new girl, who had joined Marielouise, Yvonne and the others. She 'picked me up' rather than I her – a new and most thrilling experience. The other was *Reinanken*, a local fish, smoked and speared on a stick. My devotion to both these new passions was nothing if not intense. They were duly but silently noted by the assembled family, augmented that summer by Aunt Klara and cousin Hedi. Everyone was very discreet. No comments were made. Presumably Father, who tried to hide his delight at my interest in another young lady, had warned the family not to say anything for heaven's sake. So, no noddings from Grandmother, no playful remarks from Aunt Sally, not even one word from Annitschek. Only Aunt Klara once gave way to what must have been extreme provocation, when I sat a bit too close to her in the Café Zauner after an immensely enjoyable *Reinanken* orgy. 'Your young lady must be inordinately fond of fishy smells,' she observed.

Well, my new love was indeed nothing if not tolerant. Very! She was two years older than I, experienced, and knew how to guide me to everything, short of everything. Almost, though not quite, she answered my dream of that older woman, who would come into my life one day and lead me to fulfilment. I had actually met such a woman once. That was in March or April 1936 at the birthday party of a school friend. She was an older cousin, possibly an aunt of his. She was about thirty-five, tall, had a slim but most feminine figure, wore a low-cut elegant black dress and moved with seductive grace. I see her before me leaning against a white door, smoking a cigarette through a very long, thin, black cigarette holder, her other arm lightly resting on her beautifully curved hip. It is a scene right out of a Hollywood film. The *Graduate* perhaps, with me in Dustin Hoffman's role. I, at fifteen and a half, would, of course, have been much more a man of the world. If only – ah, if only – she had taken the first step. My eyes popping out of their sockets I ogled her. She smiled. Who knows what might have happened? My script remained unwritten, my cameras never started to roll. I was suddenly called to the telephone. It was Mother. In her happiest voice she told me that Father was back from Prague. We had not expected him until the next day, but he, the Lindbergh of Pichlergasse, had done the incredible, the astounding: he had flown from Prague to Vienna in an aeroplane. In 1936 that was sensational. At one stroke my father had become a hero, someone much more fascinating than any woman could be to a fifteen-year-old.

I rushed for my coat and raced back home, all my sensuous dreams forgotten in the instant, to see that great adventurer, my father, and to hear his story. He sat beaming in his favourite armchair in his study, Mother clucking around him like an excited young chick, when I rushed in. Would you believe it, he played down his heroism, actually said that there was nothing to flying, that it was the most enjoyable form of travel by far, and that – the reckless bravery of the man! – he would do it again. How proud I was to have such a father!

This absolute hero-worship of the boy for his father ended within the year. It ended with that bitter row we had over Lisl. From then on I began to see Father more as a human being, less as the all-protective giant of my childhood. That row was the end of our old and the start of our new relationship. It never fully developed, never got beyond this beginning. We, my parents and I, were never given the time to know each other as adults. Our relationship could never mature. It ended with me still a teenager and my picture of my father and mother can, therefore, never be complete, never quite firm in its outline. It has always remained without adult perception and perspective, somewhat flat, somewhat primitive perhaps, lacking shade and shape and form, but filled with love.

I was given a considerable degree of independence by my parents

as I approached my seventeenth birthday. This was still fairly unusual for the time and also for the Viennese Jewish bourgeoisie to
which we belonged. I only became aware of it on my actual birthday. My parents were giving one of their dinner-parties on that
evening to celebrate their eighteenth wedding anniversary.

By about seven-thirty all the guests had arrived: the Mautners,
the Herlingers, assorted uncles and aunts; Herr Bloch, one of Father's
deputies at the bank and his wife and the Dr Maurers. Yes, my
parents' house-friend had succumbed at last and surrendered his
bachelorhood to a very sweet, dark-haired young woman. I had a
drink with them, and then, to their astonishment, said my goodbyes. When they heard that I was going out to celebrate my birthday with my girl-friend at Vienna's most famous cabaret, the 'Simpl',
our guests reacted with a moment's stunned silence. No one said
anything, but you could read on their faces what they thought.
'Ernst and Stella are really going a bit too far allowing their boy to
go out with a girl that late, and to a night club, of all places!'

In fact, the 'Simplicissimus', to give it its full name, was certainly
no low dive. There were no lonely blondes there waiting for lonely
men. It was run by two Jews, Karl Farkas and Fritz Grünbaum.
Farkas was one of the wittiest men in Vienna. Grünbaum, a refugee
from Hitler's Germany, had been one of the best comedians of the
German theatre. Every child knew him from the many character
parts he had played in innumerable UFA films. There never was a
more perfect partnership in the history of cabaret, an art form
which, I think, reached its highest form in the Vienna of the Thirties.
But of the many cabarets in the city the 'Simpl' under Farkas and
Grünbaum was the most superb. One must not confuse the Viennese
cabaret I am talking about with the Anglo-Saxon variant. The Viennese cabaret offered a series of politico-satirical sketches, inter-
spersed with songs, and unlike the German cabaret which dated
from the 1890s continued an old satirical tradition going back to
the great Johann Nestroy and the Vienna of the early nineteenth
century. Nestroy's work is little known outside Austria. Written in
the Viennese idiom it loses much of its charm if translated into High
German, never mind a foreign language. But to the satirical stage
Nestroy was what Shakespeare is to the dramatic one. To this native
tradition Farkas and Grünbaum added their own highly individual
mixture of Jewish humour. The result had sharpness, wit and intelligence, changed mood within seconds from hilarity to thoughtful-

ness, instantly switched back to mirth again, and gripped the audience from the first moment to the last. For its success the 'Simpl' needed the large Jewish audience which Vienna could then provide, one that understood every quip immediately, and instinctively knew the closeness of laughter and tears.

Within hours of the *Anschluss* the Nazis arrested Fritz Grünbaum. They took him to Dachau where they clubbed him to death. Farkas was more fortunate. He escaped and emigrated to the United States. A few months after the end of the war he was back in Vienna and opened the 'Simpl' again. I sometimes saw him on my infrequent visits to post-war Vienna, grey-haired, elegant and very lonely, sitting in the Café Sacher, always very respectfully addressed as '*Herr Professor*' by the waiters. The Austrian state, keenly aware that honorifics are cheaper than restitution payments, had given him a title.

The 'Simpl' show to which I took Lisl on my seventeenth birthday was called *Robinson Farkas on the Grünbaum Island*. Celebrating the cabaret's twenty-fifth jubilee, it was the best ever. Grünbaum and Farkas were brilliant. So funny were they and their script that Herr Flieder, the head waiter of the 'Simpl' and quite a character himself, so fell about laughing during the final rehearsal that he dropped the tea tray he was carrying. Herr Flieder had been carrying trays round the place for the whole of its twenty-five years, but never before had he dropped as much as a slice of lemon.

It was 21 December 1937 when Lisl and I were sitting there in the cabaret, laughing and clapping, even shouting for sheer joy, as did the others of that well-dressed, prosperous-looking audience, all of us behaving as if we had not a care in the world

Yet I cannot be far out in my estimate that about a third of the men who were there with us that evening were, before another three months had elapsed, behind the electrified barbed wire of some Nazi concentration camp. How many understood what Farkas and Grünbaum were really saying? They were not merely superb comedians, those two. At the core of many of their jokes was an almost prophetic awareness of the menace suffusing the very air we breathed. They were undoubtedly the funniest Cassandras in history. Their true message, their instinctive awareness of the tears to come after the laughter, like the messages of all Cassandras, tragic and comic, was not understood. Not even, as his sad end proved, by Grünbaum himself.

New Year's Eve 1937. We were in the study – Father, Mother and I. Father and I played a few games of chess, we talked, listened to the radio cabaret, whiled away the time till midnight. The saw-blade clock, balanced on the head of the baroque clown figurine, showed that midnight was only a few minutes away. Father opened the window to Nussdorferstrasse. We stood by it and waited for the sound of Vienna's many church bells, ringing out the Old and ringing in the New. When their booms and chimes broke the stillness of the night, we raised our glasses, drank to each other and kissed.

On New Year's Day 1938 two Viennese newspapers, read neither by Father nor myself, published messages that were out of the ordinary. Their leading articles called for government action to stop further immigration of Jews into Austria and at the same time recommend a review of all naturalisations granted to Jews after 1918. Douglas Reed, then the Vienna correspondent of the London *Times*, reported to his newspaper:

The bulk of opinion in Austria sympathises with the views of these two newspapers, which has nothing to do with anti-semitism. Of late years the Danubian and Balkan capitals have been flooded with immigrants from Germany and Poland, a fair proportion of whom have criminal records, and a closer scrutiny is inevitable sooner or later in all these countries.

Dr Goebbels could hardly have asked for a better mouthpiece than Mr Douglas Reed. Had he and his Führer not always said that Jews were criminals? Obviously the Jews were running away from Germany and Poland merely to escape the just consequences of their criminal activities.

The newspapers we read at home, the *Neue Freie Presse* and the *Neues Wiener Tagblatt*, reported the following morning what the *Wiener Neueste Nachrichten* and the *Reichspost* had written the day before. Father, after reading this, said nothing. But he was very quiet that Sunday morning and left to visit Grandmother in an exceptionally thoughtful mood.

What he had been thinking about became clear over lunch when he suddenly asked Mother and me: 'Did you read the papers this morning and see what the *Reichspost* and the *Neueste Nachrichten* said yesterday?'

We had both read it, we said.

'I would expect the *Neueste Nachrichten*, that Nazi rag, to write in this vein,' Father said. 'But for the *Reichspost*, practically a government newspaper, to write virtually the same, that does go too far. You know, Stella, I think I should ask the bank to pay me off. Let's take the money, something like 40,000 Schillings I'd get, not much, but enough for a new start, and go to Switzerland.'

There, the bombshell was out.

Mother and I looked at him in stunned surprise.

'Well, what d'you think?' he asked, turning to Mother.

Mother hesitated, so Father very quickly answered his own question – so quickly, that if I think about it now I realise that he had been merely toying with that idea, that he never seriously meant to go at all.

'What would happen to Mother and Sally if I did that?' he said. 'Who'd look after them? I'd like to go, but how can I?'

Of course, so much in him wanted to escape such a decision. He was forty-eight. Was he to give up at that age everything he had worked for, his home, his career, that comfortable existence in a city which he felt to be his home town and loved? Nevertheless all these things might not have counted for so much had his feelings and responsibilities for his mother and sister been less strong.

Father had decided to stay, although he had recognised the danger earlier than most. From that day on until after the *Anschluss* he never talked about emigrating again and with self-induced blindness ignored the danger signals increasing day by day.

Spurred on from Germany, encouraged by the growing confusion of the Austrian authorities, our local Nazis became more restive and aggressive with every passing hour. Petrol and smoke bombs landed in synagogues, creating panic among the congregations. Huge swastikas and Nazi slogans appeared on house walls overnight. Mobs of teenage boys and girls roamed the streets molesting anyone who looked the least bit Jewish in their eyes, including, much to the amusement of Vienna's Jews, a party of Italian fascist dignitaries visiting the city. These tightly organised Nazi groups were easily recognisable. They all wore white knee-length socks to show their political affiliation. Sporting the swastika badge was still illegal, but the police could hardly arrest someone because of the colour of their socks.

It was carnival time in Vienna. The Opera Ball, the most traditional and most elegant social event of the season, was as splendid as ever. Had Grandmother Julie still been looking out of the window of Opernring 3, she would have watched a scene almost as brilliant, gay and colourful as the one she saw as a young woman so many years before. At the Ball of the City of Vienna at the neo-gothic Town Hall, the second most important event in the calendar of carnival festivities, less aristocratic, more middle-class, they waltzed till the early hours of the morning, and at the Ball of the 'Fatherland Front' the 'professional' Austrians whirled under red-white-red banners over the parquet floor. Gallons of goulash, wine and beer revived the revellers when they were nearing exhaustion. Who ruled the country? The government at the Ballhausplatz or the Nazi mobs in the streets? That was an open question. But there was no doubt who reigned – Johann Strauss.

Any doubts still existing about who reigned and ruled in Germany were settled 'once and for all' – one of his favourite phrases – by the Führer. The conservative nationalists who had helped him to power had finally outlived their usefulness. So had some senior army generals. Rumours had been making the rounds for some time that dramatic developments were to be expected in Germany. On 4 February 1938 Hitler confirmed that the rumours had been well founded. He named the dismissed generals, announced that he had appointed himself supreme commander of all Germany's armed forces, that he had replaced Herr von Neurath, the conservative Foreign Minister, with the rabid Nazi von Ribbentrop, and that Germany's ambassadors to Washington, Rome and Vienna, all members of the old order, were to be recalled.

How did the disciples of the 'Hitler cannot last long' school of thought react to these changes? Well, as political pundits so often do, they refused to be confused by facts. The question is relevant, because we had one of those pundits in our own family: Uncle Paul. And his views carried a lot of weight with my father. Paul knew a number of senior men in the Schuschnigg administration, he had, therefore, the reputation of being well-informed. He was the eldest brother and a *Herr Regierungsrat* to boot. Before 4 February 1938 Paul, and those whose views he shared, had been sure that 'Hitler would not last long' because the army and the conservatives in the German civil service were bound to sabotage his radical ideas. Hence

160

he would run foul of his more fanatical followers, there would be a Nazi *Putsch* against him, countered by an army *Putsch* against the Nazis, and obviously the army was bound to win.

Now there was a new situation. The conservatives had not got rid of Hitler. He had got rid of them. His power now appeared to be absolute. Not so, explained the pundits, who adapted their views to the new situation with lightning speed: 'Hitler won't last long' now because he had over-reached himself. Freed from the restraints of responsibility Germany's conservative opposition would now act. It was only a question of months, if not weeks, till they would topple the Führer.

No one in Vienna shed any tears for Herr von Papen. There was universal relief that this arch-intriguer had to pack his bags. The relief was misplaced. Herr von Papen in office was, as events were to show, less dangerous than Herr von Papen out of office. True, the end of Austria would have come in any case. Mussolini had known what he was talking about when he had warned Colonel Liebitzky that Austria had little time left. Signs that Germany was preparing to act against Austria were multiplying. Anthony Eden warned his Austrian colleague Guido Schmidt that intelligence reports received in London indicated impending German moves to solve the 'Austrian problem'. Members of the Austrian legation in Berlin reported a change in the attitude of Nazi leaders towards them. One Austrian diplomat later summed this up in the words: 'They began to treat us like living corpses.' All this was true, but that Austria's end came when it did and how it did, that was in large measure the work of von Papen. His desperate struggle to retain a grip on influence and power, to intrigue himself back into the centre of events and above all into Hitler's favour, sealed the fate of Austria.

Before leaving his post in Vienna, the recalled Herr von Papen sent Hitler a message that he wished to make new proposals for a solution of the Austrian question. He requested permission to submit them to the Führer personally. On the evening of Sunday 6 February von Papen boarded the train that was to take him home into the Reich. Hitler's response was immediate. Shortly after his train had left Vienna the ex-ambassador was handed a telegram ordering him to report to the Berghof, Hitler's mountain chalet on the Obersalzberg near Berchtesgaden, where he was relaxing after his victorious battle against Germany's establishment. Von Papen disembarked at

Linz, the capital of Upper Austria, spent the night there and motored to the Obersalzberg early the following morning.

Twenty-four hours later the grey-moustached elegant was back in Vienna, closeted in the Ballhausplatz Chancellery with Schuschnigg and his Minister of State for Foreign Affairs, Guido Schmidt. Von Papen's return was a closely-guarded secret, but it could not be kept from the foreign press. The London *Times* reported the sacked ambassador's surprising peregrinations with an air of ever-growing astonishment. On 10 February it said:

Herr von Papen, who is still in Vienna, appears to be most anxious that if some new concessions apparent or real are to be made by the Austrian Government in the near future, it should be done before his departure, not after it, when it would appear a quick feather in the cap of his successor, who might prove to be somebody much closer to the National Socialist party than himself.

Von Papen's was a very simple argument suggesting that all outstanding problems between the German Reich and Austria could be solved in a personal talk between Schuschnigg and Hitler. It was important that this meeting should take place in the very near future, so that he, von Papen, could still take part in the conversations between the two leaders and play the part of conciliator. Surely the Austrian Chancellor appreciated the fact that he himself was not a Nazi. But very shortly Herr von Ribbentrop would take over the German Foreign Office, a Nazi would be given the Vienna embassy. These people were bound to influence Hitler towards more radical proposals which von Papen might yet be able to prevent.

Schuschnigg by now knew enough about Hitler and his methods to be very much aware that the Führer was not just another, if more boisterous, German Chancellor. But he made the same mistake Chamberlain and Daladier made in the autumn of 1938 at Munich. He still believed Hitler would, in international affairs, conform to universally accepted rules of diplomacy. In spite of many misgivings, Schuschnigg finally agreed to accept Hitler's invitation and visit him at the Berghof. That the Austrian Chancellor had doubts and was desperately trying to strengthen his hand before meeting Hitler is proved by an Austrian Government decree of 11 February, which ordered compulsory military service to be extended from twelve to eighteen months.

One wonders whether Schuschnigg and Schmidt also took another precaution, more elementary than keeping conscripts six months longer in the army. Did they, before starting on their journey to the Obersalzberg, look at the first chapter of Hitler's *Mein Kampf* and read or re-read what he wrote about Austria? Had they done this, would they still have set out on their mission to disaster?

Much of what Hitler wrote about international relations in *Mein Kampf* was carefully ambivalent. His references to Britain and France, for instance, were far from crystal clear. But his views on Austria he expressed in the first pages of his book with absolute frankness. Right at the beginning of his opening chapter, 'The House of my Parents', he wrote: 'in my earliest youth I came to the basic insight, which never left me, but only became more profound – that Germanism could be safeguarded only by the destruction of Austria ... Even then I had drawn the consequences from this realisation: ardent love for my German-Austrian homeland, deep hatred for the Austrian state.'

The Reiss-Bar was in one of the side streets off the Kärntnerstrasse. It was a very chic establishment. The long bar was made of shiny mahogany, sparkling chromium and glass, the chairs of red leather, the little tables of gilt wood and marble. Exactly the place to appeal to two seventeen-year-old 'men about town' and also, nightly, to Vienna's more glamorous and expensive whores. Fritzl Pollack and I liked to meet there on Saturday afternoons. At that time we usually were the only customers. To sip a liqueur in such exciting surroundings made us feel highly sophisticated.

On Saturday, 12 February 1938, we entered the Reiss-Bar at about five in the afternoon. Lisl was away ski-ing in the mountains near Vienna and Fritzl and I planned to follow our usual routine: a drink, the cinema and then dinner at the O.K. Stüberl.

Apart from us there was only a waiter in the Reiss-Bar at that early hour. As we came in he switched on the radio. It played the usual Saturday afternoon light music. We sat down, ordered our drinks and talked. The music suddenly stopped in the middle of a waltz. Silence. We looked up in surprise. Then the familiar voice of the announcer came on. 'Radio Vienna here. We break off for an official announcement: Following an invitation from the Führer and Reich-Chancellor Adolf Hitler. Chancellor Dr Kurt von Schuschnigg, accompanied by Dr Guido Schmidt, Minister of State for Foreign Affairs, arrived in Berchtesgaden this morning where talks between the German and Austrian leaders are taking place. We are now returning you to the studio for the second part of our afternoon music transmission.'

We paid and walked out into the street. Everything was normal. We turned into Kärntnerstrasse towards the Opernring and passed the German travel bureau with the huge Hitler portrait. No cheering Nazi crowds had yet collected there. The secret of the Berchtesgaden meeting had been well kept. Some hours were to pass before the first Nazi demonstrators assembled and the Heil-ing and shouting began.

We both knew that carrying on, going to the cinema and to dinner afterwards as if nothing had happened, was unthinkable. Grown-up or not, all we could think of was getting home, being with our families, feeling protected by our accustomed and loved surroundings.

But confusion and self-deception began when I entered our flat. Father was not nearly so alarmed as I had expected him to be. He had telephoned some of his friends and brothers, including Uncle Paul, of course, immediately on hearing the announcement on the radio. They had assured him that with a Schuschnigg in the Chancellery we were living in the best of all possible worlds. That could well be interpreted with hindsight as the blindness of people too close and too involved, who had too much at stake personally to be able to observe and interpret coolly and calmly. But so little was Hitler's true character understood and appreciated at that time that a leader writer on the Times could call the Obersalzberg conference 'an unexpected, but hopeful meeting' between Herr Hitler and Herr von Schuschnigg'. And when other British newspapers headlined their reports 'Austrian Crisis' the Times pontificated against such 'alarmist' journalism.

I did not think of asking Father whether he had also telephoned Richard Mautner, the gloomiest and most pessimistic of his friends. The richest of my parents' circle, Mautner was also the only one who did everything right when the end came, and thereby, however indirectly, saved my life.

We tried to convince ourselves that the situation was serious but not hopeless: and we became interested in everything, hard news or rumour, sounding hopeful, clutching even at the patently optimistic, self-deluding government propaganda. Again and again it stressed that the Chancellor had only travelled to the Obersalzberg in response to Hitler's invitation and it made their time together sound like a cosy tea-party. 'The meeting took place', said a leading Austrian newspaper, 'in an atmosphere of greatest cordiality and their talks lasting many hours showed the depth of the full mutual understanding between the two men . . .'

The *Wiener Zeitung*, the official government organ, spoke of 'A friendly discussion . . . amiable atmosphere . . . frank talks man to man . . . no sensational development.' The Führer had even welcomed the Chancellor on the steps of his chalet. Everything had been lovely in Hitler's mountain garden!

Then rumours started that the 'tea-party' had not been quite the friendly *tête-à-tête* we had been told. It became known that Herr von Ribbentrop, the new Nazi Foreign Minister, had joined in the discussions and finally, on Monday, 14 February, even the *Wiener Zeitung* had to name a few other gentlemen who had also taken part in those 'amiable talks': 'General of Artillery Wilhelm Keitel, Chief of the Supreme Command of the German army; Luftwaffe-General Sperrle, commander of the Munich district; General von Reichenau, commander of Army Group IV.' No explanations were given. Presumably they had been there, jack-booted and in full war paint, merely to enjoy the mountain air. Or was their presence required to further the spirit of détente which our Chancellor's visit had allegedly achieved? Yes, suddenly that magic word 'détente' was on everyone's lips.

Everybody talked about 'détente' at the ball given by the Austrian Government on Monday, 14 February. The carnival season was reaching its climax, the most lavish and sumptuous ever to be held in the state apartments of the Hofburg, the Habsburg residence in the city. Chattering and smiling they danced through the Imperial halls: the gold-laced diplomats, the Government ministers, the leading bankers and their bejewelled ladies. How many of them, deep down in their hearts, harboured sadness and fear? How many treason?

Arthur von Seyss-Inquart entered the Hofburg together with Schuschnigg, the man he was to betray. Although the Austrian Chancellor had tried to resist Hitler's demand at Berchtesgaden that Seyss should enter the Austrian cabinet as Minister of the Interior and had only given way when Hitler's threats became massive, he still believed the shy lawyer to be a loyal Austrian and a personal friend.

Except for the members of Schuschnigg's government and a few of his close confidants, no one in Austria knew that the country's most sensitive ministry, controlling all its security forces, was to be placed into the hands of Seyss, the leader of the euphemistically named 'Nationalist Opposition'.

On 15 February, the morning after the ball was over, *The Times* published a dispatch from Vienna letting the cat out of the bag. 'If Herr Hitler's suggestion that Dr von Seyss-Inquart should be made Austrian Minister of the Interior with control of the Austrian police were granted, it would in the general view of anti-Nazis in Austria mean that before long the word "finis Austriae" would be written across the map of Europe.'

Wilhelm Miklas, the Federal President, refused to sign the document appointing Seyss-Inquart and resisted for nearly forty-eight hours. Then he had to give way to Schuschnigg's pressure. Miklas signed in the early hours of 16 February and Seyss swore his ministerial oath later that morning. During his first day as minister he met the senior officials of his Ministry and then that very same evening he left Vienna on the night express to Berlin.

'That the first act of the Minister of the Interior is to pay a visit to a foreign country is a fair indication of the unusual situation in which Austria finds itself after the Hitler–Schuschnigg meeting', *The Times* aptly commented.

What had happened during these two days for that newspaper to change its tune? The truth about Berchtesgaden had come out, and even Geoffrey Dawson, editor of the *Times* and Britain's arch-apostle of appeasement, had to recognise the fact that Hitler had treated the Austrian Chancellor at Berchtesgaden like a refractory schoolboy. He had shouted and threatened, had forbidden the chain-smoker Schuschnigg to light a cigarette in his presence, and at the one point when Schuschnigg had shown some backbone and had suggested that Seyss be given a ministry other than that of the Interior, Hitler had broken off the talks screaming for his generals.

That 'friendly talk ... man to man' was the worst ordeal in Schuschnigg's life, but also one of the most superb performances the actor Hitler ever gave on the political stage. Schuschnigg, the intellectual, was temperamentally incapable of dealing with a phenomenon of this kind. The peasant Dollfuss, with his much greater intuitive political understanding might have been able to call Hitler's bluff; Schuschnigg, the academic, was not.

Though the truth about Berchtesgaden was now known, at least to the world outside and to those in Vienna privileged to enjoy the company of Herr von Papen, who, tactful as ever, gleefully told anyone who would listen to him how Hitler had treated Schuschnigg, not one man in power anywhere raised his voice to stop Hitler. The French said little themselves, but let it be known that they were shocked by Mussolini's passivity. The Poles, of all people, claimed to be neither disturbed nor surprised, and paid a tribute to Hitler's political skill. The Czechs, at least officially, behaved as if all this had hardly anything to do with them. The one exception, the one foreign politician, though far from power, who understood what was happening, saw the consequences, and warned, but, of course, was not taken seriously, was Winston Churchill.

On Tuesday, 22 February, he rose in the House of Commons to express regret at 'This tragedy of Austria and the violent pressure placed upon the Government of that country'. 'How did this show improved relations?' Churchill asked and went on to say, 'Austria has now been laid in thrall and we do not know whether Czechoslovakia will not suffer a similar fate.'

One can hear in one's mind that sonorous voice, the slurred *rs* and spluttering *ss*, as Churchill delivered his prophetic speech to a lethargic House listening to Winston once again blathering about far-away countries.

On Sunday, 20 February, Hitler addressed the German Reichstag. Austrian radio was broadcasting a Hitler speech for the first time. It was to begin at one, and Father and I were keen to listen, particularly as Hitler was expected to deal at length with the Berchtesgaden agreement and – vitally important – would once again reaffirm Austria's independence.

At one o'clock sharp we sat by the radio in Father's study, listening to the German commentator fulsomely describing the scene in the Kroll Opera, which was used instead of the burnt-out Reichstag building.

Thundering '*Sieg Heils*' greeted the Führer's arrival. A few minutes after one, Hitler's Austrian-accented, slightly hoarse and vulgar, but spell-binding voice came over the air. After outlining the recent government and army changes he spoke about the first five years of his stewardship, paying particular attention to his regime's economic performance and successes. He droned on and on about how many thousands of tons of this and that Germany was now producing and continued endlessly about coal-mines, shipyards, steel-rolling-mills and their output, like the proverbial club bore driving home the same point over and over again.

At the very end of his three-hour speech Hitler devoted four minutes, or 2½ per cent of his total speaking time to our country. He thanked Schuschnigg for the 'great understanding and heart-warming readiness with which Dr von Schuschnigg accepted my invitation to Berchtesgaden, where the Austrian Chancellor and I made every effort to find a way in the interest of both countries as well as in the interest of the whole German nation, whose sons we all are no matter where our cradle stood.'

He ended, stressing that Berchtesgaden was an example of gradual détente in Europe and how it had proved, confounding Germany's enemies, that Germany was for peace. 'Sieg Heil! Sieg Heil! Sieg Heil!'

Father and I looked at each other. We both noted that he had made few remarks about the Jews. Neither as capitalist nor as Bolshevist beasts had Hitler denounced us. A few routine curses, yes, but no more. We also noticed, of course, that Hitler had not mentioned, never mind reaffirmed, Austria's independence. But that was explained away by the newspapers next morning. It was stated explicitly in the 1936 agreement, so there was no need for it to be mentioned again, particularly as Berchtesgaden was merely an extension of that earlier treaty. We believed it, because we wanted to believe it.

Three days after Hitler's speech *The Times* reported from Vienna :

The uneasiness of last week has given way to calmer feelings in Austria, also noticeable among the large Jewish population. The Jews have been reassured by the relatively few references to them in Herr Hitler's speech on Sunday and by the fact that Herr Bruno Walter's, the conductor's, contract with the Vienna Opera has been renewed for a year.

The day before Hitler's Reichstag speech Archduke Otto von Habsburg wrote Schuschnigg a remarkable letter :

Austria's enemy through an unexplained act of brute force has succeeded in pushing your Government into a situation full of menace, which perilously undermines our further resistance. Should you feel that you can no longer resist the pressure from German or extreme nationalist circles then I would request you, whatever the situation may be like, to hand over the office of Chancellor to me. I am firmly determined to go to the utmost to protect the people and the state and am convinced that the nation will respond. The situation being such that lengthy negotiations with other powers concerning a restoration of the monarchy cannot be contemplated I will not ask for it under the circumstances. I would only ask you to hand over the Chancellorship to me.

When he replied to the Habsburg heir declining his suggestion, Schuschnigg was beginning to feel more optimistic about the future. He was buoyed up not merely by his own propaganda, but also by the true resurgence of a patriotic spirit amongst the people; not that the Austrians were beginning to see their Chancellor quite in the same light as the sycophantic *Wiener Zeitung*. Mixing metaphors from chivalry and seamanship it described Schuschnigg as 'A knight without fear or blemish steering the Austrian ship of state through the waves of our time.' Social-Democrats and trade unionists began to move towards the government camp. Although they still hated the clerico-fascist regime, and found it impossible to forget that its guns had fired on the workers' flats, they feared and hated the Nazis more. Prominent men of Schuschnigg's closer circle, like Miklas, Vienna's Burgomaster Schmitz and others, began to press for an opening to the Left. Very slowly, too slowly and too hesitantly, the Chancellor began to follow their advice.

But *The Times* was right when it reported that the atmosphere in Vienna had become more balanced. Nazi demonstrations were still taking place, but they were countered by pro-Government demonstrations. The swastika was no longer the only political symbol to decorate the walls in Vienna; the Crutched Cross, symbol of the 'Fatherland Front', was painted next to or over the swastikas during the night, and one saw as many 'Red-White-Red unto Death!' slogans as 'One people, one Reich, one Führer!' More and more red-white-red flags were coming out, Vienna was to have a festive air for the Chancellor's speech on Thursday, 24 February.

One felt the greater firmness, the greater determination to resist the threat from across the border. It reflected on the young. In my school the Nazis who had been very cock-a-hoop during the week after Berchtesgaden began to look somewhat crestfallen. Some returned to school from their demonstrations looking considerably the worse for wear. More and more workers were joining the pro-Government demonstrators, many of them old *Schutzbund* men.

On Thursday Schuschnigg was to address the Bundestag, the corporate state's pseudo-parliament, at seven in the evening. All offices closed down at two in the afternoon to enable the members of the patriotic organisations to assemble in the streets around the parliament building and give the Chancellor a rousing welcome, and others to be home in good time before the streets were blocked off by police so they could listen to his speech on their radios at home.

Once again we sat by the radio in Father's study. The Austrian radio commentator described the scene in hyperbole every bit as ecstatic as that of the German announcer four days earlier. Chancellor, like Führer, was given a standing ovation as he entered the assembly hall. The shouts of *'Heil Österreich!'* and *'Front Heil!'* sounded just as fervent as the Reichstag's *'Sieg Heils'* had done. Chancellor, like Führer, wore uniform, but all these outward similarities between the clerico-fascist Austrian and the Nazi German production ended the moment Schuschnigg began to speak. There was no ranting, no shouting, there were no threats, no accusations, but in a clear, steady voice he delivered the greatest speech of his career, a passionate plea for Austria.

The only indications Schuschnigg gave of his true feelings about Berchtesgaden were when he referred to 'that hard day, 12 February 1938' and when, taking a leaf out of Hitler's book, he also, with quite noticeable irony, listed at length figures measuring Austria's economic achievements in tons of production and millions of Schillings.

The key sentence which indicated Schuschnigg's willingness to work with the Left in future came after his call to let bygones be bygones and concentrate on the future in unity. 'If there ever should be factions,' he said, 'intellectuals on one side, workers on the other, then you will find me on the side of the workers.' That was a very clear message, because the Nazi leadership in Austria and their most dangerous and vociferous followers were largely members of the intellectual proletariat, young men with university degrees who could not find the jobs and positions to which they felt themselves entitled and who fervently believed that a Greater Germany including Austria would bring them their millenium.

Looking back, one can see that this undoubtedly great speech, expressing beliefs held sincerely and strongly, listened to by us with rapt attention, giving us new hope, but also increasing our false sense of security, was only more wool over our eyes. Had it been an open challenge to Hitler, had it been an open appeal to the world, had it been truthful about the great danger facing us all, less states-manlike, more that of a human being driven to the edge of despair, it would have ensured Schuschnigg a prouder place in history and above all it would have saved thousands of lives.

The Times wrote: 'Tonight's demonstrations [about the Chancel-lor's speech] have shown that in Vienna at all events there is a large body of opinion which has been aroused to almost passionate sup-port of the Government by fear of the threat to Austria's independ-ence.'

Strangely enough, these hectic days did not produce in us ex-cessive tension. There was excitement and fear, but we also had hope and expected life to go on in its firmly established daily rhythm. Father went to the bank in the morning as he had always done, came home to lunch after a mid-morning snack at Würstel-Biel, Mother did her shopping, checked the maid's dusting as she had always done; I went to school, took Lisl dancing or to the cinema on Saturday; indeed, on the Saturday after the Chancellor's speech I went with her to my first big ball, the famous *Kirtag in St Gilgen*, one of the top events of the carnival season. It was always held in the Konzerthaus where I had been only once before as a little boy to bring a bunch of flowers to Grandmother Adele, looking some-what wan from hunger as she fasted and prayed at the Day of Atone-ment service in the Konzerthaus, which traditionally was turned into an overflow synagogue for the faithful on that, the highest of Jewish holy days.

Kirtag in St Gilgen was a very different occasion, and though my memories of that Day of Atonement visit long ago were somewhat vague, it still seemed impossible to believe that this was the same building. Austria's best stage designers had changed it into a very life-like imitation of that famous holiday resort not far from Salz-burg. They could not, even if they wanted to, put a good part of Vienna under water and bring the St Wolfgang lake into the Konzert-haus, but the White Horse Inn, the lake-side hostelry known to operetta lovers all over the world, had been reconstructed inside the building, so had the village square, maypole and all, and on various levels there were farms with real cows and horses in their stables, country-inn gardens with buxom waitresses in old-style peasant costumes serving wine and beer, and any number of bands from the genuine 'tarara boom-deeay' to modern ones playing the swing hits from Fred Astaire–Ginger Rogers films by Irving Berlin and Cole Porter, evergreens that have outlasted my youth.

How I managed to get tickets for this ball, sold out months in advance, I have no idea. But I know that this was the ball I wanted to go to. It was known to be more fun than any other and presented no dress problems. At the *Kirtag* men did not wear dinner jackets or white tie, but *Lederhosen*, peasant jackets, open-necked shirts, in short my usual Bad Ischl summer outfit would do admirably. The ladies wore their peasant dirndls, though admittedly some were of such elegance and made of such expensive materials that no St Gilgen maiden could ever have owned them, unless – as had been known to happen – she found favour in the eyes of some princeling or rich banker.

For a seventeen-year-old at his first ball this was fairyland. Somehow in all this throng I managed to lose Lisl in the course of the evening, or, equally likely she lost me. I remember that I stood alone, at least I think I did, though vaguely there are memories of a blonde holding my arm – and Lisl was not a blonde – on the main dance floor when the Chancellor entered the box of the Federal President and Frau Miklas, Schuschnigg, wearing Tyrolean dress, was welcomed by frenetic, almost hysterical, applause and cheers. This ovation lasted for several minutes. The Chancellor had to rise again and again, bowing stiffly from the waist. Schuschnigg, though not yet forty was prematurely grey with a small moustache over a tightly-drawn mouth, the short-sighted eyes hidden by sharp glasses glinting in the strong light of the stage lamps which had been trained on him. It was clear from the way he responded to this overwhelming acclamation what a closed-in and inhibited man he was. Austria's answer to Hitler was a university don. Admittedly he had risen above himself in one great speech, but the streak of stubbornness he did possess was not enough to deal with his own problems or those of the world in which he lived.

And how much of the applause in the Konzerthaus was really an expression of confidence in him? Perhaps the cheers of that crowd – many of them Jews – were so loud only to drown its fears.

As for me, it was the first ball. I enjoyed the dancing, the drinking, the gaiety, the amazing speed and ease with which one found partners. I stayed until the band had played the last waltz.

How do I remember my few remaining days of youth and freedom, when I still felt that everything was possible, that I was special somehow, that life was only about to begin? I know that even the ever more vehement Nazi demonstrations appeared more exciting to me than threatening. I went about most of the time wearing white knee-socks, a black raincoat and a Tyrolean hat, very much the sort of clothing the Nazis liked to be seen in, not so much as a camouflage for the Jewishness in my face, but more as a sign of my own militancy, my readiness to fight. Looking like a Nazi as much as possible instilled a feeling of toughness in oneself, even gave one a more aggressive expression, and the more you looked and behaved and bore yourself as they did, the less likely were the Nazis to touch you. That changed, of course, after the *Anschluss* when they had become the masters, but during the last few days before it, when they were still unsure whether the executive, particularly the police, was for or against them, they carefully chose their victims from among the most defenceless.

On the evening of 9 March Schuschnigg, speaking from his home town of Innsbruck, the Tyrolean capital, suddenly announced a plebiscite for the following Sunday. All Austrians over twenty-four were to vote for or against a 'Free, German, independent, social, Christian and united Austria. That the result of this vote was bound to be an overwhelming victory for the Schuschnigg Government was a foregone conclusion. At least two-thirds of the adult population would vote 'Yes'. The mass following of the Nazis in Austria was not amongst the more mature. Hitler's most ardent followers were mostly under twenty-four.

During the last days of February Goebbels's newspaper *Der Angriff*, followed by the *Völkischer Beobachter*, the official Nazi party newspaper, had published reports from Vienna claiming that the Schuschnigg regime had let the Austro-Marxists off the leash, and that the 'Fatherland Front's' anti-Nazi demonstrations were led by communists and radical-socialists.

The impressions of the *Times* correspondent were different from those of his German colleagues. Under the headline 'Tensions in Austria – Triumphant Nazis', he wrote, 'If things continue in this way, the Nazis seem likely, in effect, to have a monopoly of political liberty, rather than equality with other groups.'

All this Schuschnigg had borne in silence, but then, on 9 March, in Innsbruck, came his eruption. Speaking in the same hall where ten years earlier he had delivered his first political speech, he now threw down the gauntlet to Hitler by announcing the referendum. He finished his speech quoting the words Tyrol's national hero, Andreas Hofer, had used when calling his peasant soldiers to arms against Napoleon and his Bavarian allies: 'Men – the hour has struck!' The crowds cheered Schuschnigg's words like mad.

On 10 March Vienna woke to a fever of patriotic fervour. The painting columns of the 'Fatherland Front' had been at work all night stencilling Schuschnigg's portrait, huge 'Yesses', crutched crosses and slogans on walls and streets. Everything with a large enough surface had been covered with 'Fatherland Front' symbols and with exhortations to vote for the Government. Aeroplanes showered leaflets over the city. Lorries draped in the national colours, packed with men and women yelling 'Red-White-Red unto Death!' cruised through the streets distributing more leaflets. Demonstrators were marching through every district shouting their loyalty to Schuschnigg and to Austria. The whole city was a seething, teeming hot-bed of patriotic emotion and activity. Vienna had last witnessed comparable scenes in August 1914, when its crowds acclaimed the outbreak of the war.

All day the radio played Austrian military marches, and the spoken word was entirely devoted to plebiscite propaganda. No question – on the Sunday Austria would give Schuschnigg an overwhelming 'Yes' and Hitler a resounding 'No'.

The next morning, 11 March, we all, Father, Mother and I, went about our usual business, feeling quite confident. Mind you, there were anxious questions as to how Hitler was going to react to this challenge. But when we sat down to lunch that Friday, the radio was assuring everyone that rumours about a possible postponement of the plebiscite were untrue and the work of the enemies of Austria.

Having finished my homework I took my bike to cycle to the fencing school in the inner city of Josef Losert, the Austrian foil champion. As I turned into Nussdorferstrasse I saw Robert Rosen, an old school chum, standing at the corner talking to Norbert Gewürz and Heinzi Buchwald, other Jewish fellow pupils of mine at elementary school. I stopped. Robert, a member of Betar Trumpeldor, the militant Zionist organisation, greeted me with the words: 'Are you going to fight?' Of course I was! I had thought about it a good deal during the last few days. There was no question. Walter Mitty-like, I pictured myself in the thick of battle behind a machine-gun spitting its bullets into Hitler's soldiers. All those tales of martial heroes I had read for many years in *Der Gute Kamerad* were more alive in my fantasies and day-dreams now than ever before. It was a strangely bloodless war I was fighting in my imagination, very much like the many German war films I had seen, where it is always the enemy who falls dead into the mud, never one of your own men. Having assured Robert that he, Schuschnigg and Austria could certainly count on me, I cycled off.

The fencing lesson was from four to five. My cousin Hedi went to the same fencing school. She was more experienced than I and in a higher class, but her lesson was at the same time as mine. For a whole hour I sweated out my surplus fat and aggressions, lunging forward and jumping back, like a streak of lightning, or so I thought, particularly when I made a mistake and Losert used his foil as a whip to lash me into becoming a more expert performer at his art.

Having showered and changed, Hedi and I left together, at about six o'clock. It was getting dark, and the streets, though the rush-hour was about to begin, were not quite as crowded as usual. Walking next to Hedi, I was pushing my bike, we were passing Am Hof 4, the headquarters of the 'Fatherland Front' just across the road from our fencing school. A lonely storm-corps man guarded the entrance. He was young, tall and looked very impressive in his dark blue S.S.-type uniform with high laced boots, the old Austrian military shako on his head. Seeing him I wondered why the men of the 'Fatherland Front' storm-corps had not been more in evidence recently to smash up Nazi demonstrations. That youth looked the very picture of Himmler's ideal S.S.-man. What was going on his head? To whom did his loyalties really belong? I remember that those questions went through my mind as I said 'good-bye' to Hedi and jumped on my bike.

When I rang the bell of our flat the scene that followed had a strong *déjà vu* quality. Again, as had happened on 25 July 1934, after Dollfuss had been murdered, as I put my bike against the white bench in the hall, the dining-room door opened and there, much to my surprise – it was not yet seven – stood Father with Mother close behind him.

'The plebiscite has been called off,' he said.

'Nonsense, Daddy,' I replied. 'You're falling for Nazi rumours. They're not true. There have been warnings all day not to believe those Nazi lies. The radio said so again and again.'

'I know what the radio said,' Father answered. 'It is saying the

175

opposite now. They have just announced that the plebiscite will be postponed.'

'It can't be!'

But as I said these words I looked properly into Father's face for the first time. We had started talking while I was still putting my bike straight, and I had not really looked either at him or Mother. Now that I took in the expression on his and Mother's face I knew that it was true.

We went into the study. The radio was on. It played music. Not the martial airs of yesterday, this morning and early afternoon, but a very slow, sad, classical tune.

'But it's only postponed,' said I, the optimist.

Father shook his head. 'I don't know,' he said, 'but to postpone after this tremendous build-up can only mean it will never take place. It is the end for us. If only, oh if only, I had done what I said a few weeks ago. Got my money from the bank and taken Mother and you to Switzerland!'

An announcer interrupted the music. He merely repeated that the Sunday referendum had been cancelled. Would listeners stay tuned for further announcements. The music continued. We sat at the dining-room table and ate in silence.

We had just finished when the door bell rang. We jumped. Helene, our maid, opened the door. But it was only the Ornstein family from the other side of Pichlergasse: Emil Ornstein, proud owner of the title 'Commercial Councillor', the elegant, platinum-blonde Selma, his wife, her mother, old Frau Radziwill and Ilse their daughter, now a fast-ripening fifteen.

They had come, because they could not bear to be alone at that critical hour. One needed to talk, to hear other people's views. So we sat in Father's study grasping at straws, groping for some shreds of reassurance, searching for a power – Italy, France, Britain or God – to come to our aid. The music stopped. It was about a quarter to eight. A breathless voice, more shouting than speaking, announced 'The Chancellor', and then Schuschnigg spoke, his voice trembling with emotion:

Austrian men and women! This day has brought us face to face with a serious and decisive situation. It is my task to inform the Austrian people about the events of this day. The Government of the German Reich presented a time-limited ultimatum to the Federal President demanding that he appoint a candidate chosen by the Reich Government to the office of Chancellor and also follow its suggestions when selecting the ministers to serve in that cabinet. Should the Federal President not accept this ultimatum then German troops would begin to cross our frontiers this very hour.

I wish to place on record before the world that the reports disseminated in Austria that the workers have revolted and that streams of blood have been shed, that the Government is incapable of mastering the situation and cannot ensure law and order, are fabrications from A to Z.

The Federal President has instructed me to inform the nation that we are giving way to brute force. Because we refuse to shed German blood even in this tragic hour, we have ordered our armed forces, should an invasion take place, to withdraw without serious resistance, without resistance, and to await the decisions of the coming hours. The Federal President has asked the army's Inspector-General, General of Infantry Schilhawski, to assume command over all troops. All further orders for the armed forces will be issued by him.

So, in this hour, I bid farewell to the people of Austria with a German word and a wish from the bottom of my heart: 'God save Austria!'

They played the national anthem. After the last bars of Haydn's tune we all sat in utter silence for a few moments. Then, before any of us had had a chance to say anything, the sounds of hundreds of men shouting at the top of their voices could be heard. Still indistinct, still distant, it sounded threatening none the less. Those raucous voices grew louder, were coming closer.

I rushed to the window and looked out into Nussdorferstrasse. It was still quite empty. A few moments. Then the first lorry came into sight. It was packed with shouting, screaming men. A huge swastika flag fluttered over their heads. Most of them had swastika armlets on their sleeves, some wore S.A. caps, some even steel helmets.

Now we could hear clearly what they were shouting: 'Ein Volk, ein Reich, ein Führer!' they were chanting in chorus, followed by 'Ju-da verr-rrecke! Ju-da verr-rrecke!' ('Per-rish Judah!') In English this sounds softer, less threatening, but in German, coming from a thousand throats, screaming it out in the full fury of their hate, as lorry after lorry with frenzied Nazis passed below our window, it is a sound one can never forget.

Father switched the light off so that the men on the lorries could not see us – my parents and the Ornsteins had joined me by the window – and we stood there for nearly twenty minutes watching the procession. Only when the last lorry had disappeared in the distance was the light switched on again. The others sat down, but I stayed by the window.

I was still looking out into Nussdorferstrasse when I suddenly heard a muffled shout from right below our window. I craned my neck and saw an Austrian policeman, a swastika brassard already over his dark green uniform sleeve, his truncheon in his fist, lashing out with beserk fury at a man writhing at his feet.

I immediately recognised that policeman. I had known him all my life. I had seen him on traffic duty at the nearby crossroads, had chatted with him when we occasionally met in the shops around the corner, had seen him give Father a polite salute in the street. Indeed, when I was much younger I had identified this policeman with Poldi's fictitious one, the one she had invented to get me to go to sleep in the dark. He had been, first the ogre of my childhood, then almost a friend, and now that I saw him club with all the strength of his powerful body some poor soul who had shouted out his anger at the ecstatic Nazis, not fiction but fact had made him an ogre again. Within minutes of Schuschnigg's farewell that policeman, yesterday's protector, had been transformed into tomorrow's persecutor and tormentor. That was more terrifying even than the frenzied 'Ju-da verr-rrecke!' Nothing could have driven home more clearly what had happened on this one day than this single incident.

I turned back into Father's study and joined in the conversation. I said nothing about the scene I had witnessed. Now that all doubt had gone the talk had become more animated. The certainty must have given us all a feeling of relief. We did not know what was yet to come, but we all knew that our life in Austria and a family history linked so closely with that country for so long, were over. The radio, still on in the background, now played Hitler's favourite marches.

We finally parted at about two o'clock on the Saturday morning, and the words Selma Ornstein spoke to Mother as she was about to leave have remained in my mind through all these years. They illuminated so sharply the abyss that had opened between our past and our future. They were not at all profound. But the very simplicity of what she said was an unforgettable summing-up of 11 March 1938: 'Tell me, Stella, what on earth did we talk about before? Maids, children, dresses, food? What world did we think we were living in?'

We were too tired to talk any more after the Ornsteins had gone. Everything that could be said that night had been said. We went to bed. Around us there still was the protective warmth and familiarity of my parents' flat.

But our home – it was no more.

Part Three

My parents' last shelter, two tiny rooms, one up one down, and a kitchen, dark, dank and clammy, was in St Pierreville, a mountain village in the département of the Ardèche in France. A minute patch of garden, much loved and lovingly tended by Mother, went with it. In her letters she often mentioned the joy she felt sitting there with Father, watching nature's rhythm around them, or as much of it as her myopic eyes could see through the thick lenses of her spectacles.

She had very little time for that simple pleasure. In a letter he wrote to me on 23 January 1942 Father described her unceasing efforts to make that dingy refuge into a home for him:

Life in the country is highly uncomfortable now. The freezing cold in one's soul is equalled by the freezing cold from outside. One has to do everything oneself, and it is admirable how your mother copes with everything on her own. Nothing is ever too much for her, she never complains, is utterly selfless. Her brooms, brushes and dusters she only exchanges for her pots and pans in which so many of her excellent culinary ideas are brought to life. Oh yes, she still has her thing about cleaning.

Indeed, nothing could ever make Mother abandon that passion. Her outstretched right hand armed with a wet, soapy face-flannel reached, figuratively speaking, for my face all the way from St Pierreville in Vichy France into my army camp in Britain:

Although you, my Georgerl, are now so grown-up, [she wrote] I still dare to remind you to wash with hot water as often as possible. In these times it's more important than ever. I can hear you exclaim, 'Oh God, Mother's running true to form again!' as you read this, but you must understand that my anxiety for your health or, as you will undoubtedly call it, 'Mother's besotted cleanliness', will never change.

She was right about that. But in many other ways Mother had become a different woman. The change began virtually the very moment when the ecstatic Nazi hordes swept into Nussdorferstrasse. She, who most of her life had accepted Father's guidance, suddenly began to display enormous strength of character. Her headaches, her frequent tears, her other complaints, practically disappeared overnight. That spiralling hair-line in her eye went, never to return. She, who had always tap-tapped for every kerbstone with the toe-cap of her shoe, claiming that even with her glasses she could not see that far down, suddenly walked with sure step through the streets of Vienna.

In spite of their grim existence in France, the short time, just over a year and a half, Mother and Father spent in St Pierreville was not unhappy for her. It was the only time in their whole marriage when Father was completely hers. There was no bank, no Herr Direktor Fischer, no Fräulein Blankenberg, no Grandmother Julie, no sister, no brothers – and no son. In this remote village to which the France of Pétain and Laval had assigned them – they were not voluntarily in St Pierreville – Stella at last had that total unity of soul and body with her husband she had always longed for, probably without ever allowing herself to be aware of it, but had never attained during their years of good fortune. Now, in misfortune, she had Ernst, her man, totally to herself.

I think Father sensed what gave Mother that indomitable physical and spiritual fortitude he so much admired.

In the evening, [he wrote] when everything is so quiet here that even the mice, frequent visitors of ours, hold their breath, Mother takes a volume of Goethe or some French author from the shelf and refreshes her mind and spirit. Her constant work does not permit her to do this during the day. She is a great and true human being. Had she had the good fortune of meeting Goethe, or, rather, had he had the good fortune of meeting her, he would most certainly have said, and with greater justification: 'Voilà une femme'.

This 'Voilà une femme', 'There is a true woman', not as Father would have called her in Vienna, 'a good wife and mother', seems to me to show how much more clearly he now recognised her qualities, had penetrated through the surface of their relationship. Father's comments seemed to embarrass Mother. Below his words of praise she wrote: 'If it were at all possible to blush in this ice-cold weather, I would. I am merely doing my duty and accept things as they are.'

Among my parents' belongings which I collected from the office of the Lyon Jewish Community after the war, I found a photo of Father and Mother standing side by side in their little garden. It must have been taken in late spring or early summer of 1942. Father had lost much weight. His face was much thinner than I remembered, his nose looked more prominent, his eyes were smaller and had receded into their sockets. That inner cold of which he had spoken in his letter is in the expression of his face. The sunshine in which they stand makes no difference to that. He holds his arms folded in front of his body, one hand clasping the other – a picture of loneliness. Etched in his face is the self-torture of reflecting over past 'mistakes' again and again. His eyes seem to look only inward and into the past, without expressing any interest in his surroundings. Mother had obviously gained weight since I had kissed her goodbye at London's Victoria Station on 30 March 1939 as she boarded the Paris express to be re-united with Father. She had regained her Viennese proportions. There is a smile on her face, and her pose, with her right arm circling father's waist, is one of unity with another human being. She looks at peace with herself and her environment. What a different woman from the one in the photo taken in Ireland after we had emigrated from Germany! There her near-blind eyes look almost washed away by the streams of tears she shed whilst separated from Father, who was then already living in Paris. It is the picture of a very sad, lonely and deeply unhappy woman. Yet when it was taken she was not alone. Her only child, her son, was with her, and she was also safe in a country far from Hitler's grasp. But neither I nor safety could console her. The one human being she wanted and desperately needed to be with was Father. Only he really mattered. More than her own life.

The woman in the St Pierreville photo is smilingly accepting 'things as they are'. Standing next to her husband she is complete and without fear. Yet the German troops in occupied France were at most a hundred miles from where they were, and the French minions of the S.S. and Gestapo were much, much closer.

Ernst's and Stella's way did not lead straight from Vienna to St Pierreville. But a number of events, each requiring immediate steps, which taken by themselves were, sensible and logical, inexorably forced them away from their planned direction, and led them to that village surrounded by the picturesque mountains of the Ardèche, where, as a local travel brochure states, one finds 'space on a human scale, and, in the purest of lights, freedom'.

One of my father's favourite authors, Jules Romains, described the Ardèche more aptly as 'A harsh mingling of sadness and joy'. That is what my parents found there.

We woke late and leaden-souled on that Saturday, 12 March 1938. I went into Father's study and opened the window to Nussdorfer-strasse. It was a cold, but bright and sunny day with a slight fragrance of spring in the air. As the new government had ordered schools and offices to stay closed the streets were quieter than usual. They were also much gayer with the many flags flying from roof-tops and windows, their dominant red heightened by the sunshine. Many were still the 'old' red-white-red Austrian ones of yesterday, some the proper Nazi Party flags – red with a big, black swastika in the white centre circle – but most of them were red-white-red with swastikas of various sizes and often somewhat irregular shapes hastily painted or sewn on by eager hands during the night.

Helene, our maid, had red eyes as she laid the table for breakfast. Her mother, she told me, had arrived early in the morning from Perchtoldsdorf, the small town just outside the city boundary, where she lived, and was now in the kitchen. I went to greet her. She was sitting over a cup of coffee crying her heart out. 'Oh, Herr Georg,' she sobbed, 'what are they going to do to our lovely little country? What is going to happen to our Austria?'

If only we knew the answer. We sat dry-eyed over our breakfast, but all the certainty we had felt after Schuschnigg's farewell the evening before, had gone. Emigrate? How? Where? Perhaps it would not be so bad after all? More bark than bite? Should we just sit tight? What if Austria remained a separate state though one with a Nazi government? Would they apply the Nuremberg racial laws? And even if they did was it inevitable that Father would lose his job? After all, the Länderbank was French-owned. Mother men-tioned Rosl Bartmann, her second cousin, eldest daughter of Uncle Alfred's late elder brother Ludwig. She lived in Berlin with her mother, Aunt Manya, and had a good job with Air France. How were the French going to react to the events of last night? How the British? And Mussolini? Was he really prepared to have German troops stand at the sensitive Brenner border, with the irredentist South Tyroleans on his side?

There was no clear answer to any one of these questions.

We felt worried and depressed, but not desperate, as we sat and talked over our morning coffee. We could even laugh, somewhat bitterly, but laugh we did when Father read out a report in the newspaper, which under the headline 'Successful Escape' told how poor Miss Greta Garbo, surrounded by nothing worse than a posse of journalists, had escaped from them through a secret door in the garden wall of the villa near Naples where she was staying with Leopold Stokowski, the conductor.

Where was *our* secret door to freedom?

Father's gloomy friend, Richard Mautner, had found his. Our telephone rang a few minutes after father had read out the Garbo story. Mother answered it. It was a mutual friend of hers and Käthe Mautner's, who was also a neighbour of theirs. The short message from Käthe she gave mother merely said, 'Love to you all, we have gone on a journey. Will be in touch.' The details of the Mautners' escape we only learned later. Richard, the pessimist and in this case certainly also the realist, had not only seen black, but, unlike most doomsayers, had also acted. Apparently he started to move his money secretly to Switzerland after the July 1936 treaty between Austria and Hitler's Germany. When Schuschnigg announced the plebiscite he told his wife to start packing their most important belongings.

Within a few minutes of the radio announcing the postponement of the plebiscite Richard drove up outside their Hietzing villa, his driver already wearing a swastika brassard on his left arm. Quickly the ready suitcases were flung into the car, Käthe and their daughter Dorli were bundled into it, and they were off. They reached and crossed the Swiss border before Seyss-Inquart had taken his oath of office as Schuschnigg's successor. The Austrian border guards at Feldkirch, with no clear idea as yet of what was happening in Vienna and much impressed by Richard's driver's swastika armlet and smart 'Heil Hitler' salute, let them pass without any trouble.

That Richard, by so quickly escaping through the still unlocked door in the wall, was also keeping it open for us, we only came to realise a few months later.

After breakfast I got dressed and did what was for me a surprising thing to do. I went to Grandmother Julie's flat. I visited Grandmother from time to time, and not always with Father, but that I felt a need to go to Josefstädterstrasse on this of all mornings shows not only that the old lady meant quite a lot to me, but also that I saw in her and her surroundings a permanence more firmly established than that of our own home. Our home represented the present, Grandmother's the past, and what I was really doing by going to see her was, I suppose, fleeing from our shattered present to the unity of our past.

Grandmother was quite calm. She understood what had happened and yet at the same time she did not. In another four weeks she was going to be seventy-eight, but in spite of her age she was totally alert, her intelligence was as sharp as ever. Emotionally, however, she was removed from the reality of events by at least a century. 'Look Georgerl,' she said, 'I'm so old, I have lived through so many upheavals. This is one more of them and – God willing – I'll live through that as well till my time comes.' Her generation, growing up and maturing in the heyday of European Liberalism could envisage some aspects of evil, something like Lueger's treatment of her husband, but it could neither envisage nor comprehend the brutal evil that was breaking out all over Vienna on that very day.

As usual I also spent some time with Annitschek in the kitchen. She summed up the events of the last twenty-four hours with more insight than Grandmother. 'It's the end of the Klaar family,' she said, and the way she spoke these words left me in no doubt that she also saw it as the end of any purpose in her own life. She knew that we would have to go, and that neither Grandmother nor she could come with us.

I walked home. I had gone about half way, when the first squadron of German bombers appeared over Vienna. Flying in exact formation and very low, they looked very big and very black against the blue sky, their engines throbbing menacingly. Squadron followed upon squadron, more and more Luftwaffe planes, hundreds and hundreds of them, circled over the city. I can only repeat, in describing the scene, the old cliché of the 'plane-blackened' sky, because it was literally true. Their intent was entirely friendly. All they dropped on Vienna were propaganda leaflets, but I could not help thinking, as I watched them, of my talk with Robert Rosen and my other school friends only the afternoon before and how determined we had been to fight the Nazis. What chance would we have had to withstand this mighty air force? How much of Vienna would be standing now had they dropped bombs instead of bits of paper?

'City of Frenzy and Fear' was what that Saturday morning's *Times* called Vienna. Those few words described the atmosphere in which we now lived with utter precision. The frenzy of the previous night had not yet returned to the streets. Last night's delirious revellers, exhausted by their ecstatic raving, were still in their beds or just beginning to bestir themselves. The new day's eruption of frenzy had yet to come. Fear was everywhere, all-pervasive. It was in the air I breathed as I walked home; the flags symbolised it, so did the swastika brassards on the policeman's uniforms, the shiny new swastika badges in people's buttonholes, the black Luftwaffe planes circling over my head.

The first top Nazi leader to arrive in Vienna from the Reich, Heinrich Himmler, had landed with his cohorts at Aspern airport at 4.30 in the morning. The abject surrender of Schuschnigg and his government had made Himmler's task only too easy. The Austrian police files were now in Himmler's hands.

Fear gripped most firmly those who had no deeply-held political or religious convictions. Those who had them were infinitely stronger than we were. One of them was Robert Rosen. He visited me in the afternoon. He came straight to the point. He wanted my revolver. Years before I had bought it from a fellow-pupil at the Schopenhauergymnasium, a strange character with excellent connections to Vienna's underworld. It was my most prized, most secret and most dangerous possession.

Robert's firm belief in Zionism gave him the courage to go out into the street with my revolver in his pocket. Before he left, Robert asked me to join Betar Trumpeldor to which he belonged, the militant Zionist organisation founded by Jabotinsky in which Menachem Begin, then still in Poland, held a leading position. I refused; probably because by becoming a member of a Zionist organisation I would have acknowledged that I was a Jew and not an Austrian. With my background and upbringing, I was not yet ready to renounce my claim to more than a hundred years of Austrian heritage accumulated by my family.

A short while after Robert had left, 'Sieg Heil' and 'Juda verrecke' echoing from the street told us that the frenzied crowds had fully recovered. So they had. And now they began to convert their antisemitic slogan into dire action, for no other point of the Nazi programme found a more resounding echo in Austria than its anti-

Jewish plank. Possibly only a minority of the men and women of that screaming street mob were convinced Nazis. The Austrian essayist, Alfred Polgar, once said: 'The Germans are first-class Nazis, but lousy anti-semites; the Austrians are lousy Nazis, but by God what first-class anti-semites they are!' That summed it up.

In the matter of Jew-hatred Austria's anti-semites could at last leap from the abstract to the concrete. It expressed itself in primitive sadism. Jews, businessmen and professionals, women and children, the old and sick as well as the young and healthy, were rounded up and forced to do menial and debasing work out in the streets, surrounded by the cheering and laughing mob.

We were not molested on that first evening and, wrongly as it turned out, thought that the many kindnesses, presents and generous tips our caretaker and his family had received from us over the years gave us some protection.

Vienna's first great round-up of Jews for street-cleaning ended in the late afternoon. Another evening of frenzied joy, a torch-light procession of thanksgiving, had been organised by Vienna's Nazi party bosses for seven o'clock that evening. As column after column of joyful Viennese marched towards the city centre, few Jews, as could be expected, ventured out into the streets. One of the exceptions was Uncle Paul. He and Aunt Alice came to see us. It was not really an act of courage, though Paul was certainly no coward. It was simply a manifestation of his firm belief in his special status as a senior police surgeon and highly decorated World War veteran. He just refused to believe that the world we lived in today and the one we had lived in yesterday were poles apart. He was still as convinced as he had been for the last five years that Hitler was merely a passing phenomenon.

Entering Father's study Paul switched on the radio. With its volume turned down, so that none of our neighbours could overhear it, we listened to German language broadcasts from France and Switzerland. The French, though without a government, Léon Blum's cabinet having resigned a day or so before Hitler struck, had an aggressive radio-commentator, who poured scorn on Hitler, denounced the Nazis and what he termed their 'Austrian adventure' with biting irony. His words were music in our ears. Listening to him one felt certain that the next French government would sweep the Nazis and the German army out of Austria with an iron broom. Paul believed this absolutely. By now Father was much more sceptical, but a little less gloomy than he had been during the day.

The first day of what is often referred to as the 'Rape of Austria' was drawing to its close. But while we were listening to the French station, at about 7.30 p.m., the great rapist himself entered Linz, the capital of Upper Austria, where he had spent much of his own youth. Until his arrival in Linz Hitler had not decided what to do about Austria. Should it remain a separate, but Nazi-led state – a dominion of the German Reich with its own administration? It was what Seyss-Inquart and a number of leading Austrian Nazis were hoping for. Throughout his career Hitler played the role of the strict 'legalist'. His orgiastic reception in Linz dispelled all doubts. Hitler ordered Wilhelm Stuckart, the constitutional expert in the Reich Ministry of the Interior, to report to him in Linz, and on his arrival Stuckart was told to prepare the legal document for the act of union, the *Anschluss*, the absorption of Austria into the German Reich.

Some late snow had fallen during the night from Saturday to Sunday. When I looked out into Pichlergasse from the window of my room it looked white and clean, and the Schuschnigg slogans on the pavements were blanketed by it.

Looking out of the window of my Father's study into the Nussdorferstrasse I saw the white snow turning into dirty slush under stamping jackboots and the exhaust fumes of innumerable army lorries. The German Wehrmacht was moving in. I stared fascinated at the steel-helmeted German soldiers, sitting stiffly upright and completely motionless in their vehicles, their hands clasping the barrels of their rifles.

I breakfasted, dressed quickly and raced out into the streets, all fear forgotten. I went across the road and stood under the canopy of the Collosseum cinema. A tall Wehrmacht motor-cyclist, looking the very image of the German warriors I had seen in so many war films, passed me on his way to buy some cigarettes and wished me a friendly 'Good morning'. I walked along the line of troop-carriers right to the end of Nussdorferstrasse, turned left into Währingerstrasse, the convoy stretching the whole length of it, and driven on by my curiosity to see more and more, I reached the Ring at the Schottentor, before deciding that I had better turn back. This was my first sight of the most powerful military machine of its time. I was impressed by this demonstration of perfect discipline and splendid equipment.

The men themselves were tall, young, handsome, smart and polished; and I realised, unbelievable though this may sound, that I admired these soldiers and was even proud of them. So caught was I, the seventeen-year-old Jew, in my Austro-German conditioning from childhood, so deeply ingrained was all I had read, that I could not see these clean-limbed young men as my enemies. The Nazis, the S.S., the S.A., they were my enemies, but not the young and handsome soldiers of the Wehrmacht.

If I had not been born a Jew, could I have been a Nazi at seventeen? Could I have been one of them, attracted by the power and the glory of Hitler's Reich? I was racially 'immune' to Nazism, but to this day my judgment about those youths who succumbed to Hitler is beclouded by the memory of my own sensations on that day.

Who were these men and women who surged through the streets, breaking into Jewish homes and shops, looting and stealing? What were they like, the creatures who dragged Jewish men, women and children out into the streets, forced them on to their knees, and ordered them to scrub away the Schuschnigg plebiscite slogans which had been painted on the pavements and the walls of houses – often by the very people who were now falling about with laughter and glee as they watched their Jewish victims. 'Work for the Jews, at last the Jews are working!' the mob howled. 'We thank our Führer, he's created work for the Jews!'

'Herr Karl' created by the Austrian satirist and actor, Helmut Qualtinger, in a sketch some ten or fifteen years after the war, was the classic example of that type. For this one work Qualtinger deserves a place in German literature at least on a par with Karl Kraus. Kraus's figures were abstractions from reality, they were caricatures. Qualtinger's Herr Karl is a portrait true to life, but also one into which the features of the whole Viennese mob of 1938 have been condensed. Mirrored in it are all the nastiness paired with false bonhomie, all the sham *Gemütlichkeit* with its envious vulgarity, of the thousands of Herr Karls and their wives who were now let loose to pour bucketfuls of their hatred over defenceless victims. And what did our *gemütlicher* Herr Karl look like? Not the Herr Karl of today, a benign-looking old man of seventy or more, but the Herr Karl of 1938. You can see him in contemporary photographs of Jews being led through the streets of Vienna, with Herr Karl watching over them with eagle eyes. On one of these photos he looks down at a Jewish boy of twelve or thirteen who has been forced to write 'Jew' in red paint on a Jewish shop. Herr Karl is of medium height and dressed in military style civilian clothes. His hat, to give him a more martial look, has its brim turned down front and back, he wears knee-breeches stuffed into long woollen socks and lace-up boots. His short jacket is tightly buttoned over his protruding paunch, on his left arm is the swastika armlet, and in his buttonhole a swastika badge. While bystanders grin, his expression is unsmiling, serious, official, that of a dedicated man doing his duty by his Führer.

The paradox of Vienna's volcanic outburst of popular anti-semitism was that it saved thousands of Jewish lives. The 'lousy anti-semitism' of the Germans led many German Jews to believe that they could go on living in their beloved Germany, while the 'first-class anti-semitism' of the Austrians left no Jew in any doubt that he had to get out of the country as quickly as possible.

We had talked to the Ornsteins about emigrating on Friday evening, and we had talked about it among ourselves, but it had been just talk, somehow lacking urgency and the full awareness of an inescapable truth. Now we knew that there was no alternative. We knew it not only because of the ugly incidents all over Vienna, but more decisively after we heard what had happened to the Ornsteins late on Saturday night. Emil and Selma had already been asleep in their beds, when the door bell rang. They opened the door. Outside stood the caretaker of their house, two Austrian policemen and two German S.S. men in their black uniforms. They stormed into the Ornsteins' flat, searched every nook and cranny, emptied drawers on to the floor and finally, having handcuffed Emil Ornstein's arms behind his back, they led him away. He was a prominent businessman, a Jew and a leading Freemason. Those were his 'crimes'. One week later we saw his photo together with those of other Jews in the hands of the Gestapo, on the front page of the S.S. newspaper *Das Schwarze Corps* ('The Black Corps'). He looked ill and had a week's growth of beard. They did not allow Jews to shave, in order to make them look unwholesome and unwashed.

Emil Ornstein himself we never saw again.

Early on that afternoon Father broke down. I can still see him sitting in the Louis Seize armchair in the bedroom and hear his sobbing. I had never seen my father cry before, had never heard that racking sound of pain and despair of a crying man, had never witnessed that choking struggle with which a man, overcome by grief, tries to regain control over himself. A man, brought up to believe that it is not manly to cry, does not find release in tears as a woman does. His tears do not flow freely from his eyes, but burn out of them, hotly and agonisingly, dimming sight and soul. Mother and I embraced him, tried to comfort and console him. I believed, and I think so did Mother, that Father had broken down because he had finally realised the total collapse of his world, the end of his career and that he was also afraid they might come for him as they had done for Emil Ornstein.

But when he started to speak, between sobs that shook his whole body, he said just one sentence, and he said it over and over again: 'What is going to happen to my mother? What is going to happen to my mother?' The final parting from Grandmother Julie, which he now knew to be inevitable and the knowledge that he would probably never see his mother alive again, that, not the collapse of all he had built for himself over the years, was the core of his grief.

Looking back on it I wonder whether his despairing cry, 'What will happen to my mother?' really meant what it said. Was he not really saying: 'I want to be a child again, and I want my mother to protect me from a world that I cannot face any more'?

When Father broke down and cried so bitterly I felt pity, tenderness and much love for him, but at the same time one of the certainties of my life crumbled to dust. Father, the invulnerable giant of my childhood, was vulnerable after all. How could he, a grown man, cry for his mother? I did not know then, as I do now, that the child lives on inside a man for as long as he lives. But, if I had lost my protector, I also realised that my childhood had ended, that I would have to step outside the protective warmth of the family and stand on my own.

Father's breakdown was actually quite brief. He recovered within half an hour, and when the phone rang a little later he answered it in his normal voice. He listened very attentively. His somewhat puzzled expression changed into a smile as he looked at Mother and me and then we heard him say: 'Certainly. We look forward to seeing you soon.' He replaced the receiver and announced: 'Alfred, Klara and Hedi are coming round.'

The great family feud, after twelve years of bitter vendetta, was at an end. What the three Schapira sisters had tried to bring about for so long and in vain, Hitler, by so wonderfully concentrating the minds of Jews, achieved in less than forty-eight hours. What happened when the Bartmanns arrived was quite unbelievable. The two brothers-in-law, arch-enemies for so long, fell into each other's arms.

When we had all settled in Father's study and the coffee had been served, Father's and Uncle Alfred's opening remarks reminded me very much of Selma Ornstein's question to mother: 'Stella, what on earth did we talk about?' because in everything the two men said to each other you could hear the question: 'What on earth did we quarrel about?'

The telephone rang again. This time I answered. It was Lisl. Could I come over. They had had visitors. I could hear from her voice how upset she was. I needed no description of the visitors. I went back into the study and explained that I had to go out and why. The protests were strong indeed. I must be out of my mind! What inconsiderate behaviour! Here were the Bartmanns for the first time after so many years and I had to go and see 'that girl'! Father and Mother were furious. I was foolhardy, ill-mannered, thick-headed, insensitive. I was bound to be picked up in the streets by rampaging Nazis. Only an imbecile would leave home and provoke disaster.

I listened to them for a little while and then I went.

When I arrived at Lisl's flat, after a twenty-minute walk during which nothing happened at all, she and her family had calmed down quite a bit. Their visitors, as I had expected, had been Austrian S.A. men. The whole thing was almost like a comedy, though that was not how one felt about it at the time. The men had been in the usual semi-military carnival outfits. Some wore tin hats, some had jack-boots, but more frightening, they all carried either revolvers or rifles. They had thoroughly searched the flat, liberated a few pieces of family silver and whatever cash there was, confiscated some books and helped themselves to drinks. Before they left their leader tore a piece of paper from a note-book, and with spelling errors all through the short text, he wrote out a sort of receipt. It read: 'This flat, having been searched by the S.A., its owners are not to be troubelled again. The German people knows no feelings of revendge. *Sig Heil!*' (Even the Nazi salute '*Sieg Heil*' was mis-spelt.)

The leader of that posse, a small man with a steel-helmet two sizes too large which kept falling over his eyes every time he bent down, signed his name, Kornherr, under this remarkable document, and then, clicking their heels, they all marched off.

Oh, what a lovely *Anschluss* the Kornherrs of Vienna had!

A much more distinguished gentleman than little Kornherr, one who made no spelling errors in his 'thank-you' note to his Führer, also had a lovely *Anschluss* surprise. Ex-Ambassador Franz von Papen received a telegram from Hitler that same Sunday evening ordering him to Vienna to take part in the celebrations he had done so much to make possible, while the German radio announced: 'In recognition of his valuable work the Führer has awarded membership of the National-Socialist German Workers' Party to ambassador Franz von Papen and presented him with the golden Party Badge.'

When I got home again Father, Uncle Alfred and Cousin Hedi also had visible signs of the *Anschluss* to show. They sat in the study, just as they had done when I had left a couple of hours before. The two men were very pale, their suits were dirty and full of white paint stains. Mother's hands were trembling, Aunt Klara seemed calmer, while Hedi, whose dress was also stained and dirty, had a look of defiance on her face. They all were in a state of shock, but Hedi less so than the grown-ups; but gradually they told me what had happened. I, the foolhardy one, must have left the house within a minute or two of the S.A. entering it. Our caretaker had led them to our door, and the steel bars fixed to it so many years before were no defence against them. They took Father and Alfred and Hedi, but left Mother and Aunt Klara in the flat. That was an even worse torture for the two women than if they had been ordered into the street as well. The S.A. men marched the men and Hedi off without saying anything about their fate, leaving Mother and Aunt to guess whether the three had been arrested or whether they had just been taken downstairs to scrub Schuschnigg slogans off the walls. Alfred, who was ten years older than Father, came back first. Father and Hedi were kept an hour longer on their knees, the jackboots of the S.A. men standing over them before their eyes.

I remember very clearly what we talked about during the rest of that evening, because the conversation was so typical of the many subsequent discussions at home with relatives and friends. The men, Father and Alfred, were shattered. Their talk circled eternally round their past mistakes. Father reproached himself again and again for not having asked the bank to pay him off when he had first thought of it, while Alfred blamed himself eternally for not having done what Richard Mautner did. Like Mautner he had substantial funds salted away in Switzerland. He later surrendered the money to the Nazis, who threatened all Jews who did not declare their holdings abroad with capital punishment and meant it. He had secretly bought his first car a few weeks before the *Anschluss*. It was supposed to be a surprise for his wife, but he was only going to tell Klara after he had passed his driving test which he failed every time; and his chief clerk, Herr Schreiber, an 'Aryan', had been fully prepared to drive the Bartmann family out of Austria and into Switzerland immediately after Schuschnigg's resignation.

Alfred told us how they had paced up and down, up and down, in their flat on Friday evening, trying to make up their minds. He could not bring himself to leave all his possessions behind. Now it was too late, and he beat his breast because he knew that he had lost much, much more than he would have done had he nerved himself to go there and then. And he was going to lose even more.

The women behaved very differently from the men. Klara could even talk with some wry humour about their car and how she had seen it only once, because she just happened to look out of the window as the Nazis drove it out of its garage across the road from their flat. It had happened on Saturday morning and she only learned that the car had been theirs when Herr Schreiber called to explain to uncle that he had had no alternative but to hand over the garage and car keys to the storm-troopers. Neither Mother nor Klara were in the least concerned about the past, about what happened yesterday or last year. They were only thinking of the future. Now, and during the months and years that followed, the soft and much cossetted and protected Schapira women showed what strength, what steel they had in their souls. They took over from their men. They guided and decided. It was their determination which saved their families. That was even more true in the case of Klara than in my mother's. Father regained his nerve and stopped looking only backwards after a few weeks, but Alfred did not recover so soon. He was like a walking corpse for many years, fell into a state of melancholia from which he recovered quite amazingly in his late sixties. The last four years of his life – he died in his seventy-third year in 1952 – he was a very active man and took a great interest in everything. He even tried to start an Export-Import firm again in London.

The whole city behaved like an aroused woman, vibrating, writhing, moaning and sighing lustfully for orgasm and release. This is not purple writing. It is an exact description of what Vienna was and felt like on Monday, 14 March 1938, as Hitler entered her.

And as the Führer's motorcade passed through the streets of the old Habsburg city, lined by hundreds of thousands waving jubilating Viennese, its church bells rang out their own obscene *jubilate*.

That was what Vienna was like on that day. I know. I was there. But I also know that there were many thousands, by no means only Jews, who stayed away behind tightly-closed windows in order not to hear the frenzy of the streets. Those were the men and women who had genuine convictions. Social-Democrats, Legitimists, true Catholics, Christian-Socials, who put patriotism before opportunism, as well as people who were neither this nor that but just honest human beings. What they felt during those hours, sadness, shame and defiance, and a resolve to stand together as Austrians one day, was in due course to bridge the chasms that had divided them for so long and, eventually, provide the moral foundations on which the Second Republic was built.

The Austrian Catholic Adolf Hitler, standing upright·in his Mercedes car, his right hand raised in the Nazi salute, beheld the crowds of Austrian Catholics welcoming him to their city, a city that once took no notice of him. He never forgave Vienna this original slight. He resolved that not his Austrian, but his German paladins would be the future masters here.

Meanwhile the German Catholic Franz von Papen, his brand-new gold party badge shining on his left breast, was preparing his next diplomatic master-stroke: a meeting between Cardinal Innitzer and his Führer. Not even the news he received on his arrival in Vienna, that Wilhelm von Ketteler, his loyal secretary and closest collaborator for many years, had disappeared from the city without trace, could dampen Franz von Papen's ardour to serve Hitler.

Next day, while von Papen stood with the Führer's entourage on the balustrade of the Hofburg, looking out over the sea of faces in the Heldenplatz and heard Hitler 'report to German history the homecoming of my home land into the German Reich', a corpse with shattered skull was fished out of the Danube. Wilhelm von Ketteler, murdered by the Nazis, had been found.

We returned to school on Wednesday morning. All the boys in my class, with the exception of us Jews, of course, were wearing either Hitler Youth badges or swastikas in their lapels. But before the first lesson began, Helmut Wieczorek, physically the strongest boy in my form and therefore also the acknowledged class-leader, got up and addressed us. 'What I want to say is this. There are Jewish boys in our class. They have been our colleagues and friends for years. And I feel they should remain our colleagues and friends and be treated as such!' The assent that welcomed his words was universal. Even the Hitler Youths joined in.

Another remarkable young man was Fredl Resch, the boy who had been my closest childhood friend. During the last few years, after I had left the Wasagymnasium, I had been much closer to Fritz Pollack and hardly ever saw Fredl. On the second Sunday after the *Anschluss*, at about eleven in the morning, our door-bell rang. I opened it. Fredl stood there. All he said was: 'I thought we might go on our usual Sunday walk.' He came in to greet my parents and then we went out into the street, his 'Aryan' arm linked with mine, just as it had been when we had strolled as children along the Ring. We had always said it would be re-named 'Klaaresch Promenade' one day when we had both become famous men. What Fredl did that day was an act of great courage, and more than that. It gave not only me, but also my parents, a renewed faith in human nature, and we felt the stronger for it.

Father's first experience on returning to the bank had been less fortunate than my return to school. He had entered his office, his second home for so many years, knowing full well that it would not be his for very much longer. It was a large room, or so I remember it, though here too the benevolent fraudulence of memory may have enlarged its true proportions. Its furnishings were very Austro-Victorian, very plushy, very red. Father's heavy oak desk faced a conference table with a red plush cover surrounded by four – or were there six? – red plush-upholstered chairs. Red plush curtains framed the window. A blue-patterned oriental carpet covered the centre of the parquet floor, and a book-case and hat-stand completed the furnishings.

Father had hardly settled behind his desk, when Dr Hilger entered. Dr Hilger, one of the few non-Jews in the department, had served with Father during the war. Dr Hilger was the fellow-officer who had persuaded Father to join him on that one and only, and nearly disastrous, experience of horseback riding my father had in his whole life. Like all former Austrian army officers Dr Hilger and Father used the familiar *du* instead of the formal *Sie* when talking to each other. This morning Dr Hilger did not say as usual '*Grüss Dich Gott*, Ernst!' as he came into the room, but, clicking his heels and raising his right arm, a masterfully arrogant expression on his face, he shouted: '*Heil Hitler*, Ernst!'

Father said nothing. The words that now came from Dr Hilger's lips were meant to be every bit as masterful and arrogant as his 'Heil Hitler' had been: 'I've come to tell you, Ernst, and I trust you will understand my reasons, that as from today I can no longer work for or accept instructions from a Jew.'

Father looked at the man he had known for so many years and replied: 'Under the circumstances, Herr Dr Hilger, I would prefer it if you would address me as *Sie* instead of *du*, should there be any occasion for you to speak to me again in future.'

Dr Hilger turned on his heels and left. There was no second 'Heil Hitler.'

Father had been almost thirty years with the Länderbank. This ended officially – I think he stopped going to his office earlier – with a curt letter signed by a Herr von der Lippe, one of the many German functionaries who were now the bosses in Austria. It was dated 9 May 1938 and addressed to 'Herrn Ernst Klaar, Vienna'. Without any 'Dear Herr Klaar' or even 'Dear Sir' at the beginning, it said:

In agreement with the State Commissioner for the Private Sector Economy we would inform you that we are instructed in accordance with the General Directives for Structural Re-Orientation, to withdraw from you the right to sign on behalf of the bank. The necessary amendment in the Trade Register has been implemented.

You are simultaneously suspended from all further active employment and, until further notice, will be on leave of absence.

Public interest in contemporary issues can be judged by the letters readers write to their newspapers. In Britain the best barometer for the highs and lows of public interest in any issue is the august letters column of *The Times*. During the weeks following the *Anschluss* only five letters dealt with Austria. The first appeared there on 14 March. Mr Leo Amery, Conservative M.P. and friend of Winston Churchill, wrote: 'with Austria has fallen the last home of German culture, the last citadel in which the true soul of the German race could still find a refuge'.

On 25 March a Mr F. O. Lindley wrote:

Sir – That the long expected seizure of Austria by Germany should provoke hysterical outbursts and idiotic suggestions from those whose judgment of foreign affairs has invariably been at fault was to be expected. Fortunately we have a Prime Minister and a Foreign Secretary strong enough to withstand such ebullitions.

Mr William, later Lord, Beveridge, wrote on 8 April :

Two of Austria's most distinguished scientists whose eminence has been marked by the award of the Nobel Prize have been taken from their homes and imprisoned, their families being allowed to see them for a few minutes only each week. The character, attainments and age of these men make it clear that nothing but their Jewish race can be the reason for this treatment.

The future founding father of Britain's Welfare State went on to appeal for funds for the Society for the Protection of Science and Learning to help scholars displaced from their own countries.

Another letter, published on 14 April, was also an appeal for money to help refugees. It was signed by a number of prominent British humanitarians, George Bell, the Bishop of Chichester, and Mrs Yvonne Rothschild among them.

Politically the most telling letter appeared on 4 April. Mr Edwin A. Stonor wrote :

At St Anton – a village beloved by British skiers – the railway station was a blaze of colour; even the station dog wore his swastika, but he looked unhappy and wagged a reluctant tail. Ninety per cent of Viennese now sport the swastika, popularly referred to as 'the safety pin'.

One of the strangest sights was the vast crowd struggling to get into the British Consulate in Wallnerstrasse. Many were Jews desirous of British nationality or anxious to leave a country where only Aryans are tolerated. Poor demented folk, they had little chance of success.

How right Mr Stonor was! I was one of them. Robert Rosen had heard a rumour – there was a new one every second – that the British army was going to accept young and fit Austrian Jews as recruits. Off we went to Wallnerstrasse to learn our first lesson in the British Way of Life – queueing. We stood there for hours. Finally, we were ushered into the presence of a British official. Through him we offered our hearts, souls and bodies to His Majesty, only to be dismissed with a curt : 'We don't run a Foreign Legion.' Another chance to get a visa for Britain? 'No.'

How were we to know that on Tuesday, 22 March, a few days before we went to the British Consulate, the House of Commons had decided by 210 votes to 142 against the introduction of a Private Member's Bill giving the Home Office much wider powers for the admission of Austrian refugees. After that vote Sir Samuel Hoare, the Home Secretary, explained that he would examine carefully and sympathetically applications from Austrian refugees working in science, the arts, business and industry, whose presence in the country may be advantageous to Britain. In less elegant words his message was: if you are just a Jew fleeing from Nazi persecution, keep out. If, by wealth or training you are a person useful to us, then you might come in, even if you are a Jew.

Britain, of course, was by no means the only country to react like this. Within a few hours of the *Anschluss* Czechoslovakia, long hailed as the only true democracy and the most liberal state in Central Europe, sealed its borders against Jewish refugees from Austria. Paul-Henri Spaak, the Belgian politician, reputed to be one of Europe's foremost liberal statesmen, announced in his parliament that there could be no 'wholesale' admission of foreigners into his country. And the U.S. Secretary of State, Cordell Hull, while proposing the setting up of a special international committee for political refugees, made it quite clear that no increase in the German and Austrian immigration quotas could be contemplated. Europe's oldest popular democracy, Switzerland, became so worried about the influx of Jews from Greater Germany that her police chief Dr Heinrich Rothmund, not Hitler's S.S., had his name recorded by history as the originator of the large red 'J' stamped on the passports of the Reich's Jewish second-class citizens. He justified this step with the excuse that as there were no visas required for Germans entering Switzerland, and vice versa, his border policemen often could not tell Jewish from 'Aryan' Germans.

World-wide unemployment and trade union opposition to immigrants were the most frequent excuses for keeping Jews out.

I had little hope of being accepted for the British army, but I also knew that one had to try everything. Hence I was hardly very disappointed when I came home from Wallnerstrasse. As I entered our dining-room, returning from the British Consulate, I saw a tall, very slim and handsome, grey-haired lady sitting next to Mother at the table, holding Mother's hand in hers and gently stroking it. 'Helga, this is my son George,' Mother introduced me.

When Mother mentioned her guest's name I knew who the stranger was. She had often spoken of Helga von Alvers as her closest friend at the Hanover boarding school. Although they had not met for over thirty years, Mother and her friend Helga had always kept in touch. In 1929, when my parents travelled through Germany, they had meant to visit Helga von Alvers, but something had happened at the last moment to prevent a visit to Hanover, where Frau von Alvers lived. Helga had planned to come to Vienna in 1933, but Hitler, by imposing his 1000 Marks blockade of Austria just then, stopped that. When he dropped it, after the 1936 Austro-German pact, Helga had meanwhile lost her husband, and her meagre pension did not permit the expense of a journey to Vienna.

Now she had come on the first trip to Austria organised by the Hanoverian section of 'Strength Through Joy', the National-Socialist Labour Front's leisure organisation, which cost next to nothing. On arrival she had first left her luggage at her hotel, and then, before coming to us, she strolled through the streets of Vienna for hours, witnessing the scenes of Jewish degradation, the scrubbing out of Schuschnigg slogans that was still going on, and the delight the Viennese took in this spectacle. She walked past Jewish shops with the Star of David and the word 'Jew' sloshed all over them with red paint, she saw the printed placards on the doors of shops and coffee houses saying 'Jewish customers not wanted here' or more directly 'Jews keep out!' It had badly shaken her, the German 'Aryan' of impeccable lineage. And it was not only the pleasure of seeing her friend again after so many years that made her stroke Mother's hand. Her gesture expressed love, but also pity and shame.

'I have told Stella what I felt when I saw the terrible things going on in this city,' Helga said, turning to Father, 'and I also told her how deeply ashamed I feel, not just personally, but as a German. Please believe me, nothing like this has ever to my knowledge happened in Germany.'

She paused. She looked at Mother, Father and me. And then, after a moment of hesitation, she went on: 'But I must also tell you honestly that I joined the National-Socialist Party in 1929 and that I am still a party member. That is why I was able to come on this "Strength Through Joy" trip.'

'Why did you join, Helga?' Mother asked.

'I hope you will understand,' Helga von Alvers replied. 'You remember that I was always a proud German, that I loved my nation, that I believed in it. I bitterly resented the injustice of the Peace Treaty and above all that we Germans were given the guilt for that terrible war. I did not love the Republic, but I did believe in Stresemann. I always voted for him. He was the greatest statesman we had, and I believed he would lead Germany back to her rightful place in the world.'

She stopped and took a sip of tea from Mother's paper-thin china, brought out in Helga's honour.

'But after Stresemann died in October 1929, who was there? All the other politicians did was talk and talk and fight amongst each other. The only man who seemed to have a plan, who seemed determined, was Hitler. True, he was also only talking at that stage. But all the others had had their chance. They had done nothing. Why shouldn't he have a chance too to show what he could do? And feeling that I should also do more than talk, I went and joined his party.'

'But Frau von Alvers,' Father said, 'Stella talked so much to me about you, how close you were at school, yet surely you knew that Stella was Jewish, you also knew her parents, you stayed with them in Hamburg, you could have no doubt what they were and yet you joined the Hitler party? You heard his storm-troopers shout their "*Juda verrecke!*" You heard him denounce us Jews, threaten us, revile us.'

'Yes, I did. But will you believe me, Herr Klaar, that I, and thousands like me, didn't take that at all seriously. After what I saw today I know that I was wrong. But believe me, I thought all that anti-Jewish propaganda was just rabble-rousing, something for that drunken S.A. mob. I ignored it and thought it unimportant. I felt certain all that would be forgotten once Hitler came to power, that . . .'

'And the Nuremberg laws?' Father interrupted her.

She thought a little while before replying.

'Yes,' she said, 'you're right to ask me that question. What shall I say? Of course, I know about them, but I also know now that I pushed that knowledge away from me. It won't be as bad as it sounds, I thought, and that injustice, I persuaded myself, had to be put on the scales and weighed against Hitler's achievements. Nearly six million unemployed were found jobs, Germany was strong and respected again, the shame of Versailles was wiped out. Yes, I looked for the good things and was intentionally blind to the bad. I am sorry, Stella, I wanted so much to believe.'

Helga von Alvers stayed in Vienna for three days and spent most of her time with Mother. We heard from her immediately after her return to Hanover. Her letter to Mother had two enclosures. One was a circular from the Hanover Gauleitung saying that instances of Jewish shops being smeared with anti-semitic slogans had occurred there recently, that such practices were un-German and had to cease forthwith. The other was a letter from Helga von Alvers to the Gauleitung resigning her party membership.

I have said that father's friend Richard Mautner, however indirectly, saved my life. Others who influenced my fate were Herr Direktor Schwartz of the Associated Austrian Ribbon Factories, Emil Hirsch, Schwartz's leading competitor, Maurice Witzthum, a Polish-born Jew and naturalised citizen of the then Irish Free State, and – last but not least – Sean Lemass, its Minister of Trade in 1938 and a future Prime Minister of the Republic of Ireland.

The man, who did most to protect me from concentration camp and extermination, the man who really saved my life, was my father. This was not immediately obvious because during the weeks after the *Anschluss* he seemed to live in a daze. His mind had turned inward. His eyes only saw the past and almost every sentence he spoke began with the words: 'If only I had . . .' That warm, slightly ironic smile of his I loved so much seemed wiped from his face forever. He spent hour after hour brooding in his armchair in the study over the things he should have done, but had not, over the dangers he should have seen, but saw not.

'If only I had understood what it was that Ernst Herlinger's brother told us in 1933 . . . if only I had asked the bank to pay me out . . . if only I had not been so blind . . . so foolish . . . so criminally optimistic . . . so trusting.' He went on and on like that. And even when he sat silent in his chair one knew that the words 'if only' were turning round and round inside his head.

But as he was sinking deeper and deeper into lethargic dejection, Mother became stronger and stronger. I was really observing a sort of spiritual duel between the two. Love and her well-reasoned appeal to Father's highly developed sense of responsibility were the two main weapons Mother used in this struggle. She fought with infinite patience and will-power. The first sign we had that she was succeeding, and that Father was about to face the present and the future again, was when he suggested I should be baptised. He knew, of course, that this would change nothing as far as the Nazis were concerned, but having heard that the Quakers were very actively helping 'non-Aryan' Christians to emigrate, he wanted me to grasp at any chance, however remote, to get out. I could not say how I would have reacted had Father suggested baptism to me during the Schuschnigg era, but now I absolutely refused. A strong awareness of my Jewishness had grown within me during those first weeks of rabid anti-semitism. It certainly did not come from religious conviction, but from defiance. I had been born a Jew, and as a Jew I would die.

Father now joined Mother in exploring every possible contact and connection to enable us to leave. Mother had even written to the Quaker Oats Company in Chicago to ask whether they would help me, Bernhard Schapira's grandson, to obtain an American entry permit. Father wrote to President Reuter of the Banque des Pays de l'Europe Centrale in Paris and received a reply from Reuter by return assuring him that he was trying to help as many members of his former staff as possible, that Father was high on his list and that he was hoping to find a place for him with a small private bank in London in which the Banque des Pays had an interest. That, our first gleam of hope, further restored Father's morale and self-confidence.

Herr Direktor Schwartz of the Ribbon Factories, in spite of his name, was as 'Aryan' as they came. Father had known him for years as he had always audited his firm's books on behalf of the Länderbank, which had a substantial investment in it, and he knew that he was an anti-Nazi. Richard Mautner, who had been the managing director of Austria's biggest hat factory, knew Schwartz very well indeed, and may also have suggested that Father should ask him if he had any international connection which would help us. Schwartz put Father in touch with Emil Hirsch, who had already begun negotiations with Lemass and the Irish Government through the company promoter Maurice Witzthum in Dublin about transferring his factory to Ireland.

The Irish were keen to industrialise and create employment and, I think, were already offering various incentives to foreign industrialists to establish themselves in their country – not that Jewish factory owners really needed much incentive, Hitler provided the strongest one possible.

Some far-sighted Czech Jews had already, with Maurice Witzthum's help, founded a felt hat factory in the Free State, and Hirsch's ribbon factory would naturally complement it. Hirsch, a very rich man in Austria, had no money abroad. He felt confident of getting his looms and ancillary machinery as well as a certain amount of stock out of Austria, but what he needed was a little starting capital in Ireland. Paying a fortune in bribes to various Nazi authorities, including the S.S., Hirsch did indeed obtain permission to export all the equipment he required to start again. As far as I know his was the only case in Austria where a Jewish owner succeeded in shipping virtually a whole factory out of the country after the *Anschluss*. His starting capital was to be provided by Richard Mautner through Father, on condition that Father, Mother and I could also emigrate to Ireland. The sum involved was only £1000, worth very much more then than it is now, but still not an enormous amount. It was enormous, however, as the Mautners' proof of their friendship for my parents. It was so unusual and generous that the Hirsches themselves never quite believed that the money was really Richard's. They felt sure that it was Father's own, but that for some reason he did not want to admit that he was a rich man. And for a long time I believed the same.

I simply could not understand why my father, who had been so highly paid by the standards of the time, should have had no savings whatsoever. The simple answer was that he spent a lot of money on his beloved pictures and antiques, and that he supported his mother and sister.

Maurice Witzthum came to Vienna, and negotiations were completed in Pichlergasse. Father, who did not know the difference between warp and woof, or between the front of a loom and its back, was to be given an Irish work and entry permit as a ribbon-weaver. Mother and I would be allowed into Ireland as his dependants. Witzthum said the formalities would take only a few weeks, time to prepare all the documents and pay all the taxes which the Nazi authorities required from emigrating Jews.

This was more easily said than done. The proverbial Austrian sloth was now transformed into state policy and used to harass and offend the Jewish petitioner. Surprises awaited one at every office when, after queueing for hours at the still constant risk of being hijacked from the queue by a passing S.A. or S.S. patrol for a few hours of cleaning their barracks, one finally faced the official one had come to see. In eight cases out of ten one learned then that one had done it all wrong. Back to the starting point and get a chit to another office to get a chit from another official entitling one to talk to the first one. And when one had come back, duly equipped with the required piece of paper, after queueing for another few hours, needless to say, then this stamp was not right or that document wrong and one started all over again. The inventiveness of the Nazi officials knew no bounds. There was also method in all this madness. Even better than the heady joy of sudden power, it also brought tangible rewards in the form of bribes. Outside every office you were accosted by Jews specialising in the new profession of 'documentation experts'. They had their price, but you got every document, every stamp you needed, without trouble and in reasonable time. They knew every policeman and every official, knew exactly who could be bought, and for how much. They knew every back door. It was the poor Jews who queued for hours outside the front doors.

But parallel with all this sloth which interfered with a steady outflow of Jews from Austria someone else was busy developing policies to accelerate the removal of Jews from the country. S.S. Lieutenant Adolf Eichmann, working in the old Rothschild Palace in the third district, was laying the foundations for his future career with his activities in Vienna. No one had yet accomplished what he did : to get the largest number of Jews out of a country in the shortest possible time, at the same time increasing the financial tributes demanded from those ready to go. By the time each Jewish goose was out of Austria it had laid a 'golden egg' for Eichmann and the Nazi state.

But if Eichmann was in a hurry, the Irish most certainly were not. The few weeks became very many. All sorts of complications arose and were dealt with with the speed of a snail perambulating from the shore of the Liffey to the top of O'Connell Street and beyond. But they were no great exception. No country wanted Eichmann's Jews.

We were all like screaming, helpless travellers on a nightmarish big dipper racing upwards towards peaks of hope only to plough down even more rapidly and deeply into ravines of despair. In a way it was all epitomised by the World Refugee Conference, held, following the suggestion of Mr Cordell Hull, the U.S. Secretary of State, in Evian in the summer of 1938. There was not a Jew under German dominion who did not look towards that spa with hopeful expectations. The representatives of thirty-two countries assembled there, listened to evidence, conferred and deliberated, talked and considered : and, after a few weeks at Evian, came to the conclusion that they could not – oh, so regrettably – find a place for the Jews anywhere in the world, not even for their children.

On 30 July, Father received a registered letter from the Länderbank. It contained the 'further notice' promised by Herr von der Lippe, or rather, simply Father's notice. It was not a personal letter, but a circular saying 'Consequent upon the re-organisation in the Land of Austria we have cause to terminate your employment as from 31 August 1938. In order to settle the financial questions arising from your retirement we request you to report to our personnel department during the week from 8 to 13 August, preferably on 8 August 1938, at 3 p.m.' The date and the time were stamped on the circular.

On the appointed afternoon Father entered the building for the last time in which he had spent so much of his life. All he really had to do there was to sign a receipt for 13,000 Reichsmark, 'received, at my own request, in settlement of all claims against the Länderbank arising out of my employment with that institute'. One can only smile wrily at the inclusion of the words 'at my own request'. The letter telling Father that his active employment had ceased as well as the letter of final dismissal did not even pretend that Father had been consulted in any way, but when it came to money the new powers were more careful. Even Nazi bankers protected themselves against all eventualities. Thirteen thousand Reichsmark at the Schilling to Mark conversion rate of 1.50 to 1, arbitrarily laid down by the German Reichsbank, came to 19,500 Austrian Schillings, almost exactly half of the 40,000 Schillings Father was entitled to. Actually, it was even less, as the purchasing power of the Austrian Schilling had virtually been the same as that of the Reichsmark.

Father was not too upset by this fraud. It was what he had expected. Even more important, this final act of severance from his past did not bring about a relapse in his morale, a return to 'if only I had'. On the contrary, he treated it almost with relief. A very large and very important chapter of his life was closed. What mattered now was our future, and that at last looked really hopeful. Witzthum had written that our visas had been granted. According to him all we had to do now was to travel to Berlin to the Irish Legation for Germany and Austria and present our passports. Our entry permits would be stamped on them then and there. We would be a sort of advance guard. Emil Hirsch and his family and all the others joining them to build up the new factory, including one anti-Nazi non-Jewish foreman, a real weaving expert, were to arrive in Dublin only towards the end of the year, after supervising the packing and shipping of the machinery.

The short time we still had in Vienna was full of hectic activity. Arrangements had to be made for packing not only our personal belongings, but the entire household, the pictures, the furniture, the linen, everything. The final removal of the entire Pichlergasse contents by the shippers was to take place only after our departure, and Helene, our maid, was to take charge of it. She was to marry that year and my parents, both as a wedding present and a sign of gratitude for her help, had given her their double bed.

We left on the Berlin night-express in the exciting luxury of a 'Wagon-Lits' sleeper. A bit of a problem arose at the station in Vienna when a stout German, Nazi party-membership badge in his buttonhole, entered my compartment. Not the ideal sleeping companion for a Jew. I made some excuse, slipped out and told Father. A five-Mark tip for the sleeping-car attendant solved that minor racial difficulty. In the hearing of that Prussian gentleman the porter informed me that he had unfortunately made a mistake when allocating my compartment. Mine was the next one. He gave me a wink, transferred my luggage next door, the train had just begun to move, and whispered, 'You'll have that compartment to yourself for the whole journey.'

We arrived at the Anhalter Bahnhof, Berlin's biggest railway station, around noon the following day. We were booked into the Hotel Excelsior, right across the road from the station, where my parents had stayed on their visit to Berlin in 1929. With six hundred bedrooms it was the biggest, and also one of the most luxurious, on the European continent. But what impressed me most was that the railway porter, having loaded our bags on his trolley, led us to a lift on the arrival platform, which took one down to a subterranean passage connecting the station directly to the hotel.

Following the porter on our way to the reception we walked through the Excelsior's famous beer-cellar, packed with lunching, munching, drinking Berliners. Passing a table with uniformed party-officials and S.A. men I felt slightly uneasy, but they took no notice of us whatsoever. In Vienna a few rude remarks about 'Jews being everywhere' would have been the least to expect. There was something about these Berliners which made them look different from a similar crowd in Vienna. This puzzled me. Then I found the explanation. Hardly anybody had a swastika in his buttonhole.

What also struck me a little later, after we had been received with perfect politeness and shown to our rooms, was that the hotel had retained its rather un-German international name under Hitler. In Vienna such names were out. Within twenty-four hours of the *Anschluss* Herr Hübner, Vienna's leading caterer, had changed the name of his 'Café Splendide' to 'Kaffee Berlin', and others quickly followed his example.

As I was to learn a little later that very day there were quite a number of things in which Austrians were much more thorough than Prussians. That became clear when we visited Mother's Bartmann relatives in the afternoon and I first met my second cousin Hanno, who was five years older than myself.

'What would you like to do this evening?' he asked me. 'D'you want to go to a cinema, the theatre or just for a drive round Berlin in my car?' I looked at him with the open-mouthed astonishment of the proverbial village yokel.

'But how can we?' I asked. 'We're Jews.'

'Yes, and don't I know it,' he replied. 'But what's that got to do with it?'

It seemed incredible to me, but it was perfectly true – in Berlin, in the capital of the Third Reich, in the very lion's den, Jews were still allowed in September 1938 to visit places of entertainment, coffee-houses; some even still owned patisseries, they could own cars and shop where they pleased. On the whole of Kurfürstendamm, one of the city's most elegant streets. I saw only one shop with the sign 'No Jewish customers', so universally displayed in Vienna. Indeed, many Kurfürstendamm shops were still run by their Jewish proprietors. How many became obvious a few weeks later when Jewish shops had to display the name of the owner in large white letters on their windows. But even then no words of abuse were smeared over them in red paint. Nor, as I could see for myself, did the 'Aryan' German customers keep away from those shops.

I felt even more of a provincial later that evening, when we drove back to our hotel in a taxi through crowded, busy streets, brightly lit by many-coloured neon lights and I sensed the invigorating pace and intensity of Berlin. Compared with it Vienna was a backwater, its life eddying along at the tempo of an early Hadyn minuet, while Berlin's roared forward dynamically and determinedly like a Stravinsky Suite. I was overwhelmed by that city and also breathed more freely there than I had in Vienna during the previous six months. With every additional day my impression grew stronger, and it was shared by my parents, that after Nazi Vienna one felt in Berlin almost as if one had emigrated and escaped from Hitler's rule.

Our first morning started most enjoyably in the Excelsior's breakfast room. Everything was as my parents had reported after their previous visit. You helped yourself to cold cuts, eggs, sausages, cheeses, various kinds of rolls and bread. Only butter was now rationed. After this huge breakfast we took a taxi to the Irish Legation in the Tiergarten, Berlin's diplomatic quarter. The Legation was housed in a small villa. After walking up a short flight of stairs one entered a narrow, almost suburban hall. The door on its left marked 'Private' led to the Minister's office and living quarters. Father knocked on the door on the right marked 'Passport and Visa Section'. A female voice answering in German asked us to come in and we walked into a small office containing one desk, two filing cabinets, a small round table with two chairs and Frau Kamberg, an attractive German blonde in her middle-forties, who was the 'Passport and Visa Section' as well as the Minister's secretary. The two of them made up the entire staff.

Father explained that we had come to pick up our visas. She looked at him with some astonishment. With a note of regret in her voice she told us that no instructions had come from Dublin, indeed that she had never heard of our names before. Father showed her Witzthum's letter. She read it carefully and checked though her files again. Nothing. She was ready to believe that somebody in Dublin had told Witzthum that everything had been arranged, but, unfortunately, nothing was.

The three of us – Father, Mother and I – had gained enough experience with the consular officials of various countries by that time to sense whose side they were on. Some, not too many, felt sympathy for the Jews, some, not too few, were in sympathy with the Nazis' anti-semitism; but most of them were simply indifferent. That Frau Kamberg was certainly not. It was obvious how sorry she was having to give us such shattering news. Though she was most discreet in what she actually said, she also managed to convey that she would try to help as much as she could, but that the Minister himself might be somewhat less keen. Our best hope was to contact Witzthum and ask him to cut through the red tape of the Dublin bureaucrats. Meanwhile, provided her boss agreed, she would get in touch with Dublin. Could we either ring or come to see her in another week?

So, once again, we had been taken for a ride on the big dipper. Up, up and up to what to us had appeared not merely a summit of hope, but a certainty, only to be plunged down again with totally unexpected suddenness.

A return to Vienna was unthinkable and impossible. We had no home there any more. Financially we did not have a problem. The money father had received from the bank was of course finite, but it was no tragedy if we spent it. You were not allowed to take more than 10 Reichsmark with you when leaving Germany in any case. The question no one could answer was how long it would be till we got our visas and how much money we would need till then. After the first shock of disappointment had worn off our confidence returned. Surely the whole thing would be cleared up and settled in another week or so.

Father cabled Witzthum, who confirmed in his reply that he was taking immediate action, and so we stayed on in the Excelsior, which had preserved intact not only its name, but also something of the atmosphere of Auden's and Isherwood's Berlin.

After the end of one week Frau Kamberg still had not heard from Dublin. Obviously an open-ended stay at the expensive Excelsior was out of the question, so we moved to a private boarding-house. We also from then on took the advice of one of the Bartmanns, who had pointed out that there were less expensive means of public transport in Berlin than taxis.

Pension Lurie, the boarding-house we moved to, occupied the entire third and fourth floors of a house at the corner of Wilmersdorferstrasse and Kurfürstendamm and was, therefore, in a very good and central location. Frau Lurie, its owner, was a Jewess, and all her guests were Jewish. We had two comfortable rooms, and the food was very good. Once a week lunch consisted only of a main dish, the *Eintopf* or *pot-au-feu* with which everybody in Germany had to support Hermann Goering's 'guns or butter' austerity drive. But the strict rationing of butter was the only austerity one really noticed in Berlin. The restaurants were crowded, and people looked well dressed, even elegant. The women taking their afternoon coffee at the famous Café Kranzler were not at all the frumpish *Hausfraus* I had expected, having been told so often in Vienna that all German women were born without dress-sense. Many of them were very chic, smart and attractive.

Occasional visits to the cinema, alone, with my parents, or with Frau Lurie's pretty daughter, who was my age and about to emigrate to South America, or a drive to the Berlin lakes in Hanno's tiny car, passed the time, but did not allay our overall feeling of insecurity. Of course we were not worrying all the time. My parents and I often went out to dinner together, and then we most likely discussed our plans for the future. Father was confident that he would be able to work as a chartered accountant in Ireland after a while, and I was still bent, as I had been for so many years, on a career in journalism. That I would have to write in English did not worry me at all. I had started to learn the language at school at the age of fifteen, and in a mysterious way some recesses of my mind, though planted in a foreign field, must have been forever English. The vocabulary just spilled out of me. After the first year my English master announced before the whole class that I had reached matriculation standard.

Though time passed pleasantly enough, our feeling that it was really borrowed time grew with every passing day. There was no news from the Irish Legation. Mother phoned Frau Kamberg fairly frequently, thus building up a more personal relationship with that very nice woman. On 16 September when we had been in Berlin for almost three weeks it was, however, Frau Kamberg, who phoned Mother. Could she come to see her? No, the visas had not arrived. There was something else she wanted to tell her. I remember the date of her call so exactly, because it was the day after Prime Minister Chamberlain had surprised the world by flying to see Hitler in Berchtesgaden.

Father and I waited for Mother's return from the Legation in the Jewish-owned Café Dobrin on the Kurfürstendamm. She had news for us. A policy decision and not Irish distaste for speedy action was prolonging our stay in Berlin into one *mañana* after another. A letter from Dublin had arrived at the Legation that morning explaining that the Irish authorities thought it too risky to allow a Jewish family to enter their country before they had confirmation that Hirsch's machines, which were what mattered to them, were on their way. No doubt this explanation had been couched in more diplomatic terms, but that is what it amounted to. Frau Kamberg took the risk of telling Mother – had it come out, she would have been sacked immediately – because she felt so strongly we ought to know where we stood. As we knew that the machines would not be shipped before the end of October, another six weeks or so in Berlin were now a certainty. This knowledge had unforeseen consequences for me.

Father was getting seriously worried about my fate. The growing danger of war breaking out over Czechoslovakia and my eighteenth birthday being only three months away upset him deeply. He was sure Hitler would use able-bodied young Jews as cannon-fodder.

Chancellor and Prime Minister met for the second time in Bad Godesberg on 22 September. When the news that they had failed to agree came out after Chamberlain's departure on the next day, the crisis worsened and Father was by no means the only one to panic.

I went to an afternoon performance at the Filmbühne Wien, the biggest Kurfürstendamm cinema, on the twenty-third. It was already dark when I came out. Newspaper sellers were shouting out the headlines of their papers: 'Godesberg talks fail!', 'Czechs mobilise!' People tore the newspapers out of their hands and read them there and then. They looked drawn, pale and worried, soldiers just as much as civilians. There was none, absolutely none, of that 'Hurrah, up and at them!' spirit with which the crowds in all European capitals had welcomed the outbreak of the Great War.

When I returned to the Pension Lurie I found Father almost frantic. I had to go. Immediately. The only country still freely admitting Austrian Jews was Latvia. We knew this because Lisl and her family had emigrated there. Father, who had so much wanted that relationship to end, decided to send me to her. He had already phoned the Latvian Consulate, which had confirmed that I could enter Latvia with an Austrian passport. No special permit was required. After that he had phoned the Lithuanians. Provided I could show a railway ticket to Riga, the Latvian capital, they would give me a twenty-four hour transit visa. Even the ticket for next day's evening train Father had already booked. While Mother was doing my packing he and I would collect it next morning and then get the Lithuanians to stamp my passport.

I was of course overjoyed. Not in my wildest dreams had I dared to hope to see Lisl so soon again. Any pangs of conscience I felt about leaving my parents were allayed by their argument that it was all-important for at least one member of a family to be abroad. I could do more to help them from there than if I stayed with them. In any case our separation would not be for long. Frau Kamberg had told Mother that I could get my Irish entry permit from the British Consulate in Riga as soon as my parents had been granted theirs. At that moment Father's only concern was to get me out, to save me, as he saw it, from the clutches of the Wehrmacht. It shows how much we still misunderstood Hitler's anti-semitism by thinking he could ever be guided by rational considerations. It just did not occur to Father, or to me, that to Hitler the idea of a Jew wearing his army's uniform was a grotesque perversion.

On the late afternoon of 24 September we took a taxi to Bahnhof Zoo, the railway station a few hundreds yards off the Kurfürstendamm from which trains going east departed. A German customs officer searched my luggage for valuables or other contraband I might be smuggling out. He was a little chap with a Hitler moustache, but a gay Berlin street-urchin twinkle in his eyes. 'How many golden dentures have you hidden in there?' he asked, pointing to my case. I was a little slow on the uptake because of my excitement and told him that I had no need for dentures. He grinned. 'As far as I'm concerned,' he said, 'you can have as many as you like,' and he added 'with diamonds for teeth too.' He opened my case, gave its contents a cursory glance, touched a few things very superficially and then shut it again.

My train was already standing at the platform. I put my things in my compartment and pulled the window down to say goodbye to my parents. Mother, of course, had a few final words about the importance of inner and outer cleanliness to say to her departing son. Something like 'Never eat unwashed fruit and always remember to wash your hands before and your face after meals with soap and hot water.' No one could stress quite like her the importance of one's washing water being very hot. As she repeated the words *heisses Wasser, heisses Wasser*, one felt a cleansing geyser hissing and gushing all over one's body.

The train started to pull out. This was it. None of us knew when, where or how we would meet again. I looked at Father in his dark winter coat and grey hat and remembered the days, so recent and so far away, when he had waited for me outside my school and I had run towards him so proud that this handsome man was my father. Mother wore the black Persian lamb coat she had inherited from her mother. Her arm resting on Father's trembled slightly. That was the only sign betraying how upset she was. For a few moments both stood quite still side by side. Then I saw Father bending towards her. The train went into a curve and I lost sight of them.

I settled down to the long journey stretching before me. First through the Polish corridor to East Prussia, then o' to Kaunas, the Lithuanian capital, and from there over the Latvian border to Riga, where Lisl – we had sent a wire – would be awaiting me. I was so much looking forward to being with her again. My thoughts, more with her than with what I was doing, I leafed idly through my passport re-reading the Lithuanian visa as well as the swastika stamp-adorned endorsement by the Vienna passport office stating 'Valid for one outward and one return journey only'. Every Austrian Jew knew that this 'return' entitlement was on paper only. When one collected one's passport one was told in no uncertain terms that a return journey would end in Dachau should one ever have the cheek to come back again.

But when our train stopped at the Latvian frontier station and the whole of Lithuania now lay between me and Hitler's Germany I had no feeling of liberation and deliverance.

Latvian border guards, little grey-uniformed men with huge rifles slung over their shoulders, boarded the train and collected our passports. Half an hour or so passed before they returned. I was absorbed in reading and therefore only half-heard the man's voice calling out two names. I looked up and listened. 'Passengers Klaar and Mandl, passengers Klaar and Mandl!' the man repeated. I stood up and went out into the corridor. Out of the next compartment stepped a slight-built prematurely bald man of about thirty-five.

A Latvian border guard sergeant came towards us.

'You Klaar and Mandl?' he asked in broken German.

We said we were. He opened the two Austrian passports in his hand and verified our identity from the photographs.

'Austrian passport no good,' he announced. 'Take things get out here.'

'But why? What have we done?' we asked.

'Austrian passport no good, only German good. You out,' he replied.

Mandl and I were the only travellers still using properly endorsed but Austrian passports. All the other passengers who came from Austria – there were plenty of them and nearly all Jews – had new German passports.

Of course we remonstrated with the sergeant and explained that we had checked with the Latvian Consulate, but it was no use. If he would let us go on to Riga we would surely be able to clear up what could only be some sort of misunderstanding. The man was not unkind, but very firm.

'You come now,' he said. 'I talk Riga telephone. If Riga O.K. you next train. If no, you back Germany.'

When he mentioned a possible return to Germany my stomach suddenly began to turn over. Mandl's reaction was very much more visible than mine. He began to shiver and tremble and was in such a state that I had to help him with his luggage and even support him as he climbed down from the coach to the platform. After a couple of minutes he had recovered enough for the two of us, struggling with our luggage and followed by an armed escort, to move along the platform to the border police office.

Our fellow passengers watching this miserable little procession through the train windows knew as well as we did that being a Jew was guilt enough. But even so one could read in their faces how they were calming their own permanent sense of unease with the thought: 'Those two must have done something wrong.'

It is well known that the mere fact of being arrested induces a sense of guilt in the victim. Kafka, as well as policemen all over the world, discovered this long before I did, but I can vouch for the truth of it from personal experience. I did feel guilty – of what I did not know – as Mandl and I shambled along under the watchful eyes of two armed border guards.

The sergeant kept his word. He phoned Riga. 'They ring back,' he told us. He allowed us, still under guard, to go to the station restaurant where we blew the few Marks we still had left on a pot of coffee and two brandies to steady our nerves. Riga did not phone back. Near midnight the sergeant at last gave in to our repeated requests and called Riga again. No news.

Convinced by now that we were not likely to run away he withdrew our guard and we settled down on the hard wooden station benches for a few hours of fitful sleep. At four in the morning they woke us.

'Riga no. You four-thirty train Kaunas. Get luggage.' How we would get back from Lithuania to Germany without a penny in our pockets was no concern of the Latvians. They did, however, give us a cup of coffee each and free railway tickets to Kaunas.

Had the first train to Kaunas left one hour later we would not have been deported and my fate might have been very different. Whether for good or bad, who can say?

The Berlin–Riga express, on which she had expected me, having arrived without my being on it, Lisl and her family moved heaven and earth to find out what had gone wrong. When they knew they persuaded influential Latvian Jews to intercede with the government. The result was that my name appeared on the agenda of a cabinet meeting for the first and last time in my life. The Latvian ministers deliberated for many hours what to do with Mandl and Klaar. Their final decision was positive. We could proceed to Riga. But it took hours, with most officials being asleep in their beds by then, for the news to filter through channels. When the sergeant of the border guard was at last phoned and told to let us go, the two of us, travelling in the opposite direction, tired, hungry and afraid, were back in Lithuania.

It was mid-morning when we arrived in Kaunas. Surrounded by our luggage we stood in the station and I, on my own, would not have known where to turn next.

Now Mandl took over. His family had left Galicia for Vienna during the Great War. Still a traditionalist, he knew that no eastern Jew would ever refuse help to another Jew in trouble, and he also spoke fluent Yiddish. Finding a Jew in Kaunas main railway station, or, for that matter, anywhere in the Lithuanian capital, was no problem. With a large percentage of its population Jewish, Kaunas really was just an overgrown *shtetl*.

Mandl went up to the first caftaned and side-locked Jew he saw and told him about our plight. From then on we were looked after. The man got a porter to move our things to the Left Luggage, paid him and the storage fee out of his own pocket and then walked with us to the near-by office of the 'Joint', the American-Jewish financed international aid organisation.

A bearded Jew in western dress received us. After listening to our story he said: 'I'm sorry, but I must tell you that you have no option. You can't stay here. You must go back to Germany.' He saw the desperation on Mandl's face. 'I'll explain why,' he continued. 'Your Lithuanian transit visas expire at midnight. If you stay longer the police will get you. Although I would wish no one to see a Lithuanian prison from the inside, that would not be the worst, for when they deport you they won't just take you to the border and wash their hands of you like the Latvians. They will hand you over personally to the Gestapo. Once they've got you, you have no chance. As ordinary passengers on the train you might be lucky and slip through.'

He turned to me. 'You say your parents are in Berlin. Wire them from Königsberg and ask them to send you the money for the rest of your journey. I can only buy you tickets as far as Königsberg. Rail tickets for foreigners must be paid for in U.S. dollars and there are plenty of others I must help.'

We said we understood.

'Your train leaves at three. You two must be starving. My secretary will take you to a Jewish eating-house and later she'll bring you your tickets there.'

Starving we certainly were, but when I sat at the neatly-laid table and they put a huge plate of Jewish caviare before me, one of my favourite dishes, a delicious mixture of finely-chopped goose-liver, eggs and onions, I could only nibble at it. My stomach, though it had meanwhile stopped turning, now seemed to be filled with lead. I managed to get down a few spoons of the chicken soup that followed, but the main dish, roast goose, red cabbage and potatoes, I could not touch.

Two hours later we sat in the train to Königsberg, and I did not know what worried me more: our likely fate or Mandl's utter loss of nerve. I had tried to steady him by pointing out that there was some reason to hope that our next stop might actually be Königsberg and not Dachau concentration camp. I reasoned that, though the Austrians' threats had been most explicit, Austria, or 'the Ostmark' as it was now called, was a very long way from East Prussia. There was a chance that the Austrians, indulging in the pleasurable game of making Jews squirm, had merely bluffed. I tried to convince Mandl that all was not lost and that it was essential to behave as naturally as possible in order not to arouse attention, but he could not control the terror within him. He sat silently opposite me in our compartment – other passengers had joined us and we did not dare speak – looking deathly pale. His hands were white at the knuckles, he held them so tightly clasped in a vain attempt to stop their trembling.

Outwardly, I think, I looked calm enough, but the nearer we came to the German frontier the louder my heart beat; and the blood did not pulse, but sledge-hammered through my brain.

The compartment door was pushed open. Framed in it stood a tall German in a dark suit, a small S.S. badge in his buttonhole. 'Deutsche Grenzkontrolle, your passports, please.' We handed ours over. He added them to the pile of passports he was already carrying and closed the door.

Mandl, his hands still tightly clasped, sat there with his eyes closed. I was not looking at the face of a thirty-five-year-old living man any more, but at a wax-coloured death-mask, its expression unblessed by the serenity of final release.

I held a book in my hand and pretended to read, all the time listening for the sound of men in heavy boots marching towards our compartment. Then I noticed the silence around me, only interrupted by the hiss of steam escaping from the standing train. Nobody spoke. I prayed silently. Perhaps twenty minutes passed like this. Then I heard compartment doors being slid open and the voice of the S.S. man again saying: 'Your passports, Dankeschön.'

He came closer. Mandl opened his eyes and gave me a look so full of despair that I almost wanted to touch him consolingly, though feeling at the same time anger that he was in such a state of fear that he might suddenly do something crazy in his terror, like falling on his knees and pleading for mercy, and thus give us away.

Then our turn came. The door was opened. 'Your passports, *Dankeschön*.' He handed them back, closed the door and was gone.

We did not dare to show the immense relief we felt, to talk, to sing, to shout, to dance, to praise and thank God, not only because of the others in our compartment – how did one know that no Gestapo spy was among them – but also because we still could not quite believe that we had really escaped, that I had been right, and that frontier control in East Prussia simply accepted 'valid for one outward and one return journey' to mean what it said.

We arrived in Königsberg about ten at night, were given the address of a nearby boarding-house by the information desk and, repeatedly asking people in the street for directions, eventually found it. A tall, blonde woman answered our ringing. I told her that we had no money, requested permission to use her telephone to send a wire asking for money to my parents, and she, asking no questions, showed us into a large, clean double room. Minutes later Mandl and I, buried deep under huge duvets, were exhaustedly asleep.

The ringing of the door-bell followed by a stentorian '*Heil Hitler*' woke us at six the next morning. Mandl nearly fell out of bed. 'They've found us. They've come for us,' he whispered. I went and opened the door of our room. Our landlady and a green-uniformed postman stood in the corridor. 'Are you Herr Klaar?' he asked. I nodded. 'I've got some money for you. Sign here, please.' He handed me two hundred Marks from my parents, *Heil Hitler*-ed and left.

The nightmare of my flight from the Wehrmacht was over. The nightmare of life in Hitler's Germany could continue.

I met my parents again on the late afternoon of 27 September on the arrival platform of Bahnhof Zoo. They were greatly relieved to have me back again, safe and sound, after an adventure which might easily have ended in disaster. Father gave Mandl the money to buy his ticket back to Vienna, and I parted from the companion of the most traumatic journey of my life without too keen a feeling of regret.

While I was travelling, either with intent, or being shunted involuntarily around Eastern Europe frontiers, the crisis over Czecho-slovakia had reached and passed its peak. Nothing had yet been finally decided, but with the news that the powers, at Benito Mussolini's suggestion, were to meet in Munich in another two days, some of the heat had gone out of the situation. Hitler had assured the world that the Sudeten were definitely his last territorial demand, and only three days after my return to Berlin Mr Chamberlain, waving his famous piece of paper at Heston airport, was assuring the world in his turn that it was 'Peace in our Time'.

German troops were preparing to move again, and so were we. They were to enjoy yet another triumphal entry, this time into what used to be Czech territory, while we were facing a somewhat hang-dog return to our home territory – Vienna. Nothing is more pathetic than the 're-immigration' of the would-be emigrant. After the tearful 'goodbyes' the almost shame-faced 'hellos'. And then, after a few days, we knew we were only going to stay a very short while in Vienna before returning to Berlin, with the harrowing partings all over again. But our journey to Vienna was unavoidably necessary. My passport, having been used for a return trip, had lost its validity, but even without my escapade we would have had to get German passports now that Switzerland's police chief Dr Rothmund had prevailed. From 5 October 1938, all passports issued to Jews had to have the large red 'J' stamp.

Back in Vienna Father and Mother stayed with Uncle Paul and Aunt Alice. I slept at the Bartmanns'. Cousin Hedi gave me her room and moved into the now empty maid's room next to the kitchen.

The morning after our return we went to the passport office. A very fat and apparently genuinely good-humoured official issued our new passports and shook his head in disbelief when he learned that we had come back all the way from Berlin to get them. 'Why did you bother? If you had paid me the journey and bought me a goulash and a beer I would have brought them to you. I've always wanted to see Berlin. Oh well!' Shrugging his shoulders as if to say 'that's life', he stamped our 'Js' neatly and carefully, as if they were some sort of special adornment, on the top left-hand corner of the first inside page of our new passports and handed them to us. 'Have a good journey,' he said with a wink, and no 'Heil Hitler' came thundering after us as we left his office.

That night – or, to be more exact – at about three in the morning, I was woken up by a shrill scream. Jumping out of bed, I raced into the corridor. At its far end I saw Aunt Klara half supporting, half dragging her husband Alfred back to their bedroom. I only saw his back, but there could have been no more pititful sight than that of this once elegant man in his white nightshirt, his head lolling limply on his neck. His figure in near-collapse expressed a dejection, a more total defeat, than even a Goya could convey when he painted the victims of tyranny and darkest despair – and I am not forgetting his 'black paintings' either.

The smell of gas was all-pervasive. I stormed into the kitchen, but Klara, with great presence of mind, had already switched off the gas cooker – the door of its baking oven was still open – and torn open the window. I quickly went into the maid's room where Hedi slept. I opened her window and woke her. She was woozy and felt sick, but came round quickly.

I returned to the corridor. Klara, her shivering son Fritzl by her side, was on the telephone. She was talking to my Uncle Paul.

In less than half an hour Paul, Alice and also my parents had joined us. Paul, having given Alfred a sedative, assured Klara that he would be all right. Klara had been asleep, but her instinct must have been very alert. She woke barely a couple of minutes after Alfred had quietly slipped out into the kitchen, immediately went to look for him and thus saved him and quite possibly us as well.

My parents told me to get dressed and pack my things. They felt that Klara could not be burdened with me after this. We stayed with her for another hour. By then the worst of her shock had worn off and we walked back to Uncle Paul's flat in Blindengasse, only a few streets away from the Bartmanns'.

It was not only because he had been torn out of his sleep that I remember noticing a change in Paul Klaar that night. What he said still sounded confident and optimistic, but underneath it all there was a nervous tenseness, which had not been there before. He was still fully paid as a police-surgeon, but had been suspended from active service. The civil service moving more slowly than private enterprise, such as father's Länderbank, he was not retired, on three-quarters of his pension entitlement, until 31 March 1939. The letter telling him this was, however, not signed by some obscure Herr von der Lippe, but by Seyss-Inquart himself.

Thus did the state 'honour' its own.

In the summer of 1947, on my first visit to post-war Vienna, I saw Uncle Paul for the last time. He and Aunt Alice had survived the holocaust – first in Vienna until the end of May 1943, and then as numbers IV/14 – 692 and 693 in the Theresienstadt ghetto where Paul worked as Medical Officer.

The Dr Paul Klaar I saw in 1947 had been awarded the style of a Hofrat, 'Court Councillor', by the President of the Second Republic, and as Chief-Surgeon of Vienna's police, which he then was, he ranked as a full general, but as a human being he had virtually ceased to exist. Physically the big, fat, cheerful and bouncy uncle of my childhood, with his boyish love for small cameras and huge fountain pens, had shrunk to a third of his former size. His soul had withered and shrivelled to less.

He functioned. He went for walks with me, took me to his office in the Police Presidium, he talked, though but little and very slowly, he ate, also little and slowly, but as I sat next to him at table, as I walked next to him through the streets, I sat next to an automaton, walked next to a robot. His face was without animation, his voice monotonous, his eyes were without life.

His profession, his past police status and high World War decorations saved Paul from physical destruction, and had, at the same time, destroyed him psychologically. Others survived Theresienstadt and the even worse hell of Auschwitz, yet, after a while, they integrated themselves again among the living; at least in their waking hours – God knows what frenzied visions haunt their dreams – and walked upright among their fellow-men. That Paul could not do, for he was bent down by the enormous burden of guilt within himself, no less heavy for being more imagined than real – indeed perhaps all the heavier for that.

Because of his standing and seniority he worked as a 'medical assistant' – Jews were forbidden to call themselves doctors – for Vienna's Jewish community for the three years before he and Alice were deported. It was his responsibility to examine those about to be deported east and attest their fitness for transportation. He did not know what fate awaited these unfortunates. People feared deportation because of the uncertainty and mystery in which their destinations were shrouded. And they had heard rumours about the harshness of existence in the ghettos of Poland and German-occupied Russia, but they did not know about the conveyor-belt death installations of the extermination camps or the mass-shootings. The S.S. succeeded so well in guarding its secrets within Hitler's realm that even the Jewish administrators of Theresienstadt did not know the ultimate destiny of the transports leaving that ghetto for the east until early 1943. They too kept silent.

But had he known the truth could Paul have saved a single life? The man responsible for transporting the Jews from Vienna, the Austrian Gestapo official Anton Brunner – called Brunner II to differentiate him from his boss, S.S. Captain Alois Brunner, known as Brunner I – saw to it that any Jew removed from his deportation lists was immediately replaced by another one.

In any case, Brunner II, one of the worst bloodhounds in Austria, only allowed those about to die to be removed from his collecting points. When Paul begged him to let him take some of the very sick to the Jewish hospital, Brunner replied: 'You can put them there only if you are sure they'll kick the bucket in less than fifteen minutes. Otherwise they go.'

But in spite of this a nagging doubt must always have remained with Paul, as did the knowledge that he had prolonged his own life by – however unknowingly – helping to cut short that of others.

Quite possibly it was this doubt which motivated Paul's sudden and violent outburst against some of the Jewish nurses in the Vienna assembly camps, who, driven by their own fears, treated the deportees – I am quoting Paul's own words – 'worse than the S.S. bandits themselves'. He shouted this while testifying in court against Brunner II, who was tried and hanged in Vienna in 1946.

No one dare judge the behaviour of another human being in extremity, but no one can stand by either and see another defiling his humanity without his own becoming defiled and contaminated as well. And within Paul's self-imposed burden of guilt, within his self-disgust, there was perhaps also another more personal and therefore even more soul-breaking sorrow. He, her first-born, had not saved his mother, my Grandmother Julie, from deportation to Theresienstadt. She died there in misery and squalor on the last day of October 1943, having survived her eighty-second birthday by six months. The wedding ring on her dead hand was not made of gold, but of iron. She had exchanged her gold ring for the iron one during the Great War to help Austria.

I have spoken to a number of people who knew Paul during those tragic years in Vienna and in Theresienstadt. From no one did I hear one bad word about him. Everyone spoke well of him, everyone that is except his own conscience. He returned to Vienna from the ghetto in 1945, received dignities, honours and high office and tried three times to end his own life. Aged sixty-two he was run over by a tram on the Ringstrasse, and two days later, on 12 September 1948, he died of his injuries. Did he walk into this tram absentmindedly or intentionally? Does it matter how he found his peace?

Our plan to stay another two days in Vienna before returning to Berlin had to be changed very suddenly. Red-headed Helene changed it for us. She was still living in our Pichlergasse flat, but when my parents called there no one answered the bell. Helene was out. Father still had his keys and he and Mother let themselves in. They walked through the flat. All the rooms were empty, as they had expected, except, and that they had not expected, for their bedroom. Helene had not only kept the double bed which they had given her, but also the big wardrobe, tallboy, chaise-longue, wing armchair, Mother's dressing-table, the bedside tables and a few other bits and pieces.

My parents were still in the bedroom when Helene returned. When she saw them her face flushed as red as her hair, but soon cool and calm again, she blackmailed them. Either we left Vienna that very evening never to return, or she would go to the police and accuse me of having forced her to submit sexually and tell them I had infringed the Nuremberg Laws by committing acts of 'racial shame'. If she carried out her threat and claimed that she, being economically dependent on my parents, had no choice, I could protest all the way to the nearest concentration camp.

As a sort of farewell message she told my parents that her boyfriend, an ardent Communist for many years, had recently joined the S.S.

We were on the night train to Berlin.

Returning to Berlin and the Pension Lurie felt more like a homecoming than the visit to Vienna had done. And as it turned out, when Father opened the mail that had been awaiting us, Helene had really done us a good turn by chasing us helter-skelter out of Vienna. There was a letter from President Reuter in Paris. He was offering Father a position at the Banque des Pays. He explained that this had been intended for a Direktor Rie, senior to Father, who with his wife had committed suicide in Vienna. Father's deputy Bloch would be given the job in London instead of Father, who was to take Rie's place at the bank's headquarters in Paris. Reuter did not do things by halves. On receipt of this letter Father was to go to the French Embassy where his visa would be issued. He would be given that most precious of all documents for Jews who fled to France and the most difficult to obtain, his *carte de travail*, his work permit, on arrival in Paris. Would he please settle the formalities and travel as soon as possible? Reuter regretted that he had not yet been able to get Mother's and my visas approved, but that was purely a formality and should be settled shortly.

Together with the letter Reuter sent Father his contract of employment. His monthly salary was to be 3,333 French francs. It was such an odd figure that I never forgot it. It was of course much less than Father had earned in Vienna, but quite apart from the fact that beggars can't be choosers, it was enough to live on. Many refugees in France would have regarded it as a princely income.

I had not seen Father so happy for a very long time. The bank, his bank, wanted him! Never mind if he had to start lower down the scale. As soon as his French had improved a more senior position would follow. Cheekily I pointed out that he had a hell of a lot of improving to do as his French language was pretty near zero. Father was much too cheerful to be upset by this saucy remark, though he knew it was true.

Of course we would not give up our Irish visas. They could be issued just as well in Paris as in Berlin. Neither the Hirschs nor Witzthum could blame Father for accepting the first chance he was offered to get out of Germany. We had sat in Berlin, waiting for the Irish to make up their minds, long enough. There was no question that Father would leave as soon as possible and on his own. Once he was in Paris he could do something to speed up things and see that Mother and I got our entry permits for France quickly. In a fortnight, at worst in three weeks, we would be a united family again and one privileged to live in Europe's most glamorous capital.

From the minute Father had opened Reuter's letter everything had changed. We had arrived in Berlin depressed and with Helene's threat hanging over us. Now we were euphoric. Where would we find our flat in Paris? At which Lycée would I take my baccalaureat? How long, considering that my French was not all that brilliant either, for there never had been any French recesses in the depths of my mind, till I reached the Sorbonne?

After a while euphoria gave way, at least to some extent, to realism. We weighed the pros and cons of France or Ireland as our final refuge. Ireland was the safer, but also very much duller. And how did Hirsch Ribbons compare where Father was concerned with the Banque des Pays? That was not a difficult question to answer.

Was there really a choice between Ballymena or Galway or some other Irish town, even Dublin, and Paris? True, France had a land border with Germany while Ireland was so remote from her, an island separated from the continent by an enormous sea-filled moat. There was the Maginot Line though, the biggest man-made defence works since the Wall of China, to stop German troops from ever entering France again.

Everything worked as President Reuter had said it would in his letter. Within twenty-four hours Father had the French visas in his new German passport, and the following afternoon we were saying goodbye yet once again. It was not my final goodbye, I was to see Father twice more, but thinking back to that Berlin station in 1938 and writing down these words, there is a great sadness in me as if the embraces we exchanged there, Father and I, had been our last. I was not sad then. It was all so exciting: trains arriving, trains departing, whistles blowing, doors slamming, people rushing, people shouting to each other to make themselves heard above the rhythmic hissing of steam from the waiting locomotives, the shiny long coaches of the Paris Express on which Father was about to journey to freedom; and soon, very soon, Mother and I would be joining him.

No, there was no sadness then, but much upon looking back, for in that Berlin railway station my life with Father ended in the sense that nothing can ever replace the intimacy of the close continuous relationship of routine daily physical presence, taken for granted and rarely treasured at the time, which is so inevitably lost once every meeting becomes an occasion and a vain attempt to bridge the gap of distance and separate experience.

The French, as we soon discovered, were in no more of a hurry than the Irish. Father telephoned from Paris at least once a week to tell us of the new promises and assurances he had been given, but every time Mother and I visited the French Consulate we were dismissed with a gallic shrugging of shoulders and a cool 'We regret, Madame. *Demain, peut-être. Merci.*' Frau Kamberg did not shrug her shoulders, but, as of course we had every reason to expect, her message was the same.

I idled my time away. One afternoon – it was towards the end of October – I strolled along Kurfürstendamm, looking at shops, doing nothing in particular, when I saw a group of men, a hundred or more, Jewish-looking and handcuffed in pairs, being led through the street by a police and S.S. escort. I cannot tell how, but I knew that these were Polish and stateless Jews about to be deported from Germany. Possibly steps against these people had been announced in the newspapers and I had read it, or I overheard someone in the street saying it to someone else. In any case the point is not how I knew, but that I knew and my reaction. I felt slightly sickened and threatened by this sight, but quickly consoled myself with the thought that Polish Jews after all had a country of their own to go to. I turned my head from them and looked away.

Certainly there was nothing I could have done, but nevertheless basically I behaved no differently from the way in which most Germans behaved later, when the deportation of German Jews began. Many did not like what they saw, but consoled themselves with the thought that these people were merely being 're-allocated' to places in Poland.

Some dates remain indelibly fixed in one's memory. Where one was and what one did on that particular day is remembered in detail even decades later. For me such a date is 7 November 1938. At about four-thirty that afternoon I entered the Palm Garden of the Hotel Eden in Budapesterstrasse and sat down at a small table for three. Mother and one of the Bartmann ladies were to join me there at five.

The Palm Garden, as the lounge of the Hotel Eden with its two potted palm trees was somewhat grandiloquently called, was Berlin's favourite 'five o'clock tea' rendezvous. One went there for the *thé dansant* and watched lonely ladies gliding over the parquet floor in the arms of professional dancers, young couples swaying cheek-to-cheek to the rhythms of the band, professional ladies demurely – more or less – glancing at lonely gentlemen with that *heure bleu* look in their eyes. The service was excellent, the ambiance very chi-chi. I thought it superbly elegant and sophisticated.

Mother and her guest arrived punctually. We ordered our tea, enjoyed the dainty little cakes, Mother moaning about her figure, limiting herself to 'only' two, and chatted away quite happily.

It must have been at around six o'clock when the man selling the late edition of the *B.Z.*, Berlin's leading evening paper, came in. He held a copy of his paper up high so that everyone could read its banner headline. The news was sensational. One Herschel Grynszpan, a seventeen-year-old Polish Jew whose parents had been deported from Hanover, had shot the German diplomat Ernst vom Rath at the Germany Embassy in Paris that morning. Vom Rath was still alive, but his injuries were very serious.

At the neatly-laid tea table with its shiny silver, the band still playing and people still dancing, we read this story and knew that it

227

was bound to have serious consequences for us Jews. But none of us would have guessed, even then, what was to come: the best-organised centrally co-ordinated pogrom in history. The *Reichskristallnacht*, sparked off by the shots of this desperate Jewish youth, was the Nazi's first major tactical exercise in their overall strategy against the Jews. More than anything they had done before it involved all aspects of state and party power, showed how far it was now possible for them to go and where there were still obstacles, psychological, financial and legal that had to be overcome before the annihilation of the Jews could be accomplished.

The Hungarian communist leader Rakosi coined the phrase 'salami tactics' to describe how almost any political aim can be achieved if one does not greedily swallow the sausage whole, but slices off one bit after another. In that way neither your opponents nor your victims notice what is happening until it is too late. But Rakosi only invented the phrase, not the technique. All along the Nazis had used 'salami tactics' for their anti-Jewish policies. They carefully observed and noted how the German nation, the Jews themselves and – more important – world opinion, let them have slice after slice. Now was the time: and Grynszpan, as they saw it, had given them the excuse to cut off one large chunk all in one go and swallow it whole. It had no lasting ill-effects on their digestion.

Two days later the *Reichskristallnacht* erupted. In Vienna they arrested and maltreated all my uncles; even little Fritzl, aged fourteen, Klara's and Alfred's son, was locked up; while I slept peacefully through the night, only vaguely knowing that some sort of anti-semitic rowdyism was sweeping through Berlin. Mother and I stayed in at the Pension Lurie on the evening of 9 November. We sat in the small lounge, saw other Jewish guests pale-faced, whispering to each other, heard the crash and tinkle of breaking glass, muted by distance, from the streets, and soon retreated to our room. After Father's departure Mother and I now shared one bedroom. I still read a bit before switching off my light, while outside the Goebbels-directed vandals and hooligans, mostly Hitler Youth kids led by S.A. toughs, played at 'spontaneous outburst of healthy popular reaction' against Grynszpan's murder of vom Rath by burning down the synagogues and smashing the plate-glass windows of Jewish shops. And at the same time the S.S. and Gestapo rounded up Jews in their homes and led them away, some being lynched on the spot, others never to return, the majority to expiate the deed of one single Jew by several weeks in Dachau or Buchenwald before being released. Either by a miracle or through inefficiency they did not call at the Pension Lurie. It may well have been that S.S. and police had their hands so full with all the Jews arrested in their homes; their catch numbered many thousands, they did not bother to comb through hotels and boarding-houses as well. But I do not really know why we escaped scot-free.

The telephone at the Pension Lurie rang at nine o'clock the following morning when Mother and I were sitting at breakfast. The call was for her, and when Mother took the receiver, she heard Frau Kamberg's voice at the other end saying 'Would you please come to the Legation immediately, your visas have been granted.' Overjoyed, Mother came back and told me. The next thing she did was to go back to the telephone and ring her hairdresser for an urgent appointment later that morning. Mother was not only Mother, she was also Stella, the woman, who was not going to emigrate with her hair in a mess.

This was not a day for public transport. From now on it was taxis only and damn the expense.

Frau Kamberg, the German, was, I think, almost as happy as we were when she stamped the visas into our passports. I have always had a suspicion, but never any proof, of course, that our visas had actually been granted by Dublin some days earlier, but that Mr Bewley, the Minister, for whatever reason, had sat on them. I believe that Frau Kamberg persuaded him that morning to issue them without further delay. It just seems too pat somehow that authority from Dublin should have arrived on the very morning after the *Kristallnacht*.

With the visas in our passports, we parted from Frau Kamberg. Mother actually embraced and kissed her, taxied to the Lufthansa offices, produced our passports and visas proudly, and bought two tickets for next day's midday flight to London. We ought to have had British transit visas as well, but Frau Kamberg, warning us that that would take a few more days, said we would be allowed to land in Britain with our Irish visas. British displeasure certainly was less of a risk than spending even one more hour in Berlin than we had to.

After that, Mother, wading through broken glass in Wilmersdorferstrasse, went to her hairdresser, while I went to a hatter's in Kurfürstendamm. I have no idea why it was essential for me to have a new hat for flying to London. Possibly, as we could take no more than ten Reichsmarks each with us anyway, it was just to get rid of some money usefully. Whatever it was, it led to an experience I should not like to have missed. When I walked into that hat shop all three assistants were busy with customers. But as I came in one of the saleswomen looked up, saw me, recognised my Jewishness – of that I am certain – left the customer she had been speaking to and immediately attended to me. Neither the customer so abruptly abandoned nor anybody else in the shop said one word. He waited patiently till I had found the hat I wanted, had paid for it and left.

Mother had an even more surprising experience at her hairdresser. Just before she left the shop the girl who had done her hair turned to Mother and said: 'Madam, I want to apologise to you for the terrible things that happened last night. Believe me, we didn't want this.'

Berlin's Tempelhof airport, then the most modern in the world, was our gateway to freedom on the morning of 11 November 1938. You did not just check in your luggage and walk through to your plane. In those days, when international terrorism was not the work of small groups of fanatical men and women, but neatly organised by whole states and their servants, the terrorists themselves carried out the security checks. With all my luggage I was led into a small room, where I and my suitcases were searched. Not by a good-humoured customs man either, but by two tall Gestapo officers in civilian suits, S.S. badges in their buttonholes, who would have cared greatly if I had had any golden dentures hidden amongst my stuff. Everything was searched. Much to their surprise, and also to mine, for Mother had done my packing, they found a box of toilet paper in my case, not a toilet roll, but one of the zigzag ones, where each sheet pulls out the next through a slit in the package. The S.S. men did not exactly yell 'tally-ho!' when they discovered it, but you could see from the triumphant look in their eyes how they thought 'now we've got that Jew-boy'. They were certain that I had hidden banknotes between the absorbent sheets. They pulled out one sheet after the other till the packet was empty and a neat stack of toilet paper adorned their desk. Dear Mother, with the sacred cause of hygiene always uppermost in her mind!

The senior of the two men had a good line in sarcasm, and he tried to provoke me. He was very much at his ease and enjoyed himself. I was not and did not.

'Glad to get out of here, aren't you?' he asked.

What was I supposed to say to that?

'No, I'm not,' I replied. 'I like Berlin, but I don't seem to have much choice, do I?'

'It's not often I agree with a Jew,' he answered. 'Now's the exception. You'll be better off out of Germany and we'll be better off without the likes of you. All right, take your things and get on the plane.'

I felt slightly dizzy. I did not give a huge sigh of relief, but kept the poker-face I hoped I had shown throughout these proceedings. Until our plane was in the air – no, until it had actually landed in London – the S.S. could still pounce and get me. Not till then could I allow myself to feel safe.

The plane we were to fly in was on the tarmac. It was one of the famous Junkers 52s, the universal work-horse of the pre-war Lufthansa, a curiously square-shaped aeroplane, its fuselage and wings made of a corrugated metal giving it something of the look of a flying Nissen hut. But no Nissen interior – and I not only helped to build some, but lived in a lot of them during the war – could compare with the comfort and luxury inside the Ju 52. Nor could any modern plane. One did not sit in aircraft seats, but in wide, soft armchairs with fixed tables in front of them. Vases with fresh flowers were fastened to the inside of the fuselage, and flouncy curtains framed the windows. Each passenger – I do not think the plane held more than twenty – was welcomed by a steward with the manners of a most experienced high-class butler, and courteously shown to his seat.

I settled down in my luxurious chair feeling most uncomfortable and highly nervous. My security check had taken a good half-hour and I had been sure that Mother would be in the plane before me. But she was not there. It was ten minutes to take-off time.

Take-off time came and passed. Still no Mother. I began to feel as I had done as the train from Kaunas approached the East Prussian frontier, outwardly controlled, but my heart pumping and beating away so loudly that I was sure everybody could hear it.

Ten minutes after take-off time! We were still on the tarmac. I suddenly remembered that Mother had all her jewellery on her. Had she been arrested? Should I get off the plane and look for her? Again and again I craned my neck to look out of the window to the passenger exit in the airport. Nothing! What was I to do? What could I do?

Twenty minutes after our scheduled departure time Mother, accompanied by a Lufthansa stewardess, comes through the exit and towards the plane. The paralysis of fear thaws from my limbs. Calmly she boards the aircraft. Only the redness of her nose, glowing through the layer of face-powder she always put rather thickly on it, betrays the emotional stress she must have gone through. She kisses me, but says nothing until the plane's doors have been closed and its engines started, their noise making it impossible for any of the other passengers to overhear what she tells me.

Like me she had been led into a small room to be searched. In her case the search had been carried out by a woman customs officer. Mother wore a tweed skirt, a blouse and a cardigan over it. On to that cardigan she had pinned all her jewellery till she looked something like Hermann Goering in his Sunday best. Over all this glitter she had put a thin silk scarf, which, though not really hiding them, did to some extent cover her baubles. That customs woman examined Mother most thoroughly, far more thoroughly than the S.S. men had searched me. Mother had even had to take off her skirt and her corset for the woman to investigate her body. She did this very closely indeed, but she never lifted mother's silk scarf although it is hardly possible to imagine that she did not notice what was underneath it.

The flight to London, the first in my life, took over four hours. We landed at Croydon, and in a world very different from the one I had known, most stylishly just before tea-time. The British immigration officer hummed and hawed a bit because of the missing British transit visa, but when we had firmly promised that we would continue to Ireland within four weeks he stamped our passports and handed them back. We had arrived. We were free.

A former school colleague of mine and his elder sister, both of whom had been living in London for some time, awaited us in Croydon. We had wired them that we were arriving. Neither Mother nor I had ever been to London before, and we would have felt lost without their help. They had also booked us into the boarding-house in Swiss Cottage from where, later that evening, I set out on my ecstatic liberation promenade.

The sister had a little car and drove us to the boarding-house, stopping at a Lyons Tea Shop on the way, where I had my first set 'English' tea. A Lyons Tea Shop was a fairly unusual setting for great emotional experiences, but one of the greatest in my life took place right there.

How do I explain and put into words that surging, joyful relief I felt at being finally out of Germany after so many false starts? I knew, but was unable to assimilate in my mind, that the people sipping their tea around me could not care less whether my nose was hooked or snubbed, whether it slanted this way or that, or whether the colour of my eyes was red, yellow or green or all three together; I knew, but could not comprehend, that these English people were totally indifferent to what I thought or said; I knew that Mother and I were safe at last, that nobody would persecute us here, and yet I kept staring surreptitiously at the door wondering when it would open and a couple of jackbooted brown or black-uniformed men would come through it; I was intoxicated by English tea, on a happy 'trip' induced by tiny cucumber sandwiches, and yet I was still afraid that on sobering up I would look into the grinning face of a man with an S.S. badge on his jacket.

And that smell of London, when we were out again in the street, that unforgettable smell of pre-war London! It remained forever in my nose. That tangy, smoky, foggy air possessed for me the fragrance of freedom.

What a strange sight London was for the youth from the continent! Rows and rows of little houses, all looking alike, packaging the citizens of the most individualistic nation on earth. Every preconceived idea I had then about Britain and London was contradicted and confirmed at the same time by the evidence before my eyes. It was almost a Hegelian journey, that drive through the streets of London in that little car, but the synthesis, an understanding of the English, took a much longer time in coming than the journey from Croydon to Swiss Cottage, even though we had to stop once more on our way – at a pawnbroker's

Mother and I had no money, and some time would pass before Father could send any. So the big diamond brooch, inherited from Grandmother Adele, was exchanged for a pawnshop ticket and ten crisp white five-pound notes. That little ticket was, as far as I know, all that remained of Mother's heirloom. There never was enough money to get her brooch out of hock again.

Father, who had meanwhile also received his Irish visa from the Legation in Paris, arrived in London towards the end of November, joyfully embraced by wife and son; and the day after his arrival we boarded the Irish boat train at Euston Station. A young Irishman joined us in our compartment, and we soon bombarded him with questions about his country and Dublin. I and Mother, who spoke English fluently and beautifully, though in a somewhat old-fashioned manner with her 'u's' having a slight dipthong sound, translated his replies for Father. Well, we were not journeying to yet another country, but straight to paradise. And Dublin, his eyes rolled heavenwards at the mere mention of that city, the most 'beauthiful' in the whole world. Oh, the width of O'Connell Street, the elegance of Grafton Street, the grace of St Stephen's Green and on a 'foine dhay' you could see the Wicklow Hills. 'Paradoise, I tell yer, paradoise!'

Beauty, as they say, is in the eye of the beholder. What my eyes beheld in Dublin was without doubt influenced by the shabby third-class hotel in which our scarce means forced us to stay, but convince myself as I would, and I wanted to because I was going to live there, paradise it was not. Small and confined it was, slums and poverty such as I had never seen, not even in the poorest districts of Vienna, surrounded O'Connell Street, dirt and drunkenness almost everywhere one looked. True, I was too young and foreign to appreciate the mellow elegance of Merrion and other graceful Georgian squares, but never having spoken to an Irishman before, never having heard of 'blarney' before, I had believed everything our travelling companion had told us, and my disappointment was all the greater for that.

It was settled that I would become a 'bed and breakfast' boarder in the house next to the Witzthums, but would live and have my meals with them. I do not know whether I ever showed them the gratitude they deserved for their kindness, so let me, however late, record it here. The Hirschs were to arrive in a few weeks. I would work for them, at first as interpreter, and further arrangements would be made then. Father would return to Paris via London, where Mother would stay till she finally got her French entry permit, which according to what Father had been told, should be very soon now.

On the morning before my parents' departure a remark of mine triggered off the last and probably also the most furious row I ever had with my father.

We were sitting over breakfast, which had been served in our room. 'You do know, Daddy,' I said, 'that I am not going to stay here if a war starts.'

Father looked at me surprised, his eyes turning dark and angry.

'Say that again,' he said.

'If a war starts I will not stay here. I shall join the British army at the first opportunity,' I replied.

He reacted so violently that, if I look back now, I do not think that his worry for my safety and his love for me alone, strong as they were, caused such an outburst. After all, I had not said anything which could not have been discussed reasonably, nor had I been cheeky or offensive in any way. But that remark of mine must also have released tensions, worries and fears he had bottled up in himself during the last few months.

'You must be stark staring mad!' he roared. 'There, I have done everything to ensure your safety. You are in the one country far enough away from everything and one that is going to remain neutral, and you tell me you want to go and fight. You don't know what you're saying, you stupid boy. You fool, you haven't seen a war. I have! No, no, no! You stay where I've put you. Don't you dare!' He stood up and paced angrily through the room.

I got up too and repeated calmly: 'Daddy, it's going to be our war. Nobody else's as far as I'm concerned. I shan't sit here and look on. To hell with Irish neutrality. How can I be neutral?'

'You will do as I tell you. I'm still your father. You've your life before you. D'you want to throw it away? You're eighteen. Not even that yet. When you're twenty-one you can do as you please. But now you'll obey!' he shouted back at me.

Mother tried to calm the two of us down, but without much success.

By now I was also shouting.

'To hell with that nonsense about my age,' I yelled. 'I'll go if they take me, and how are you going to stop me. Just how. You tell me! The moment war is declared, I volunteer!'

'For God's sake, Ernst, don't get so excited,' Mother said. 'The war hasn't started yet, and before it does we'll both be here and then you two can talk again.'

Undoubtedly she was right, and Father's great anger was probably also due to a feeling of being confronted, very suddenly and unexpectedly, by a son wanting to make his own decisions and who stubbornly refused to accept his authority. And, of course, he could not bear the thought of his little boy, armed to the teeth, sitting in a trench somewhere in France with shells exploding all around him.

The row between Father and me ended with him storming out and walking the streets of Dublin for a while. When he came back he had calmed down. We never talked about that subject again, neither in Dublin nor at our last meeting in London in January 1939.

Father then returned to Paris via London where Mother remained waiting for her French visa. She had to sit around in London for the whole of December with nobody much to talk to, very lonely and unhappy. The French officials in London were every bit as good at shrugging their shoulders as their colleagues in Berlin. Nobody either refused or granted her her entry visa. Nothing whatever happened, and she was kept in a state of suspended animation. But animated she was not. By the end of December Father had spoken to President Reuter again, who promised that he would intervene either with the Ambassador himself, M. Corbin, or with his Conseilleur, M. Cambon, whom he knew personally. Father, who also had had more than enough of that long drawn-out separation from his wife, came to visit her in London during the first or second week of January, and the Hirschs, who had meanwhile arrived in Dublin, and I was now working for them, very kindly gave me leave to go to London and be with Father.

Altruism, however, was not their only motive. Father had some of their valuables in his possession, which had been smuggled out of Austria and handed to him. I was to bring them with me when I returned to Dublin.

We went out to dinner to a Lyons Corner House, very plushy, very palmy and with a band of mock-gypsies, mostly Jewish refugees in Hungarian outfits, playing music in the background. Father was a bit hesitant about going out at first, because he was rather unshaven. Even a life without the daily visit of Herr Lippert had not yet convinced him that a safety razor was a useful instrument.

I see Father very clearly sitting next to me in that Corner House restaurant, the bristles of his beard having grown well beyond a five o'clock shadow. I see him so undimmed by time, smiling a little shyly in these, to him, rather strange English surroundings. He loved Paris. That city had very quickly become even more than a home from home for him. He said that he asked himself quite often why he had always believed that he could only be happy in Vienna. But London was a different world, still very English then, much more so than it is today.

I can most certainly see not only Father, but also Mother, in many remembered scenes, yet my picture of her, though not less precise, is somehow flatter. Father I see more in the round, more whole, more complete, as if, if I stretched out my hand, I could touch him. Mother is more shadowy, has less substance. But then, as is probably natural in a man, I have never had the feeling that my Mother lives on inside me, but I do know, in a sort of *déjà-vu* sense, that my Father does. It is not just that my movements are very much like his, or that our bodies have the same structure. No, that is not it. Nor do we look much alike. We also have very different personalities. Many of my character traits are much more Mother's than his. But, for instance, when I smile at my children I know that it is the same smile with which he looked at me, and it feels as if not I, but he, were smiling at them from inside me. It is a curious feeling, slightly eerie perhaps, but never a sad one, because not the dead, but the living father continues in the son.

Father could only stay two days, and Mother and I accompanied him to Victoria Station. Our parting, my final parting from Father, is not nearly so sharply fixed in my mind as our farewell in Berlin. My mind may have been less concentrated because Mother and I were leaving for Ireland that same afternoon. We all, including Mother herself, thought it would be much better for her if she did not spend the time until she got her visa alone in London, but together with me Ireland.

I was no longer living in Dublin, but in Galway, which had once been described to me as lying on the other side of the edge of the world. It did, as far as I was concerned. Galway was an ideal location for someone looking for a quiet refuge, for peace away from it all. Mother could have been very happy there if Father had been with her. I, who had hardly seen anything of the world, hated Galway.

To bring Mother there was a very bad idea. Seen from London, Paris is only just on the other side of the Channel, but from Galway it seems light-years away. With every mile we travelled away from London Mother's mood saddened. And then in Galway she became very unhappy indeed. Her exile there lasted for nearly two months. She lost weight, her face became haggard, and her myopic eyes were tear-reddened most of the time. She was terribly lonely, more so than she had been in London. She had very little in common with the other Austrian ladies, members of the Hirsch family and their senior employees, who were also in Galway, and I must have been a disappointment to her. I was neither good nor truly sympathetic company. I was in love with Lisl, much too absorbed with myself, and rather impatient with her all too frequent crying.

We returned to London in late March. Whether Father had written that her visa was coming through at last or she had made up her mind to storm the French Embassy I cannot recollect exactly, but in any case we went and stayed again at the familiar boarding-house in Swiss Cottage. And there on the telephone in the basement I had a conversation with Father, which left me with a sense of guilt for the rest of my life, even though I have no way of knowing whether anything I said to him did actually affect any of the decisions he made later.

Father first spoke to Mother and then asked to speak with me.

'What do you think I should do, Georgerl,' he asked, 'stay in Paris or come to Ireland?'

'What would you do with Hirsch Ribbons? Daddy, the bank has been your life. You love Paris. Of course, you want to stay,' I replied.

'All that is quite true. But Ireland is safe. What will happen to us here when the war starts?'

Our conversation took place after Hitler's troops had marched into Prague and when speaking of the next war one no longer said 'if', but only 'when'. Before I could reply, Father added, 'And if it does, the French will intern me.'

'But that's ridiculous,' I said. 'They can't intern Jewish refugees.' Father's next question was, 'What if the Germans win? What if Hitler occupies France?'

At eighteen I was suddenly cast in the role of military analyst. 'But he never will,' I replied. 'That's quite impossible. They didn't get further than the Marne last time and the French didn't have a Maginot Line then.'

Actually, I was no worse military expert than most senior British and French generals of the time. I too was fighting the last war all over again.

All this sounds harmless enough, and I did believe what I said. But I also knew – and that is what has haunted me ever since – that I had an ulterior motive, which influenced what I said to Father. I wanted to bring Lisl to Ireland and marry her, and I was afraid that Father, if he were there as well, would do everything in his power to prevent it. I did not really want my parents to come to Ireland.

Knightsbridge is renowned as one of London's most elegant districts, but hardly for miracles. Yet in late March 1939 I saw one performed there. A sad-faced fifty-year-old woman, my mother, entered the French Embassy in Knightsbridge, but a happily smiling young bride, my mother again, but with the French visa in her passport, came out.

The following morning Mother waltzed by my side, she most certainly did not just walk, along the boat-train departure platform at Victoria Station. Without any nervous tap-tapping for its steps she climbed surefootedly into her coach.

When I had settled her in her compartment and there were only a few moments left, tears came into her eyes, but they were very different from those bitter ones she had shed in Ireland. These were soft ones, tears one could smile through, tears of love and care for me, warm but not burning, and they flowed without sobs gently and tenderly.

Once again a train moved away from me and disappeared into the distance with a much-loved human being aboard. Ostensibly that train's destination was the same as Father's had been three months earlier: Paris, the City of Light. But the true, the final destination of both trains, the destination my parents were travelling to, was that gate with the words '*Arbeit macht frei*' ('Work makes you free') written over it, the entrance to Auschwitz.

The door-bell rang at the tiny furnished flat my parents rented at 10 rue de Trevise, Paris 9. Mother opened it. Outside stood two policemen. They had come for Father. It was 4 September 1939. War had been declared the day before, and all male German nationals were now being rounded up. Father was taken to Beslay internment camp, from which, having finally established that he was not a Nazi, he was released towards the end of October.

After the Germans broke through the Maginot Line the French arrested Father again and sent him to an internment camp in the vicinity of Biarritz. Mother must have found out very quickly where Father was, for she packed her things and travelled to that famous seaside resort just ahead of the stream of French refugees flooding all road and rail links to the South.

The commandant of Father's camp was a decent and humane man. When France collapsed he released all his prisoners. By no means all French internment camp commanders behaved as he did. Some kept their Jews behind barbed wire till the Germans arrived and took them off their hands. But Mother and Father were re-united even before the Pétain government had signed the armistice. They left Biarritz and went to Oloron Ste Marie, a little town close to the Pyrenees. From there they sent me a postcard. It was the first sign of life I had from them after the fall of France. I did think at one time that they might have intended to cross into Spain, but that obviously was a question I could not ask in my letters, all, of course, opened and read by the Vichy censors.

From Oloron, probably because the Banque des Pays had a branch office there, my parents went to Marseilles. We now corresponded again regularly. Our letters were routed through neutral Portugal. A second cousin of Mother's, Renée Schwartz, had married a Portuguese and now bore the magnificent name of Renée de Maghalaes Cardoso, and she was our link, not only between my parents and myself, but also between them and Lisl, who was my wife now. Father had long since not just accepted her as his daughter-in-law, but he took much comfort from the fact that she had followed me to England from Riga and from knowing us to be together and happy.

Financially my parents were supported by that remarkable man, M. Reuter, the bank's president. He had brought no less than twenty-two Jewish employees of the Austrian Länderbank to France. With the exception of my parents every one of them survived the war hidden in the countryside, and they all received financial support from Reuter, the money first coming from the bank, but eventually out of his own private funds.

I met Henri Reuter when I was still a soldier and visited France in the summer of 1946. He received me in his elegant flat in Avenue Foch. A most distinguished-looking man, a personality of great inner authority, then in his late sixties, he was resting on a chaise-longue during our talk. He was ill, exhausted by the war years, and only a few months away from death when I saw him. I believe he was of Jewish descent and came from the same family as Baron de Reuter, the founder of the famous British news service. I was, of course, much too shy to ask any personal questions, indeed I was so over-awed at being in the presence of my father's much admired and venerated chief that I am sure I was quite unable to show M. Reuter my gratitude properly. He gave me all the letters and documents concerning my parents that he had, and when I left he handed me a tidy little sum as a personal present, saying, 'I know that you are here on a sad mission, but you are a young man – go and enjoy yourself!'

Father and Mother lived in Marseilles for about six months, from the end of June or beginning of July 1940 until early January 1941. Then they were forced by the Vichy government, which was pushing foreign-born Jews out of the cities to have better control over them, to take up what was termed *résidence assignée* in St Pierreville. As I knew from their letters their life there was hard, but no harder, except for the fear gnawing away at Father's soul – he described it to M. Quinkal, a young carpenter with whom he often chatted, as a constant dumb anxiety – than that of the other people living in that remote mountain village. Father also believed himself to suffer from a glandular malfunction. This may have been more imagined than real. A friend of Father's referred to it in a letter he wrote in April 1942 when replying to one from Father, in which he must have mentioned his worries.

'I hope very much you have heard meanwhile from your son,' Father's friend wrote, 'so that one of the causes of your being so nervous will have been eliminated. As far as your fears of being ill are concerned, do please remember that you come from a medical family. This is a very grave handicap. One knows more about diseases than most other people and all too easily imagines that one is ill oneself.' That letter also refers to Mother's bad rheumatic pains, something she herself never talked about in her letters to me, but not surprising in that damp, cold place where they lived.

The people of St Pierreville were kind to my parents and liked them. A letter to me from Mother, written on 2 May 1942, begins with the words: 'As is the local tradition, a little girl brought us a posy of lilies of the valley this morning. You pin them on your dress and wear them all day, and they bring you good luck.'

The people of St Pierreville were really good to them. They knew that they came from backgrounds very different from their own and pitied them for all they had lost. Except for having to report to the local gendarmerie from time to time, Father and Mother were free to pass their days as they pleased. They could go for walks whenever and wherever they wanted to and were permitted to have a radio. The food situation in the country was not good, but certainly better than in the cities. There was no real shortage of meat, though mostly that of old cows and of poor quality. Potatoes were freely available. Supplies of butter and oil were short, but there was a well-organised black market. Coal was tightly rationed, but one only had to walk a few hundred yards into the woods to get as much wood as one wanted.

In that same letter Mother stressed yet once again that I must on no account fail to record carefully the depot number and warehouse address in Paris where our Viennese belongings were stored. That I was sure to know it was of greatest importance to my parents, probably less because of any presentiments, but more out of their general sense of insecurity. They loved every single stick of furniture, every sheet, every cup and saucer more now than they had ever done.

These things were all that remained of their years of happiness, home life and, above all, security, so sadly absent from their lives now.

Since we left Pichlergasse to travel to Berlin they had not seen them again. There had been endless trouble to get the transport out of Austria. New payments for this, that or the other were suddenly necessary, new documents were required, until Ernst Lamberg, Aunt Lisa's husband, who dealt with these problems on our behalf, at last got the final release stamp. Some eleven months after we had left Vienna, on 3 August 1939, exactly one month before the outbreak of the war, it arrived in Paris and was promptly seized by the French customs authorities. This stopped my parents, just in time, from signing the lease for a flat. The French customs demanded proof that Father had official authority to establish permanent residence in France. It was granted – a few days before German soldiers paraded down the Champs Elysées. But at least, stuck away in the mountains of the Ardèche, my parents had an official document stating that what had always belonged to them was now theirs in the eyes of the French state as well.

I was having a cup of tea in our regimental canteen sometime in late August 1942, the radio was on and I listened to the B.B.C. news. 'Recent rumours that foreign-born Jews were to be deported from unoccupied France,' the announcer said, 'have been confirmed by French sources in London. No further details are known as yet.'

I was greatly alarmed, but calmed my own fears eventually with the thought that my parents were living in such a small village so far removed from the main stream of events. A few days later I read a report in *The Times* which gave more background information:

Because of the small number of persons who volunteered to work for Germany, Laval decided at the end of July that the deficit should be made up by Jewish refugees constituting the first quota of 10,000 deportations. The first arrests were made in Marseilles on August 3. On August 6 the first 1,000 Jews left a camp at Les Milles for an unknown destination: by August 10 another 2,000 had gone and another 1,600 from other camps were due to leave the following day. About one-third were to be drawn from internment camps. A number of protests were made, including one by the Papal Nuncio to Marshal Pétain, but apparently they were without effect.

Next day *The Times* had a follow-up from a special correspondent on the Spanish side of the Pyrenees frontier with Vichy France. Headlined 'Virtual Death Sentence', it said:

The round-up of all Jews of foreign nationality who have entered France since 1936 and are now living in the unoccupied zone must be completed today, states a *Petit Parisien* message from Vichy. The persons arrested are being assembled at Dijon, pending deportation to Eastern Europe.

Simultaneously, complying with instructions from the occupying authorities, Vichy ordered the mayors to erase immediately from the national registers the names of all Jews, whether of French or other nationality, who were arrested, interned, or deported to the occupied zone. Once their names are removed from the register the persons concerned cease to have any legal existence. Moreover, their whereabouts will be subsequently untraceable. The Jews in the unoccupied zone who are still free fear that this amounts to confirmation of the rumour that the arrested Jews have been virtually sentenced to death.

I could no longer, after reading this, pretend to myself that Father and Mother were safe. But, strange as it may seem, a subsequent report from the same *Times* correspondent describing the horrible circumstances of the deportations gave me some hope again :

Eye-witnesses have described the harrowing scenes at Nice, Marseilles, Lyons, when the French police rounded up for deportation Jews of foreign origin. Many were over 70 years old, many were young children. They were put into closed vans and taken to railway stations, where, after a cursory examination they were herded into trucks and sent across the demarcation line to Dijon. Mothers were separated from children and wives from husbands. Many French people, particularly young students sympathising with the Jews, tried to intervene, and it is reported that hundreds of Jews were received into hiding in spite of the penalties for such actions.

It was this last sentence, which made my hopes rise again. And as I discovered after the war, when I was told that my parents were the only members of the Länderbank staff not to survive while the others had been secreted from the Vichy gendarmes by courageous Frenchmen and women, such hopes had not been mere folly. Indeed, but for circumstances which I shall tell later, it very nearly happened.

That Laval's orders to deport the Jews were resisted in France was confirmed by a report in *The Times* on 7 September. It said :

M. Laval dismissed General de St Vincent, Military Governor of Lyons, who refused to co-operate in the mass arrests of Jews. Laval has also ordered the arrest of Roman Catholic priests, who are sheltering the children of Jews in the unoccupied zone. Episcopal letters recommending French Roman Catholics to give every help to persecuted Jews are being read out in the pulpits all over France.

Late in September a letter arrived from Portugal addressed in the familiar writing of Renée Cardoso. My heart leapt. I had been right. They were safe! I tore the envelope open – and all hope was shattered. What I held in my hand was the last letter I had sent to my parents. It was unopened and an unknown hand had written: '*Adressé inconnu*' on it in indelible pencil.

My parents, my beloved Mother and Father, had disappeared with the many millions of *inconnus* in the gruesome anonymity of impersonal mass-murder.

Ernst and Stella's lives had been erased.

I wanted to cry, but could not. For many years I tried to close my mind and lock my heart. I wrote a letter to one of Father's brothers, Uncle Fritz, in which I said: 'My parents are dead and I do not want to know how they died or where they died.' Whenever I had reason to look at a map of France I avoided looking at that part of it which showed Ardèche, because I did not even want to see the name of St Pierreville. It took over thirty years after my parents were deported before I went to St Pierreville to find out what had happened to Ernst and Stella Klaar.

According to M. Quinkal, a former member of the Resistance in St Pierreville, M. Lascombe, my parents' landlord was woken up by Chef de Brigade Chandolas at midnight on Tuesday, 25 August 1942 and ordered to accompany him and his gendarmes to my parents' house. When my father had heard their knocking he knew why they had come. He climbed on the bedroom window and threatened to jump down and kill himself. Chandolas shouted back that the window was too low for that. He would probably break his leg, but he, Chandolas, would arrest and deport him just the same. The gendarmes then entered the house and left a few minutes later with my father between them.

Next morning, when the news of my father's arrest had spread, indignant villagers went to the Gendarmerie and remonstrated with Chandolas. Chandolas replied that he was merely carrying out his orders. In any case M. and Mme Klaar had already been transferred to Privas during the night. There was nothing he could do.

Attempts were immediately made to save Father and Mother.

M. de Juan, a Spanish Civil War veteran and friend of my parents, wrote to Henri Reuter from St Pierreville on 28 August. 'I assume you have already heard the news about M. and Mme Klaar, who left here the other night for Privas, well accompanied. As I know your friendship for them I beg you to let me hear immediately you have news from them.' By the time Reuter received de Juan's letter he already knew. The first news possibly came from Father himself, who cabled Reuter, also on 28 August, 'Please send 7,000 francs by cable. Thank you. Ernst Klaar, Camp de Venisseux near Lyon, Baraque 2.' A second cable was sent by a M. Eisen. It was dated 30 August and said 'Please help M. and Mme Klaar. They are in Dijon.' That meant that they were already in the hands of the German police.

Reuter appealed for help to an official of the Vichy government, M. Couve de Murville, later Prime Minister, after many years as Foreign Minister, of Charles de Gaulle. That Couve de Murville had also tried to help in other cases became apparent from Reuter's letter to him of 12 September.

Dear Sir,

I thank you most sincerely for your kind help. I know how difficult it is to intervene effectively in these sad affairs and I know that you certainly have done everything humanly possible to save the lives of these poor people, who have done nothing wrong.

This gives me also the courage to let you know that an old colleague of mine, a deputy director of the bank, is mentioned on the enclosed list. It is M. Klaar and his wife who according to the latest news I have received are now interned in Drancy. Would mentioning the services M. Klaar has rendered the bank, and with that French interests in Central Europe, perhaps help to save them?

I think that you will forgive my insistence in view of the grave danger in which these unfortunates find themselves.

When Reuter wrote to Couve de Murville it was already too late. By 12 September the train in which Ernst and Stella travelled to their destination was either still on its way or had already arrived in Auschwitz, and my parents were dead.

Drancy, which Reuter mentions, was the big assembly camp outside Paris from where the transports left. Father – he and Mother were still together – found an opportunity to send a postcard to Reuter from Drancy. Possibly one of the French guards smuggled it out for him. It is in some ways a remarkable document showing as it does, how even in such a desperate situation, the social and personal habits of a lifetime are maintained. Father's style on this post-card, dated Paris, 8 September 1942, was formal and controlled as it has always been:

Dear Mr Director-General,

I hope that one of my recent communications reached you. Until now I have not heard anything. Help is of the essence. We shall be leaving today and so I want to use the opportunity which has arisen to transmit to you once more my devoted farewell greetings. Although I do not know when I shall be able to report to you again I do not want to give up the hope that this may happen one day. I beg you, most esteemed Mr Director-General, to keep in contact with M. Wouters as soon as he arrives in Nice and to pay him the monthly storage rental for our furniture, so that I, I mean my son, does not lose the last of his parents. Further I beg you once more to keep, give instructions to keep, the contact with M. Valla in St Pierreville, who is looking after the things we left there and if possible to take them into your hands. My most heartfelt thanks. I hope that others have been spared our fate. With my most sincere good wishes for you and your family's future and once more with heartfelt thanks I always remain yours devotedly, Ernst Klaar.

Mother wrote Renée Cardoso's address on that card, mentioning that I could be reached through her and adding:

Let us hope that we shall overcome this trial as well. Unfortunately pointing out our special situation had no effect. Regards, yours, Ernestine Klaar.

But this postcard was not Father's last message. That was written the following morning on a scrap of paper with Reuter's address on it. It was either smuggled out of Drancy or, more likely, thrown out from the lorry taking them to the train, possibly from the train itself, and picked up by someone, who mailed it to Reuter. One can see from Father's handwriting, normally tiny and extremely even and neat, now larger, the letters unsteady, that he wrote that note in great haste and excitement; it says:

Esteemed Mr Director-General, Unfortunately we are being taken away. I wrote you again yesterday. I do not know whether it will arrive. M. de Juan, well known to the Gendarmerie St Pierreville, has some jewellery and all the correspondence with Wouters. I beg you, dear Mr Director-General, to have arrangements made to take these things into your

246

possession. I should be so happy to save all this for my son. Unfortunately we are travelling without any money. What is going to happen is not difficult to guess. I thank you for all the kindnesses you have bestowed on me over the years.

Father was so desperately anxious that I should be able to surround myself with the contents of our family home that he scribbled on the back of that piece of paper yet once again :

I beg you to pay the depot rental of fr. 215 per month to Wouters. If possible I want to save everything for my son. These lines are also my authorisation to Wouters to put everything at your disposal.

But even that last pitiful wish of his was not to be fulfilled. I was not ever, as he so fervently hoped, to use his favourite armchair where he had always taken his little 'cat-nap' after lunch before returning to the office, or sit in Mother's where I had been on her lap as a little boy and she had told me stories in what she called 'our twilight hour' as dusk fell in the evening. Nor was I ever to look at the paintings he had so lovingly collected or touch again the bronzes or the painted baroque clown with the saw-blade clock. The Nazis were much too efficient for that. Their system of murder and robbery was well practised and functioned with precision. German soldiers arrived at M. Wouters' depot on 5 February 1943 and requisitioned everything. A proper receipt – there had to be good order in everything – was issued. It stated, 'Depot M 596, Ernst Klaar requisitioned completely and removed. This receipt does not constitute an entitlement for compensation. For disposal : S.S. Obergruppenführer (Lt. Gen.) Lorenz. Authority : Field-Post No 43071W.'

There was no joy in my heart, only sorrow, as I drove to St Pierreville for my first visit almost exactly thirty-two years after my parents were deported from that village. Around me was the scenic beauty of the Ardèche. I did not see it.

For decades I had blamed St Pierreville and its people for Father's and Mother's fate. I could not even bear to see its name on a map. Very early on I had had evidence that this was unjust and unwarranted, but it had not clicked in my mind. This evidence had been in my hands since the summer of 1946 when I collected my parents' belongings, including Mother's jewellery from the Lyon Jewish Community. Everything my parents had left behind in St Pierreville had been sent to its officials, every single item accounted for, by M. de Juan and M. Valla, in whose safe-keeping Mother had left it all for me. Mother's jewels were modest, but by the standards of the villagers they were worth a fortune. It would have been so easy to say that Mother had taken everything with her. Honesty about possessions deportees left behind was much more the exception than the rule in those times.

As I said, I did not intentionally ignore these facts. I just did not see that my firmly held conviction of St Pierreville as a veritable hornets' nest of Vichy fascists was wrong. As I saw it the village's mayor was a Judas who had betrayed my parents for Vichy's pieces of silver, and the local gendarmes were more callous than the S.S. itself. How else could I explain to myself that my parents were the only ones of the Länderbank people in France not to survive? It never occurred to me that nothing worse than human frailty and ignorance might have been the reason.

How unfair I had been I learned only when I read the letter from Michel Valla, the grandson of the M. Valla who had been my parents' friend and who was now himself mayor of St Pierreville. I had written to the Mairie in preparation for my visit, asking whether they still had any documents concerning my parents.

We have none [Michel Valla replied] but my dead grandparents were close friends of your parents and held them in the highest esteem. I have spoken to several people here, after receiving your letter, who remember the circumstances of their arrest, particularly M. Quinkal, who only this morning told me a lot about it.

Our local resistance group organised discreet surveillance of your parents till about nine o'clock every evening in order to intervene should they be threatened with deportation. That a sudden arrest could be made in the middle of the night nobody ever thought of. After it had happened, your parents – they were already at the Gendarmerie then – asked to see my grandfather and gave him whatever they still had.

I can assure you that the people of St Pierreville have a most touching memory of your parents and that they experienced much pain and revulsion when the tragic news became known.

As I drove through the curves of the mountain road leading to St Pierreville under a bright blue sky my mood was determined by a passage I could not get out of my mind from Professor Raul Hilberg's

The Destruction of the European Jews. It describes the final moment
in the gas-chamber.

The gassing was a short process in Auschwitz. As soon as the victims
were trapped in the 'shower-room' they recognised in a flash the whole
pattern of the destruction process. The imitation shower facilities did
not work. Outside, a central switch was thrown to turn off the lights. A
Red Cross car drove up with the Cyclon [the gas], and a masked S.S.-man
lifted the glass shutters over the lattice, emptying one can after another
into the gas-chamber. Untersturmführer [S.S. Lt.] Graebner, political
chief of the camp, stood steady with stop watch in hand.

As the first pellets sublimated on the floor of the chamber, the law of
the jungle took over. To escape from the rapidly rising gas, the stronger
knocked down the weaker, stepping on the prostrate victims in order to
prolong their own life by reaching the gas-free layers of air. The agony
lasted for about two minutes; then the shrieking subsided, the dying
slumping over. Within four minutes everybody in the chamber was dead.

As dry an account as one could give, but just because of its matter-
of-factness more terrible than any literary description can be. It left
me with the forever unanswerable question: did Mother's and
Father's agony last two minutes or more? How long are two minutes
in a gas-chamber? Or four?

It was mid-morning when I arrived. St Pierreville, for my parents
the peaceful ante-chamber to man-made hell, is a typical Ardèchois
village, surrounded by green-wooded mountains, its air indeed harsh
and bracing. It has the obligatory château, one steepled church, a
camping site with a *boules* patch and one inn, which also lets rooms
to holiday-makers and proudly calls itself L'Hôtel des Voyageurs.

Most of its houses, including that in which my parents lived, are
built of big slabs of honey-coloured local stone, as is the building of
the Gendarmerie Nationale with its tricolour, its entrance flanked by
two flower urns. The village, one street and a little market square
with a fountain, is laid out along a cleft in the valley, and, though
the mountains around it looked friendly and inviting on that
summer's day, I could easily imagine their dark and menacing appearance in winter, when they would hold the whole village in their
dank, clammy grip, the damp cold seeping into its houses through
the porous stone. That was what Father had written about when he
talked about the cold from the outside oozing into their rooms and
merging with that in his soul, and what Mother had meant when

she added that it was too cold even for her to blush after reading Father's words of praise.

Immediately I had parked my car I went to the Mairie. It was closed. A little note on the door said 'Fermé pour vacances'.

I walked over to the village inn and asked for a coffee. Mme Sabarot, the proprietor's wife, a stout, blonde, pretty woman in her early forties, brought it. I told her that I was the son of M. and Mme Klaar, who had lived in St Pierreville during the War and asked if she, by any chance, remembered them. 'Most certainly, Monsieur,' she replied, 'I remember them well. Such nice people. I remember how happy your mother looked when I brought her a little bunch of lilies of the valley. It's a local custom, you know, we always wear them for luck in early May.'

'Alas,' she went on, 'they did not bring much luck to your poor mother.'

'Can you perhaps recall, Madame, how my parents were, how they lived?'

'No, unfortunately not,' she replied. 'You see, I was only ten years old and too shy to talk much to them. But they always had a smile for me.'

Mme Sabarot then directed me to the house where my parents had lived. Like everything in St Pierreville it was just a few paces away. I walked up the stone steps from the main road, saw Mother's little patch of garden, and knocked on the door. It was locked.

An old woman, having heard my knocking, looked out from the kitchen next door and asked what I wanted.

I introduced myself. 'Ah, quelle tragédie!' she exclaimed. Would I like to have the key? The place now belonged to a family in Lyon who came here for their holidays. But it was still exactly as it had been when my parents had lived there.

I unlocked the door and entered. The kitchen where Mother had created her 'excellent culinary ideas' was immediately on the right and behind it was the tiny sitting-room where she had read Goethe. But for three small volumes, which she probably took with her, I had found his collected works, a very old edition Father had bought in Paris, among the things my parents left for me. I climbed up the rickety wooden staircase and stood in the bedroom with the heavy Victorian bed in which they had slept. The washstand with its two earthenware jugs each side of the lavoir was in the corner. In spite of myself I could not help smiling as I thought how, for Mother, it must have been the most important item of furniture in the whole house.

I did not stay long. It was midday by now and the street lay empty in the sunlight as I walked over to the Gendarmerie. Perhaps they still had some documents. But the office, when I entered it, was empty. After all, it was lunch-time and the security of France needed strengthening.

I do not know why I, instead of turning round and leaving, just went on into the corridor behind the office. I did, and unexpectedly found myself – the door with its iron-bar grille standing open – looking into the local prison cell.

I looked at its grey walls with a feeling of cold dread and recoiled when I saw the dirty straw palliasse on the bunk and the tiny barred window high up on the far wall.

For the first time in my life I understood what it must mean to lose one's freedom, to be locked up in such a cell, and how easily, having been thrown into it, psychological pressure exerted by such surroundings could break a man's morale.

Did they lock up Father and Mother in this cell before they took them to Privas? Did my despairing Father sit on this bunk, hardly hearing the loving words of encouragement spoken by Mother's calm voice as she tried to give him back a little strength again? He did not have much any more. I could see her sit there next to him, her whole body trembling with nervous exhaustion, but her mind clear and her thoughts assessing their situation with absolute realism. Why else did she leave her jewellery behind? She knew they were without money. But she left everything in St Pierreville for me. Would she have done that had she not known what awaited them at the end of that journey? She probably knew sooner than Father that they would never return.

I was shaken by that 'somebody must be walking over my grave' shudder. Shivering, I walked out into the sun and went down the road to the house, which had been pointed out to me as M. Quinkal's.

His wife opened the door. She knew who I was. Her husband had told her to expect me. I would find him on the camping site down by the river. He was looking after it.

I drove down there. I asked the men playing *boules* whether they knew where I could find M. Quinkal. A little man with a blue beret, his body twisted by arthritis, walked towards me.

'I am Quinkal, monsieur,' he said, 'you must be M. Klaar.'

It was the first time for very many years that anyone had addressed me by that name.

He looked at me and said: 'I can see you are the son of M. and Mme Klaar. Your parents spoke so much about you. You were constantly in their minds.'

Quinkal came and sat in my car next to me.

I told him what Michel Valla had written.

'Yes, that is all quite true. He got most of it from me in any case,' he said. 'The local resistance group was led by our schoolmaster. It had fifteen members. I was in charge of a sub-section of five men. We did keep your parents observed. At the first sign of danger we wanted to take them to a remote mountain farm. We had made our preparations. After that we would have contacted the Maquis. The gendarmes would never have found them. I don't think they would have wanted to, anyway.'

'But I had always thought that their sergeant, or whatever his rank was, must have been a fascist, an anti-semite,' I said.

'Oh, Chandolas,' Quinkal replied, 'wasn't a fascist. Not at all. Fear for his own job, even for his own safety, that was what made him trick us. You see, he had four men under him. Two were in the resistance, two were not. He knew it, of course. So, when he got the order to arrest your father he didn't say anything. But he made sure that the resistance men were not on duty that night. He didn't tell the others either. Now you must understand that in a village like this people go to bed early. By nine o'clock practically everybody is in bed and asleep. Even in summer. And it was war-time too. So, as we did not think your parents in any danger our surveillance finished about that time. He waited, and then late at night he did it. Getting Lascombe out of bed, too.'

Quinkal then told me how Father had threatened to jump from the window, and Lascombe, his landlord, had dissuaded him.

'And you really believe that only fear made Chandolas behave so deviously and carry out his orders even after that terrible scene?' I asked.

Quinkal nodded his head. 'You can't imagine what a frightened man he was,' he said. 'He was scared stiff of his superiors and just as scared of the Maquis. But if Chandolas had known what was going to happen to your parents, if he had known about extermination camps – none of us did, you know, we only heard after the liberation and even then could hardly believe it – I think he would have tipped us off.'

For a minute or so we sat in silence.

'Well, M. Klaar, that's really all I can tell you. It was after all a very long time ago,' he said and he reached for the car door.

Then he turned to me again and said: 'Your mother could have stayed here till the end of the war. She would have been quite safe. Chandolas was only ordered to arrest your father. Your mother went of her own free will. She needn't have gone. She didn't want to leave your father.'

I could not believe that I had heard right. My French is not all that good, and Quinkal had spoken quickly. I asked him to repeat it and say it slowly.

He did.

My reaction, when I had really taken in what he had said, was not that of an adult. It was totally instinctive and childlike. How could she do it? Abandon her child – me! Why did she not stay alive for me?

I had to shake my head, as if I wanted to throw these thoughts out of it, before I regained my balance.

How she must have loved my father! I was deeply ashamed of my first reaction. Her life was linked to his, not to mine. I had my own. She had given it to me. Me she gave the gift of life, Father she gave her own.

'That is all,' Quinkal repeated. 'All the people who knew your parents more intimately, were closer friends of theirs than I was, are dead.' There was a slight note of reproach in his voice as he added, 'You waited too long, Monsieur. *Maintenant c'est trop tard pour être à la recherche des parents perdus* – too late now to search for lost parents!' I do not know whether Quinkal had ever read Proust. I should rather doubt it, but, so help me, that is what he said.

In one sense he was right, of course. In another sense he was not. It took some time for me to understand, to think out and absorb what he had told me, and to find the link between Mother's decision to choose death by Father's side and a recurring dream I had had about my parents which I remember in great detail, though I cannot remember when I dreamt it last.

This is how it goes: My phone rings. I answer it and hear my mother's voice at the other end. She tells me that she and Father have survived and where I can find them. Overjoyed I race off to the place she has named to take them into my arms. When I arrive I see Mother in the foreground, very clearly, and she looks exactly as she always had done during the happy days. Her face, her smile, her voice are exactly as they were. Father is in the background. Mother talks to me, but she never replies to my repeated question – why did she only tell me now that they were still alive, why had she waited for so many years before letting me know? She ignores that. Father in the background does not say one single word, does not welcome me, does not look at me, turns his head away from me. And he does not look as he used to. He is unshaven, as he was on that evening in Lyons Corner House, but much thinner. His skin seems ghostlike, almost translucent, has a yellowish pallor and his movements are unnatural, uncoordinated, jerky like those of a puppet. I try to talk to him, call out to him, but there is no response.

That is the dream. What is it trying to tell me? First I thought that Father's attitude towards me in this dream might be determined by the guilt I felt ever since our telephone talk in 1939 when I had advised him to stay in France. Then I wondered whether it showed that I, subconsciously, had felt Mother's love for Father to stand between him and me, that it was she who was pushing him away from me. My conscious mind would certainly deny that she did this. But then it struck me that the opposite interpretation, that I was pushing Father into the background to have Mother to myself, sounded just as plausible. My instinctive reaction to Quinkal's revelation would seem to confirm this. However, not only do these interpretations cancel each other out, but neither of them takes into account how my Father looks in my dream. Though his body is moving, his appearance is that of a gas-chamber corpse.

Father will not talk to me because I feel the subconscious guilt of the survivor. I know, if I know anything, that my survival was my parents' only consolation, and yet, at least as long as that dream haunted me, there must have been in me a feeling of guilt for surviving, for escaping, for not having shared the destiny of my parents and in a wider sense that of my people.

Epilogue

If, say, in Easter Week, in hundreds of cathedrals and churches, in town and country, a large picture were put up overnight above the altar, showing a thirty-year-old Jew as Jesus racked with pain, there would be a cry of horror and indignation. And this would be because it had laid bare the profound concealment and repression which attaches to the Jew Jesus and the whole Jewish tribe. For many clerics and laymen, princes of the church and pastors, such a picture of a young Jew — say, a photograph taken shortly before the victim was gassed in 1944 — would appear a terrible blasphemy.

These words were written by the Austrian Catholic historian Friedrich Heer. In large measure they provide the answer to a question I have been asking myself for decades:

Why did my parents, why did Ernst and Stella Klaar, and the millions who, like them, were destroyed like vermin, have to die? Who is responsible?

The simplistic answer is more than obvious: because of Adolf Hitler. Although true, it is a hollow truth, one without content, just as Hitler himself was a hollow vessel filled not with his own, but with other men's ideas.

Hitler was never an originator. He was merely the terrible executor of other men's hatreds, which he made his own. Through Adolf Hitler exploded the accumulated Jew-hatred of two thousand years. He was like the crater of a volcano through which the seething, searing masses of molten earth, so long contained in the darkness below, finally burst into the open.

Xenophobic dislike of the Jews as foreigners existed before Jesus, but the venomous hatred of the Jewish people began with the dejudaisation of Jesus by the early Fathers of the Church. They knew that by robbing Jesus of his Jewishness they were destroying the very essence of his identity, for Jesus was a Jew, lived as a Jew, preached as a Jew, and the Father he prayed to and served was the God of the Jews.

Nevertheless they tore the dead Jesus from his Jewishness and thereby inflicted wounds on his memory, which were deeper and more agonising than those his body suffered on the cross.

There is no greater crime than the murder of a man's soul. It weighs even heavier on the human conscience if it is done posthumously to a defenceless victim. There is no greater punishment than the guilt it instils in its perpetrators.

Man's instinctive defence against overwhelming guilt is to project his own sin on to those he has wronged. And this is what the early Fathers and many of their successors did by pointing at the inherent wickedness of Jewry, by painting on it the hook-nosed grimace of the devil, and eventually creating a man who never was: the light-haired, straight-nosed, gentile Jesus.

Religious Jew-hatred is the root of the tree from which racial anti-semitism grew. Although it also murdered Jews, it did, at least occasionally, allow them a chance of survival through baptism. Racial anti-semitism became the death-trap, for taken to its logical conclusion, as it was by Hitler, it could only lead to one result: mass-murder of the Jews.

Like the word 'anti-semitism' itself, racial anti-semitism is an invention of the nineteenth century, a by-product of the spirit of nationalism and chauvinism which began to infect Europe as a result of the Napoleonic wars.

Friedrich Grillparzer, the great Austrian poet and dramatist, who witnessed its growth during his lifetime, summed up the new nationalism and its deeper meaning in one prophetic sentence: 'From humanitarianism through nationalism to bestiality.'

Racial anti-semitism thought of the 'final solution' long before Hitler carried it through. At the time of the Dreyfus trial, Edouard Drumont in France accused the Jews of having infected Russia with syphilis and proposed that they should all be drowned in the Seine. In 1935 the English anti-semite Arthur Leese wrote: 'It must be admitted that the most certain and permanent way of disposing of Jews would be to exterminate them by some humane method such as the lethal chamber.'

There were many others of many nationalities. Most outspoken amongst German Jew-haters was the nineteenth-century historian Paul de Lagarde, who described the Jews as 'usurious vermin' and suggested that they should be exterminated 'like trichinae and bacilli'. Lagarde was one of Hitler's favourite authors. He adopted Lagarde's 'vermin' terminology.

But this must be said: racial anti-semitism was not a German, it was an international phenomenon. It still is. However, it was the Austrian Hitler – no matter how often and how loudly he screamed *Deutschland* he never became a German – who was fated to achieve the power to exploit German efficiency and thoroughness (as well as the all too willing co-operation of men from many nations) to accomplish what a Lagarde and a Leese had proposed.

Not only Jews were murdered. Poles and Russians were murdered in their tens of thousands, and we grieve for them as we grieve for the Jews, but there is one all-important difference: Hitler never had any intention to exterminate all Russians or all Poles. The Jews were the only people selected for total genocide. Even the Gipsies, though they shared the fate of the Jews in large measure, were not all condemned to die. A number of them, who had served in the German army before they were arrested and sent to Auschwitz, were returned to their army units, provided they agreed to sterilisation.

My parents had to die because they were Jews, because they belonged to the people that gave the world Jesus and a code of ethics which the world has never been able to live up to.

The Church teaches that all mankind shares in the guilt for Jesus's death on the cross. And so does all mankind share in the guilt for the death of my parents and millions of Jewish men, women and children in the gas-chambers.

The world and its leaders knew very early on what was happening. It knew about the mass-executions in Poland and Russia, about the gassings in Maidanek, Treblinka and Auschwitz. And the world, we, all of us, let it happen. We did nothing.

Perhaps this book, by telling a true story of human despair, by telling the story of the destruction of one family, can have an infinitesimal influence on at least a few. That is the hope with which it was written.

Or shall the last word on us all forever be Voltaire's verdict: 'History never repeats itself, man always does'?

Family Trees

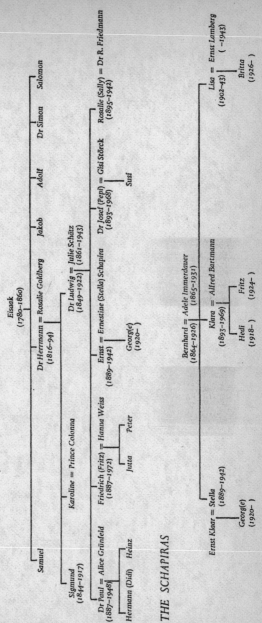

THE KLAARS

Eisaak
(1780–1860)

Samuel   Dr Herrmann = Rosalie Goldberg   Jakob   Adolf   Dr Simon   Salomon
(1816–94)

Karoline = Prince Colonna

Dr Ludwig = Julie Schätz
(1849–1922)   (1861–1943)

Dr Josef (Pepi) = Gisi Störck   Rosalie (Sally) = Dr R. Friedmann
(1893–1968)   (1895–1942)

Sigmund
(1844–1917)

Ernst = Ernestine (Stella) Schapira
(1889–1942)

Susi

Dr Paul = Alice Grünfeld
(1887–1948)

Friedrich (Fritz) = Hanna Weiss
(1887–1972)

George
(1920–)

Hermann (Didi)   Heinz

Jutta   Peter

THE SCHAPIRAS

Bernhard = Adele Immerdauer
(1864–1926)   (1865–1931)

Lisa = Ernst Lomberg
(1902–43)   (–1943)

Klara = Alfred Bartmann
(1893–1969)

Britta
(1926–)

Hedi   Fritz
(1918–)   (1924–)

Ernst Klaar = Stella
(1889–1942)

George
(1920–)

Bibliography

Adam, Uwe Dietrich: *Judenpolitik im Dritten Reich* (Droste, Düsseldorf, 1972)

Adler, Hans Günther: *Theresienstadt 1941–1945. Das Antiltz einer Zwangsgemeinschaft. Geschicte, Soziologie, Psychologie* (Mohr, Tübingen, 1955)
—: *Die verheimlichte Wahreit. Theresienstädter Dokumente* (Mohr, Tübingen, 1958)
—: *Der verwaltete Mensch. Studien zur Deportation der Juden aus Deutschland* (Mohr, Tübingen, 1974)

Akten zur deutschen auswärtigen Politik 1918–1945. Aus dem Archiv des Deutschen Auswärtigen Amtes. Serie D, Band I. Von Neurath zu Ribbentrop (Sept. 1937–Sept. 1938) (Imprimerie Nationale, Baden-Baden, 1950)

Allmayer-Beck, Johann Christoph: *Die K. (u.) K.-Armee 1848–1914* (Vienna, Bertelsmann, Gütersloh, 1974)

Améry, Jean: *Jenseits von Schuld und Sühne, Bewältigungsversuche eines Überwältigten* (Klett-Cotta, Stuttgart, 1977)

Andics, Helmut: *Fünfzig Jahre unseres Lebens. Österreichs Schicksal seit 1918* (Molden, Vienna, Munich, Zürich, 1968)
—: *Das österreichische Jahrhundert. Die Donaumonarchie von 1804–1900* (Molden, Vienna, Munich, Zürich 1974)
—: *Der Staat den keiner wollte. Osterreich 1918–1939* (Herder, Vienna, Freiburg, Basle, 1962)

Barea, Ilsa: *Vienna* (Weidenfeld & Nicolson, London, 1966)

Blumenkranz, Bernhard (ed.): *Histoire des Juifs en France* (Collection "Franco-Judaica" 1). (Privat, Toulouse, 1972)

Botz, Gerhard: *Wohnungspolitik und Judendeportation. Zur Funktion des Antisemitismus als Ersatz national-sozialistischer Sozialpolitik* (Geyer, Vienna, Salzburg, 1975)

Brook-Shepherd, Gordon: *Anschluss* (Macmillan, London, 1963)
—: *The Last Habsburg* (Weidenfeld & Nicolson, London, 1968)

Clary-Aldringen, Alfons: *Geschichten eines Österreichers* (Ullstein, Berlin, Frankfurt-am-Main, Vienna, 1977)

Cole, Hubert: *Laval* (Heinemann, London, 1963)

Crankshaw, Edward: *The Fall of the House of Habsburg* (Longman, London, 1963)

Danzer, Alfons: *Unter den Fahnen* (Tempsky, Vienna, 1889)

Dimont, Max I.: *The Indestructible Jews* (Signet, New York, 1971)

Elon, Amos: *Herzl* (Weidenfeld & Nicolson, London, 1976)

Fest, Joachim C.: *Hitler* (Propyläen, Berlin, Frankfurt-am-Main, Vienna, 1973)

Fraenkel, Josef (ed.): *The Jews of Austria. Essay on their Life, History and Destruction* (Vallentine, Mitchell, London, 1967)

Franzos, Karl Emil: *Die Juden von Barnow* (Hallberger, Stuttgart, Leipzig, 1878)

Friedell, Egon: *A Cultural History of the Modern Age* (Knopf, New York, 1930)

Fromm, Erich: *An Anatomy of Human Destructiveness* (Cape, 1974)

Fuchs, Albert: *Geistige Strömungen in Österreich. 1867–1918* (Globus, 1949)

Gedye, George Eric Rowe: *Fallen Bastions* (Gollancz, London, 1939)

Grange, Henry Lovis de la: *Mahler* (Gollancz, London, 1974)

Gunther, John: *The Lost City* (Hamilton, London, 1964)

Habe, Hans: *All my Sins* (Harrap, London, 1957)

Hasek, Jaroslav: *The Good Soldier Swejk* (Penguin, Harmondsworth, 1974)

Hay, Malcolm: *The Foot of Pride* (Beacon, Boston, 1950)

Heer, Friedrich: *Gottes erste Liebe* (Bechtle, Munich, Esslingen, 1967)
—: *Das Wagnis der schöpferischen Vernunft* (Kohlhammer, Stuttgart, Berlin, 1977)

Hilberg, Raul: *The Destruction of the European Jews* (Allen, London, 1961)

Himmler, Heinrich: *Geheimreden 1933 bis 1945 und andere Ansprachen* (Propyläen, Berlin, Frankfurt-am-Main, Vienna, 1974)

Hitler, Adolf: *Mein Kampf* (Eher, Munich, 1925)

Jäckel, Eberhard: 'Hitler und der Mord an den europäischen Juden', *Frankfurter Allgemeine Zeitung*, 25 August 1977

Jagchitz, Gerhard: *Der Putsch. Die Nationalsozialisten 1934 in Österreich* (Styria, Graz, Vienna, Cologne, 1976)

Kaindl, Friedrich: *Die Bukowina in den Jahren 1848–1849* (Pardini, Czernowitz, Vienna, 1900)

Kassner, Salomon: *Die Juden der Bukowina* (Loewit, Vienna, 1917)

Kochan, Lionel: *The Jew and his History* (Macmillan, London, 1977)

Kraus, Karl: *Die letzten Tage der Menschheit* (Kösel, Munich, 1970)

Lang, Jochen von: *Der Sekretär. Martin Bormann: Der Mann, der Hitler beherrschte* (Deutsche Verlags-Anstalt, Stuttgart, 1977)

Langbein, Hermann: *Menschen in Auschwitz* (Europa, Vienna, Zürich, Munich, 1972)

Lucacs, John: *The Last European War* (Routledge, London, 1976)

Maderegger, Sylvia: *Die Juden im österreichischen Ständestaat 1934 bis 1938* (Geyer, Vienna, Salzburg, 1973)

Magris, Claudio: *Der habsburgische Mythos in der österreichischen Literatur* (Müller, Salzburg, 1966)
—: *Weit von wo. Velorene Welt des Ostjudentums* (Europa, Vienna, Zürich, Munich, 1974)

Mann, Thomas: *Gedanken im Kriege* (1915), in *Gesammelte Werke in 13 Banden, Bd. XII, Nachtäge* (Fischer, Frankfurt-am-Main, 1974)

Marek, George Richard: *The Eagles Die* (Hart-Davis, London, 1974)

Mitchison, Naomi: *Vienna Diary* (Gollancz, London, 1934)

Molden, Fritz: *Fepolinski & Waschlapski* (Molden, Vienna, Munich, Zürich, 1976)

Moser, Jonny: *Die Judenverfolgung in Österreich 1938–1945* (Europa, Vienna, Munich, 1966)

Ottawa, Theodor: *Mein Österreichbuch* (Donauland, Vienna, 1953)

Pearlman, Moshe : *The Capture and Trial of Adolf Eichmann* (Weidenfeld & Nicolson, London, 1961)

Picker, Henry (ed.) : *Hitlers Tischgespräche im Führerhauptquartier 1941–1942* (Athenäum, Bonn, 1951)

Popper, Sir Karl : *Unending Quest* (Collins, Glasgow, 1976)

Pulzer, Peter G. Julius : *The Rise of Political Anti-Semitism in Germany and Austria* (Wiley, New York, 1964)

Qualtinger, Helmut and Herz, Carl : *Der Herr Karl* (Langen-Müller, 1962)

Reitlinger, Gerald : *The Final Solution* (Vallentine Mitchell, London, 1953)

Roth, Joseph : *Werke in drei Bänden* (Kiepenheuer & Witsch, Cologne, 1956)

Schnitzler, Arthur : *Jugend in Wien. Eine Autobiographie* (Molden, Vienna, Munich, Zürich, 1968)
—: *Der Weg ins Freie*, in *Gesammelte Werke. Die erzählenden Schriften*, vol. i (Fischer, Frankfurt-am-Main, 1961)

Scholder, Klaus : *Die Kirchen und das Dritte Reich*, vol. i (Propyläen, Berlin, Frankfurt-am-Main, Vienna, 1977)

Schuschnigg, Kurt von : *The Brutal Takeover* (Weidenfeld & Nicolson, London, 1971)
– : *Austrian Requiem* (Gollancz, London, 1947)

Speer, Albert : *Erinnerungen* (Propyläen, Berlin, Frankfurt-am-Main, Vienna, 1969)
—: *Spandauer Tagebücher* (Propyläen, Berlin, Frankfurt-am-Main, Vienna, 1975)

Stern, J. P. : *The Führer and his People* (Collins, Glasgow, 1975)

Stewart, Desmond Stirling : *Theodor Herzl* (Hamilton, London, 1974)

Stoeger, Michael : *Darstellung der gesetzlichen Stellung der galizischen Judenschaft* (Kuhn und Millikowski, Lemberg, 1833)

Tietze, Hans : *Die Juden Wiens. Geschichte, Wirtschaft, Kultur* (Tal, Leipzig, 1933)

Villiers, Douglas : *Next Year in Jerusalem* (Harrap, London, 1976)

Wagner, Dieter and Tomkowitz, Gerh   . *Ein Volk, ein Reich, ein Führer! Der Anschluss Österreichs 1938* (Piper, Munich, 1938)

Waite, Robert G. L. : *The Psychopathic God – Adolf Hitler* (Basic Books, New York, 1977)

Warner, Geoffrey: *Pierre Laval and the Eclipse of France* (Eyre & Spottiswoode, London, 1968)

Watt, Richard M.: *The Kings Depart. The Tragedy of Germany: Versailles and the German Revolution* (Weidenfeld & Nicolson, London, 1969)

Weigel, Hans: *Karl Kraus oder Die Macht der Ohnmacht. Versuch eines Motivenberichts zur Erhellung eines vielfachen Lebenswerkes* (Molden, Vienna, Munich, Zürich, 1968)

Weinzierl, Erika: *Zu wenig Gerechte* (Styria, Graz, Vienna, Cologne, 1969)

Wistrich, Robert Solomon: *Revolutionary Jews from Marx to Trotsky* (Harrap, London, 1976)

Zweig, Friderike Maria: *Spiegelungen des Lebens* (Deutsch, Vienna, Stuttgart, Zürich, 1964)

Zweig, Stefan: *The World of Yesterday* (Cassell. London, 1943)

Acknowledgements

My thanks go to Dr H. G. Adler (London) whose advice helped me to find the right sources concerning the Nazis' extermination policies and who also introduced me to Mrs Gwyn Moser (Vienna) who was my indefatigable researcher, helper and critic. Mrs Maria Bontoft typed the manuscript, but over and above that she also thought about the text she was typing and pointed out to me my occasional muddles.

Index

Rosie Boycott
A Nice Girl Like Me £1.95

Rosie Boycott was a nice girl. She was also an alcoholic. This is her story, a frank and moving account of a girl who made it from the top to the bottom – and all the way up again.

'It is the story of growing up the hard way in an easy age, with a round-the-world ticket in one hand, a glass in the other, and fear and loathing down below'   SUZANNE LOWRY, SUNDAY TIMES

Carol Gino
Rusty £2.95
A True Story

Rusty has more to forget than most. One moment she was cheering her high school football team, the next, she woke up in hospital – diagnosis: epilepsy. But nobody explained to her what epilepsy was, and terrified, she tried to commit suicide – only to find herself misdiagnosed as a psychiatric case, and shut off from the world in a mental institution reminiscent of something out of *The Snake Pit* or *One Flew Over the Cuckoo's Nest*.

Through sheer courage and willpower she is released. Carol Gino meets Rusty on her first day at a new hospital – but Rusty isn't a patient, she's the nursing assistant whom all the patients trust. Although only nineteen, Rusty can calm their fears without patronising them. She also makes Carol laugh, and when Carol's young children meet her, they adore her. Rusty overcomes seven-year-old Lynn's painful shyness, teaches her to dance, and opens up a whole new world of make-believe for Jeremy. But in spite of Carol's determination to help Rusty, and make the medical world sit up and help, the nightmare is only just beginning. Through Rusty, Carol learns that there are different kinds of healing.

Max Hastings
Das Reich £2.50

June 1944: within days of the D-Day landings, the 'Das Reich' Panzer Division marched north through France to reinforce the defenders of Hitler's Fortress Europe. They were veterans of the bloody fighting of the Russian front, 15,000 men, hounded for every mile of their march by saboteurs of the Resistance and agents of the Allied Special Forces. Along their route they took reprisals so savage they will live for ever in the chronicles of war atrocity.

'My literary VC goes without doubt to Max Hastings for his *Das Reich* . . . the story of a march that left behind a trail of blood and death, torture and heroism' SUNDAY TELEGRAPH

Élmer Bendiner
The Fall of Fortresses £1.75

August 1943: target – the vital ballbearing factories at Schweinfurt, southern Germany. 300 US Eighth Air Force B17 Flying Fortresses are sent to cripple the Nazi war machine. But across the enemy coast the Messerschmitts are waiting. More than a hundred bombers and almost fifteen hundred men were lost in two daylight raids that barely dented the armouries of the Reich.

'Ranks among the outstanding air memoirs of the war' MAX HASTINGS, STANDARD

Theodora Fitzgibbon
With Love £1.95

Paris in 1938. A young girl arrived from England in search of life and love in the fabled City of Light. Theodora Fitzgibbon found all she was looking for and more. She fell in love. She met Picasso and Cocteau.

As the Nazis swept across Europe, she made her desperate escape by bicycle home to England and wartime London. Working as a mannequin by day and in the voluntary forces by night, she struggled to make ends meet round the rent book. In the bohemian world of the Chelsea pubs she made friends with Dylan and Caitlin Thomas, with Augustus John and Donald Maclean, and she met the man who was to become her husband.

'Vivid record of a bohemian life' GUARDIAN

Karen Armstrong
Through the Narrow Gate £2.95

At the age of only seventeen Karen Armstrong entered a holy order of nuns. Turning her back on the world, her family and friends, on any possibility of becoming a wife and mother, she embraced vows of poverty, chastity and obedience. While her generation enjoyed the swinging sixties, Karen suffered indignity, squalor and emotional anguish in a nightmare that could have come out of the Middle Ages. This is a nun's own story of a life that most of us could never imagine.